Jerusalem of Lithuania:

THE RISE AND FALL OF JEWISH VILNIUS

A PERSONAL PERSPECTIVE

JERUSALEM OF LITHUANIA:

THE RISE AND FALL OF JEWISH VILNIUS

A PERSONAL PERSPECTIVE

BY

N.N. SHNEIDMAN

Mosaic Press
Oakville, ON - Buffalo, NY

Canadian Cataloguing in Publication Data

Shneidman, N.N.
Jerusalem of Lithuania: the rise and fall of Jewish Vilnius

Includes bibliographical references and index.
ISBN 0-88962-659-6

1. Jews - Lithuania - Vilnius - History. 2. Holocaust, Jewish (1939-1945) -
Lithuania - Vilnius. 3. Vilnius (Lithuania) - History. 4. Shneidman, N.N.
I. Title

DS135.L52V54 1998   947.93'004924   C98-931143-0

Published by MOSAIC PRESS, P.O. Box 1032, Oakville, Ontario, L6J 5E9,
Canada. Offices and warehouse at 1252 Speers Road, Units #1&2, Oakville,
Ontario, L6L 5N9, Canada and Mosaic Press, 85 River Rock Drive, Suite 202,
Buffalo, N.Y., 14207, USA.

Mosaic Press acknowledges the assistance of the Canada Council, the Ontario
Arts Council and the Dept. of Canadian Heritage, Government of Canada, for
their support of our publishing programme.

MOSAIC PRESS in the UK and Europe:
DRAKE INTERNATIONAL SERVICES
Market House, Market Place,
Deddington, Oxford. OX15 OSF

MOSAIC PRESS, in Canada: **MOSAIC PRESS**, in the USA:
1252 Speers Road, Units #1&2,   85 River Rock Drive,
Oakville, Ontario, L6L 5N9   Suite 202, Buffalo, N.Y., 14207
Phone / Fax: (905) 825-2130   Phone / Fax: 1-800-387-8992

E-mail: cp507@freenet.toronto.on.ca

This book is dedicated to the memory of my parents, relatives, and friends, the innocent victims of the Nazi genocide.

ALSO BY N.N. SHNEIDMAN

Literature and Ideology in Soviet Education
D.C. Heath and Company, Lexington, 1973

The Soviet Road to Olympus: Theory and Practice of
Soviet Physical Culture
OISE Press, Toronto, 1978

Soviet Literature in the 1970's: Artistic Diversity and
Ideological Conformity
University of Toronto Press, Toronto, 1979

Dostoevsky and Suicide
Mosaic Press, Oakville, 1984

Soviet Literature in the 1980's: Decade of Transition
University of Toronto Press, Toronto, 1989

Russian Literature 1988 - 1994: The End of an Era
University of Toronto Press, Toronto, 1995

JERUSALEM OF LITHUANIA:
THE RISE AND FALL OF JEWISH VILNIUS
A PERSONAL PERSPECTIVE

PREFACE

The Holocaust, and the destruction of the Jewish communities in Eastern and Central Europe have become today an important part of contemporary history. An impressive body of evidence has been accumulated to corroborate the atrocities, plunder, and destruction in the Nazi occupied territories all over Europe. The calamity, however, was of such magnitude that no single study could do justice to the subject, and cover all aspects of this horrendous disaster. I was fortunate to survive the war and the Holocaust, but for fifty years I remained silent. The memories of my ravaged youth were too painful to touch, but my past haunted me all these years. Today, motivated by the desire to help repel the insolence of those who falsify history and deny the Holocaust, I am ready to tell my story.

The proposed narrative places my personal account of survival, and the story of the destruction of the Jewish community of Vilnius, or as it is called Jerusalem of Lithuania, within the general context of the history of the city and its Jewish population. Special attention is paid to the existing annals of the resistance to Nazi tyranny in the Vilnius ghetto, and to the events which took place on 1 September 1943 at the school premises of 12 Strashun Street. This was the only place in the ghetto where the Nazis were faced with armed resistance.

My past, and my mental, emotional, and spiritual development are inexorably linked with the past of Vilna and its Jewish community. Hence, I resort in this book to the unconventional combination of historical data, academic analysis, and autobiographical material, some of it based on reminiscences and memoirs written during the war in 1943-44. It is well known that with the passing of time, accounts of personal experience inadvertently turn into important historical evidence.

My memoirs relate the first hand experience of a young man whose perception had not yet been tinged by political, economic or other considerations. My observations and experiences described here are intimately personal. I do not pretend to be objective. As anyone else, I have observed life from a peculiar vantage point, and my conclusions are personal to the core.

Chapter One of the proposed book gives a brief outline of the historical past of Vilnius and its Jewish community. It provides also a personal view of life in the city between the two world wars. In Chapter Two the Nazi occupation of Vilnius, and Jewish resistance to Nazi oppression are discussed. In Chapter Three my war experiences in the Soviet Army are described. Chapter Four deals with Jewish life in Vilnius after liberation from Nazi occupation. It covers the period between 1944 and 1998.

Names of places are usually given in the book in the version commonly used in the English language, and appropriate for the historical period under consideration. I use the designation Vilna, Vilno (Wilno), and Vilnius interchangeably to reflect the historical realities of the times discussed. One has to bear in mind that with the frequent changes of rulers the name of the city would change as well. To avoid confusion it is worth noting that under Russian control the city was called Vilna; under Polish administration - Wilno (Vilno), and under Lithuanian rule - Vilnius. In Hebrew it is Vilna, and in Yiddish - Vilne.

All translations from other languages, unless quoted from English language sources, are my own. I have adopted in the book, with minor exceptions, the widely used transliteration system of the Library of Congress.

I hope that this book will shed some new light on the life of Jews in pre-war Vilno, on the history of Nazi oppression in Lithuania, and on the relationship between resistance and survival under Nazi occupation. It will also stimulate a better understanding of the intricate processes that determine the behaviour of people placed in conditions of subjugation, tyranny, and extreme cruelty.

A note of thanks is due to all my friends and colleagues who read earlier versions of the manuscript and offered constructive criticism. I acknowledge with gratitude their assistance and advice, but I accept sole responsibility for any inaccuracies, biases, or mistakes which may exist in the book.

N.N.S.
Toronto, Canada. 1998.

CHAPTER ONE

VILNIUS AND ITS JEWISH COMMUNITY

A. VILNIUS AND ITS PAST

Lithuanians were among the tribes which inhabited the region to the south-east of the Baltic Sea in the beginning of the common era. The name "Lithuania (Lietuva) was first mentioned in a German chronicle, in 1009."[1] According to archaeological findings the region of the confluence of the Neris (Wilja) and Vilnia (Wilenka) rivers, where the city of Vilnius is presently located, was populated as early as in the ninth century. In 1323 the name Vilnius was for the first time mentioned, as the capital city of Lithuania, in a letter by Gediminas, the Grand Duke of Lithuania, to west European cities.[2]   The Lithuanian state was at that time a loose confederation of principalities under the supreme rule of the grand duke. In 1385 Lithuania established political links with Poland, and in 1386 Grand Duke Jogaila, the grandson of Gediminas, was baptized in Krakow (Poland), and married there the Polish Queen Jadwiga. Jogaila concluded thus a personal union with Poland, and was crowned king of the Polish-Lithuanian commonwealth. While a Lithuanian sovereign ruled over the united kingdom, a grand duke was in charge of affairs in Lithuania proper. In 1387 Lithuania adopted Christianity.

For close to two hundred years, from 1386 and until the death of the childless King Sigismund Augustus in 1572, the Polish-Lithuanian state was ruled by a descendent of the Gediminas-Jogaila line, with the king providing the formal bond between the two nations. In order to avert the possible disintegration of the Polish-Lithuanian kingdom, after his death, Sigismund Augustus urged representatives of the two nations to reaffirm and formalize their union. On 4 July 1569 the so-called Lublin Act of Union was signed. It confirmed the bond between Poland and Lithuania, and the existence of a commonwealth of the two nations. The two countries however, did not merge into a single state. Each remained autonomous, with its own treasury, army and judiciary, and no joint federal government was created. A single ruler, however was to be elected jointly by both states.[3]   The Union between Poland and Lithuania stimulated economic growth, and exposed Vilnius to a number of new cultural and intellectual influences. Moreover, its location at the crossroads of the east and west, north and south, turned the city into an important centre of trade, culture and migration.

Over the years social and economic strife in the Polish-Lithuanian kingdom undermined its political stability, and its neighbours did not fail to take advantage of this precarious situation. By 1795 the Polish-Lithuanian state ceased to exist. It was partitioned between Russia, Germany, and Austro-Hungary. Vilnius was occupied by Russian troops and it became a

3

Russian provincial town on the outskirts of the tsarist empire.

Poland and Lithuania recovered their independence as separate states only after the end of the First World War, in November 1918, and both claimed Vilnius for themselves. During the civil war and hostilities that followed Vilnius changed hands many times. In October 1920 the city was captured by Polish legions, commanded by General L. Zeligowski, and it remained under Polish rule until the beginning of the Second World War in September 1939.[4] In Poland Vilno was a provincial town. It was overshadowed in size, and economic significance, by cities such as Warsaw, Lodz, Krakow, Lwow, and Poznan. Nevertheless, it was an important centre of political and cultural relevance, as well as an outpost in the north-eastern regions of Poland which bordered with Lithuania, Latvia, and the USSR.

Between the two world wars Lithuania did not relinquish its claim to its ancient capital Vilnius and it did not recognize Polish sovereignty over the city. Unable to recover the city by force, Lithuania treated its more powerful neighbour with disdain. In March 1938 Polish troops were massed at the Lithuanian border and Poland presented the Lithuanian government with an ultimatum, demanding recognition of Polish sovereignty over the Vilno region, and the normalization of diplomatic relations between the two countries. Unable and unwilling to go to war, the Lithuanian government yielded to pressure and signed an agreement restoring diplomatic relations with Poland.

The German army invaded Poland on 1 September 1939. A week earlier Germany and the USSR signed a non-aggression pact which gave the Nazis a free hand to pursue their aggressive designs of territorial conquest. It also provided for the division of spheres of influence in Eastern Europe. Polish resistance to the onslaught of the overwhelming Nazi forces was minimal and, by the middle of September, most of western and central Poland were in the hands of the Wehrmacht. That was when the Red Army entered Poland from the east and occupied the eastern regions of the Polish republic. The Soviets captured Vilno on 17 September 1939. Initially, they turned the newly acquired areas into western parts of Soviet Belorussia and Ukraine respectively, incorporating thus most of eastern Poland into the USSR.

Early in October, independent Lithuania signed a mutual assistance agreement with the USSR which provided for the transfer of Vilnius and vicinity to Lithuanian jurisdiction, and the establishment in Lithuania of Soviet military garrisons for its alleged protection from potential foreign invaders.[5] On 28 October 1939 Lithuanian army units entered Vilnius. The Lithuanian civic administration followed behind. The Lithuanian people were happy to recover what they regarded as their ancient capital. Yet most did not trust their giant eastern neighbour and suspected that a high price will have to be paid for this Soviet generosity. Indeed, the ominous Lithuanian saying: "Vilnius musu, Lietuva jusu," which literally means "Vilnius is ours, but Lithuania is yours," had soon proven to be correct.

By August 1940 independent Lithuania practically ceased to exist. It was forced "voluntarily" to join the Soviet Union, becoming thus a constituent part of the USSR. Despite political turmoil, and rapid economic and social change, connected with the introduction of communist rule in Lithuania, Vilnius was fortunate to escape, at least for a while, the fate of the rest of Poland which was occupied by the Nazis since early in September 1939.

Soviet rule in Vilnius did not last long. On 22 June 1941 the German army invaded the USSR, and two days later Vilnius was in the hands of its new occupiers. For three years the city was under the control of the Nazis, and their local Lithuanian collaborators. On 13 July 1944 the city was liberated by advancing Soviet troops, supported by pro-Soviet partisans roaming the nearby forests and creating havoc to German military installations. Vilnius once again became the capital of Soviet Lithuania.

The social and economic situation in Vilnius evolved over the centuries slowly. Until 1385 there were yet no sharply defined hereditary castes in Lithuania, and one could change one's social status at will. One's social situation was usually determined by occupation, calling, official position, and the amount of taxes paid. There was no concept of hereditary slavery in Lithuania at that time as yet. After 1385, Polish influence in Lithuania became evident and the social picture began to change. Exclusive castes of prelates, nobles, and gentry rose to prominence, and a mild form of limited serfdom made slow inroads.[6] By the sixteenth century a functioning feudal system was in place.

In the middle ages many Lithuanians still lived in individual homesteads. The capital Vilnius was populated by members of the nobility, gentry, local town folks, as well as by foreign immigrants, among them many Germans and Jews. City dwellers enjoyed the right of self-government. They could establish local trade and crafts regulations and they had their own system of justice. Some of them were merchants and shopkeepers, others traders, craftsmen, and artisans.[7]

Over the years social stratification and the influx into the city of members of the privileged aristocracy, nobility, landed gentry and clergy fostered the development of culture, architecture, and the arts. The penetration of different religious and cultural influences have even left a mark on the outward appearance of the city. Old Vilnius is rich in soaring

5

masterpieces of different architectural schools, and the imposing structures of churches, cathedrals, and synagogues in Vilnius have become famous all over the world. The churches of St. Anne and Bernadines, constructed in the sixteenth century, are excellent examples of Gothic architecture. The churches of St. Peter and St. Paul, and of St. Casimir (seventeenth century), bear the mark of the diverse and rich heritage of the baroque. The features of the Renaissance style are represented in the Dawn Gateway (Ausros Vartai, Ostra Brama). Its chapel has become a Catholic shrine for it holds the famous sixteenth century image of the Virgin Mary. In the eighteenth century neoclassicism made its contribution to the architectural opulence of the city. The most outstanding example of this period is the Cathedral, located in the centre of the city, at the foot of the Castle Hill (Gedimino Pilis, Gora Zamkowa). Originally built in the fourteenth century, the Cathedral was reconstructed several times. Its final version was shaped in the eighteenth century by the Italian sculptor , Tomasso Righi.[8]

The intellectual life in the city was affected by historical and political change as well. Vilnius University was the oldest institution of higher learning in the former USSR. Originally founded as a Jesuit College in 1570, it was transformed into a university in 1579. Its faculty of law was opened in 1641, and a medical faculty was established in 1773.[9] After the partition of the Polish-Lithuanian Kingdom the university was transformed by the tsarist government, in 1803, into a Russian imperial university. It was closed in 1831, after an anti-tsarist insurrection, and was reopened only after the end of the First World War.

The fate of many world famous personalities is connected with the city of Vilnius. Among those who lived, studied, and worked in the city were M.K. Curlionis (1875-1911) and S. Moniuszko (1819-1872), Lithuanian and Polish composers respectively; the Polish writers J. Kraszewski (1812-1887) and E. Orzeszkowa (1842-1910); the Belorussian poets Iakub Kolas (1882-1956) and Ianka Kupala (1882-1942), as well as the Ukrainian bard Taras Shevchenko (1814-1861). The famous polish poets A. Mickiewicz (1799-1855) and J. Slowacki (1809-1849), and the Lithuanian historians T. Narbutas (1784-1864) and S. Daukantas (1793-1864), were students at the Vilno university. The 1980 Nobel Prize winner for literature, Czeslaw Milosz (b. 1911) spent his formative years in Vilno, and graduated from the local university.

The geographical location of Vilnius and the historical circumstances of its development greatly affected the cultural and intellectual evolution of its population. At different times the city was exposed to Polonization, Russification, the infiltration of abhorrent Nazi values, and forceful communist indoctrination. It was also subjected to vigorous attempts to inculcate its inhabitants with the basics of Lithuanian national culture and tradition, and with the notions that justify Lithuania's claim to the city and its environs.

The multinational and constantly fluctuating composition of the city's population was conducive to the creation of important Polish, Lithuanian, Jewish and Belorussian educational establishments. The city's population was paralleled by the representation of a variety of different religious denominations. Most Poles and Lithuanians were catholics. The Belorussians were either Greek orthodox or catholic. Most Russians belonged to the Russian orthodox church, but some were old believers, or members of a sect outlawed and persecuted by the tsarist government. There were several Lutheran churches in the city, attended by Germans and Balts, as well as a Karaite temple, a mosque, and many synagogues.

In the nineteenth century, under Russian rule, the economy of Vilna developed rapidly and its population grew. In 1796 Vilna was inhabited by 17,451 people,[10] by 1897 there were already 154,532 residents in the city.[11] In 1860 a railway connection with the outside world was established and Vilna became a major trading centre. By the end of the century, 336 industrial enterprises operated in the city and the formation of a proletariat was taking shape.[12] At that time artisans and workers still composed the majority of city dwellers, but over twenty per cent of the total city population was formed by the clergy, nobility, merchants, and military people.[13]

Before the First World War, in 1914, 235,000 people lived in the city. During the war the population of Vilna was decimated, and by 1920 only 128,000 continued to reside in the city.[14] In the twenty years of Polish rule the population of Vilno grew steadily. In 1939, just before the beginning of the Second World War, there were 215,000 inhabitants in the city. Close to sixty per cent of the total were Polish; the others were Jewish, Lithuanian, Belorussian, Russian, German, and some Karaites, originally members of a Jewish sect that rejected the rabbinical tradition, and interpreted the bible literally. Between the wars the situation in Vilno was complicated. Economic life was unstable. Some businesses were thriving, but competition, unemployment, as well as political instability and national strife hampered economic development.

NOTES

[1]. Jonas Zinkus, ed., <u>Lithuania. An Encyclopedic Survey</u> (Vilnius 1986), 87.

[2]. J. Jurginis, V. Merkys, A. Tautavicvius, <u>Vilniaus Miesto Istorija</u> (Vilnius 1968), 23-35.

[3]. Adolfas Sapoka, <u>Vilnius in the Life of Lithuania</u> (Vilnius 1962), 34-6.

[4]. B. Vaitkevicius, ed., <u>Istoriia litovskoi SSR</u> (Vilnius 1978), 344.

[5]. Zinkus, 127.

[6]. Constantine R. Jurgela, <u>History of the Lithuanian Nation</u> (New York 1948), 367-9.

[7]. Jurginis, Merkys, Tautavicius, 50-3.

[8]. Adolfas Medonis, <u>Vilnius</u> (Vilnius 1977), 16.

[9]. A. Bendzius, J. Kubilius, J. Ziugzda, <u>Vilniaus Universitetas</u> (Vilnius 1966), 295-300.

[10]. Jurginis, Merkys, Tautavicius, 214.

[11]. Ibid., 303.

[12]. Ibid., 277.

[13]. Ibid., 214.

[14]. G. Agranovskii and I. Guzenberg, <u>Litovskii Ierusalim</u> (Vilnius 1992), 6.

B. THE JEWS OF VILNA

Wars, persecution and foreign conquest had driven the Jews from their original homeland in ancient Israel. Having lost their country they were scattered all over the world, becoming in the process the people of the book. The bible and the Talmud, or a body of Jewish civil and ceremonial law and legend, helped them preserve their faith and traditions, and retain their unique identity. The winds of destiny carried them east, west and north, in search of peace, a home, and a place they could call their own. Some turned up in the lands ruled by the grand dukes of Lithuania as early as in the twelfth century.

The first Jewish communities in Lithuania were established in the thirteenth century and the first Jewish settlers arrived in the region of Vilnius more than six hundred years ago. According to unofficial sources, a firm Jewish presence in Vilnius was established in 1326. After the 1349 plagues and persecution in Western Europe many Jews moved to Czechia and Poland, and from there to Lithuania, seeking protection of the local princes.[1] The first documented mention of a Jewish community in Vilnius dates back to 1487. It is found in a draft of a title deed referring to a Jewish cemetery.[2] It is assumed that the first synagogue in Vilnius was built in 1440. However, only in 1573 were the Jews officially permitted to build a house of worship within the boundaries of the city.[3] In 1592 a street next to the synagogue was named "Zydowska," or Jewish Street. The same year the synagogue was damaged and partially destroyed in an assault by local tradesmen and hoodlums. In 1633 permission was granted to construct a new brick synagogue. By 1635 a new imposing structure, able to accommodate 3,000 worshippers, was erected. It has become known as the Great Synagogue.

Originally Jews in Lithuania enjoyed a considerable degree of religious and economic tolerance. They provided a useful service and the dukes and kings, with insignificant exceptions, were benevolent and sympathetic to the plight of their Jewish subjects. "In the 14th century Grand Duke Vytautas granted privileges to the Jews. They were made free and were accountable only to the grand duke."[4] Vytautas officially endorsed the existence of Jewish communities in the grand duchy and granted the Jews a charter which provided them with personal and religious security, and presented them with opportunities for economic growth.

The fortunes of the Jews in Vilnius were affected, however, by the constantly fluctuating political and economic conditions in the country and their treatment was often a reaction to internal pressures. Thus, enraged by Jewish competition, and fearful for their own well-being, gentiles often blamed Jews for all their afflictions. Accusations of ritual murder swept through the gentile community, time and again, and Jews were often the subject of looting, bloodshed, and murder. Gentile shopkeepers, workmen, and Jesuit students often joined hands with the city's rabble, in their attacks on synagogues and Jewish homes.

In 1527 King Sigismund I granted a charter to the burghers of Vilnius which prohibited Jews from living and trading in the city.[5] Several years later Sigismund I changed heart, and in 1533 issued a decree enjoining Lithuanian local authorities "to maintain the rights and liberties guaranteed to the Jews, and to lighten their heavy burden of taxation."[6] A new charter issued in 1633 by King Wladyslaw IV allowed Jews to reside in Vilnius and occupy themselves with commerce, trade, and crafts, but it also identified, for the first time, a special district where, ostensibly for their own safety and protection, Jews were advised to dwell.[7] Jewish residence, however, was not confined to this area only and gentiles were permitted to live in this so-called Jewish quarters.

In 1655 Vilnius was overrun by Muscovite and Cossack troops, and Jews were forced to leave in terror. Under temporary Russian rule, until 1661, no Jews were permitted in the city. Those who stayed behind were slaughtered pitilessly. The Cossacks set the city on fire, which raged for seventeen days. Most of the city, including the Jewish quarters, was destroyed by fire.[8]

Jewish life in Vilnius was managed by the so-called *Kahal*, or Jewish community council, which dealt with the gentile authorities, and collected taxes for the royal treasury. It was also in charge of internal community affairs, and it monitored the religious and moral behaviour of the city's Jewish population. The simple Jewish masses, however, showed little respect to the *Kahal*, because it was composed mainly of representatives of the upper classes. The *Kahal* in Vilnius joined the council of Lithuanian Jewish communities, established in 1623, and maintained contacts with Jewish people in other cities. In 1844 tsar Nicholas I dissolved the *Kahals* all over Russia and abolished the institution of Jewish self-rule in Lithuania.

In the 17-18th centuries the Jews of Vilnius were allowed to trade, peddle merchandise in the streets, and work as craftsmen. They could perform any type of work for fellow Jews, but when working for Christians they were restricted to specialized trades for which no guilds existed. On behalf of the nobles, they were permitted to deal in skins, fur, linen, silver, gold, and other commodities. They could also sell alcoholic beverages, but to Christians only in the cities and wholesale.[9] Some Jews were involved in money lending and import-export trade. Others served the nobles in the capacity of tax collectors and custom inspectors. A number of Jewish financiers and merchants became very prosperous, but most Jews were poor. They lived in the segregated and stifling quarters of the Jewish district, located in the narrow streets in the centre of the city, and close to a third of them received some kind of social assistance.

After the partition of the Polish-Lithuanian Kingdom the Jews of Vilna lived under tsarist rule. The Russian tsars were reactionary, intolerant, and fanatical foes of Jews and Judaism. Russia itself never had an indigenous Jewish population and Jews were usually driven out from areas conquered by the Russian army. In 1791 the Russian tsar Catherine II (1762-1796) established the Jewish pale of settlement in an area delineated by the boundaries of the former Polish kingdom. By 1794 all Jews in the Russian empire were confined to the pale of settlement and forbidden to own land. After 1795 the Jews of Vilna shared in many respects the fate of Russian Jews.

Life on the pale was isolated, stifling, and oppressive. It was particularly difficult under the rule of tsar Nicholas I (1825-1855) who was dubbed "the gendarme of Europe." Under his rule Russian youths were drafted into army service for twenty-five years. In 1827 an order was issued to conscript Jewish boys, at the age of twelve, for an additional six year period of preliminary cantonment before regular army service. The *Kahal* was usually given a quota, and it was supposed to provide the required number of Jewish recruits. Parents with money often saved their children from conscription by bribing local Jewish officials, but the total number of recruits was to be delivered regardless.[10] During the years of cantonment many Jewish youngsters were forcibly baptized. As they grew older some of the converts turned into rabid anti-Semites, and were used by the tsarist government to disseminate anti-Jewish propaganda.

The new tsar Alexander II (1855-1881) appeared to be more liberal. In 1856 he abolished the canton rule and military service was reduced to sixteen years for all conscripts. He refused, however, to dismantle the pale of settlement, or abrogate the restrictions established by his predecessors. And yet, large scale Jewish merchants, skilled artisans, and professionals with university education were permitted to move outside the pale. Some Jews were even granted the right to buy land.

Despite poverty and oppression Jewish life in Vilnius was intense and vigorous. Over the years the city became one of the most important centres of Jewish religious and secular learning in the world and many new settlers and migrants were attracted by local Jewish scholars and educational institutions. Since early in the seventeenth century Vilna has become known as the Jerusalem of Lithuania.[11]

The number of Jews in Vilna fluctuated over the years, yet in relative terms the Jewish population grew much faster than the city's total population. In 1645 Vilna and its suburbs were inhabited by 12,000 Christians and 2,620 Jews. In 1662, after the Russian Cossack invasion, only 415 Jews remained in the city. By the end of the eighteenth century almost 7,000 Jews resided in Vilna and its suburbs.[12] According to the official census of 1897, during the nineteenth century, the number of Jews in Vilna grew to 61,847 comprising 40 per cent of the city's total population.[13]

Vilnius was the home of the Gaon - or eminence - Elijah ben Solomon (1720-1797). He was a man of great intellectual prowess, highly versed in both talmudic and secular studies. The study of the Talmud has always been synonymous with pietism in the Jewish tradition. In the eighteenth century, in the oppressive conditions of life in Poland and the Ukraine, a new mystical movement, named *Hasidism* - from the Hebrew word *hasid*, pious or godly - pervaded the downtrodden Jewish settlements. It advocated the idea that fervent prayer was more important than study and that the unity with God was accomplished through the heart rather than the mind. *Hasidism* as such was not a theology, but rather an anti-intellectual way of life. It had a great following because it was easily accessible to simple and uneducated Jews, and it expressed the joy of life and prayer through song, dance, and common fraternal feeling.

The Gaon of Vilna regarded *Hasidism* as a threat to the Talmudic tradition, and became the leader of the so-called *Misnagdim*, or those who opposed *Hasidism*. Vilna was the centre of the struggle between these two groups, and in 1781 the Gaon reaffirmed the ban of *Hasidism*, and the excommunication of its followers. Despite this formal ban, however, *Hasidism* continued to flourish, and by the middle of the nineteenth century there were in Vilna various *Hasidic* congregations, tracing their roots to *Hasidic* rabbis in the small settlements on the Jewish pale such as Lubavich or Koidenov. It took a while before the internal schism in the Jewish community narrowed, and the adherents of *Hasidism* were recognized as a legal Jewish sect all over Russia.[14]

In the second half of the nineteenth century Jewish life in Russia was influenced by several contradictory factors. On the one hand, a degree of political and social liberalization was evident, and the Jewish upper classes benefited from this change in the socio-political climate. On the other, the few limited freedoms granted to the oppressed Jewish minority generated a new wave of xenophobia. The Russian ruling class still viewed Jews as aliens, while the middle class feared Jewish competition. Consequently, relative liberalization raised the social awareness of Jewish young people and many have become involved in radical political activity. Some joined the rapidly growing anti-tsarist revolutionary groups, while others linked their fate with the emerging Zionist movement.

The secularization of life in Vilna was influenced by the evolution of social democracy and populism within Russia proper, as well as by the development of west European humanism in general. It was also advanced by the so-called *Haskalah* movement which advocated enlightenment and modernism in Jewish life. The *Haskalah* fostered a return to the Hebrew language and aimed at introducing Jews to the culture and civilization of the western world. The literature of the *Haskalah* referred explicitly to the Jewish yearning for a return to Palestine. Judah L. Gordon (1830-1892), a native and resident of Vilna, was the greatest poet in Hebrew since the middle ages, and an influential figure in the *Haskalah* movement.[15]

Vilna was one of the main centres of the newly emerging Zionist activity in Russia. In 1889 a conference of *Hovevei Zion*, or the lovers of Zion, took place in the city. The members of this organization were the forerunners of modern Zionism. They advocated the use of Hebrew and *aliya*, or immigration, to Palestine. The founding conference of the Zionist religious organization *Mizrachi*, which later gave rise to the Jewish National Religious Party, gathered in Vilna in 1902,[16] and in 1903 a conference of *Poalei Zion*, or the Socialist Zionist Party, took place in the city. The same year Theodor Herzl, the father of modern Zionism, visited Vilna on his way to St. Petersburg. He was greeted enthusiastically by the Jews of Vilna, but was appalled by the poverty of most of them.[17] In 1905-1911 the Central Bureau of the Zionist Organization of Russia functioned in Vilna. In 1907 the tsarist government suppressed all Zionist activity, and all Zionist organizations were forced to operate clandestinely.

Vilna was the cradle of Jewish socialism. The first Jewish secret anti-tsarist revolutionary circle in Russia was established in a rabbinical seminary in Vilna. Many young Jews joined the ranks of the Russian socialist-revolutionary and social-democratic parties. Others had connections with outlawed terrorist and anarchist groups. Among the 566 defendants in political trials in Russia, between 1880 and 1891, 88 were Jews, or 15.5% of the total.[18]

In October 1897 a socialist union of Jewish workers, *Bund*, was established in Vilna. Its main purpose was to protect the rights of Jewish workers, and assist them in their struggle with their Jewish employers. Some of its members, however, followed in the steps of the violent adherents of Russian populism, and resorted to extreme terrorist measures. In May 1902, incensed by the brutality of Von Wahl, the governor of Vilna, Hirsh Leckert, a twenty-two-year-old shoemaker and a member of *Bund* fired several shots with the intent of killing the governor. Von Wahl was only slightly injured, but Leckert was tried, sentenced to death, and executed.[19]

The *Bund* opposed Zionism, and recognized Yiddish, rather than Hebrew, as the national language of the Jewish people. Initially, the *Bund* was part of the Russian social-democratic movement, led by V.I. Lenin, but it soon parted ways with the future Bolsheviks. It refused to relinquish its demands for Jewish national cultural autonomy which the Bolsheviks refused to grant. When the Bolsheviks gained power in Russia they outlawed the *Bund* in 1921 and purged most of its leaders.

At the dawn of the twentieth century Russia was in a state of turmoil. Industrial decline and agrarian riots increased discontent which resulted in renewed terrorism. Public unrest and a revolution that followed reached its peak in a general strike in October 1905 in St. Petersburg. The revolution ended in defeat, but it marked the beginning of constitutional government in Russia. An imperial manifesto proclaimed the inviolability of the principle of autocracy, announcing at the same time that a legislative assembly, the so-called Duma, elected by popular franchise would be summoned in the near future.

Five hundred twenty four deputies representing different Russian political parties were elected in 1906 to the first Duma. Among them were twelve Jews. One of them, Dr.Shmarya Levin, a well known preacher from Vilna, distinguished himself by his eloquence, but all efforts by Jewish deputies to improve the lot of the Jewish masses were in vain. P.A. Stolypin, Russia's Minister of Interior, did express a desire to abolish some of the less important legal restrictions on Jews, but tsar Nicholas II refused even to consider such a move. The first Russian Duma was soon dissolved. Four Jews were elected to the second Duma, but only two represented the large Russian Jewish community in the third and fourth Dumas. No wonder the Dumas produced no practical gains for the Jews of Russia.[20]

The outbreak of the First World War in 1914, and the ensuing hostilities between Russia and Germany, created new problems for the Jews of Vilna. Thousands of Jews served in the Russian army, yet they were abused, victimized, and accused of spying for the enemy. Moreover, they were under the constant threat of expulsion from the western regions of the Russian empire. No wonder some eagerly awaited the arrival of German troops, hoping that their lot would change for the better.

The German army occupied Vilna in September 1915, but high Jewish expectations were hardly met. The Germans repealed all anti-Jewish laws, but they were mainly preoccupied with the advancement of their own cause. The economic situation in the city was at that time extremely difficult and the Jewish community was ravaged by a typhoid epidemic raging in the city. Moreover, many Jews were conscripted to do forced labour in the coal mines of the Ruhr and Silesia regions in Germany. During the war the Jewish population of Vilna was decimated. It dropped from 98,700, its highest pre-war level in 1914, to 46,507 in 1919.[21]

Between the two world wars, under Polish sovereignty, the situation of Jews in Vilno was precarious. Some were successful merchants, manufacturers, and professionals, but most were poor blue-collar workers, petty shopkeepers, and artisans. Economic difficulties, including unemployment and business competition, stimulated anti-Jewish fervour. Influenced by the rise of Naziism in Germany, Polish neo-fascist political parties advocated the elimination of Jews from gainful employment. They attacked Jewish ritual methods of slaughtering cattle, called for a boycott of Jewish businesses, and incited thugs to desecrate synagogues, cemeteries, and destroy Jewish property.

Anti-Jewish discrimination in Vilno was vehement. The Polish civil service and the army officer corpus were virtually closed to Jews, and quotas for admission into certain professions and institutions of higher learning were established. Thus, the number of Jews admitted to Vilno university fluctuated from year to year, and it depended on the political and economic situation in the country. In 1932 4,553 attended the university. Among them were 1,209 Jews. By 1938, out of a total of 3,041 university students, the number of Jewish students dropped to 448.[22] Most Jewish students, however, were admitted to the faculties of law and humanities and an "unofficial" *numerus clausus* precluded their admission to the faculty of medicine and other attractive professional programmes.[23] In 1937 the Polish government acquiesced to the demands of neo-fascist students and authorized universities to segregate Jewish students from the rest. Special benches were placed at the left side of each classroom, thus creating ghettos for Jewish students all over the country.

Despite the economic difficulties and the lack of peace and stability in the city, Jewish social, political, and cultural life in Vilno was active and vibrant. The Jewish community council was in charge of Jewish life in the city, providing social services to the needy. The community, however, was fractured along party lines, and infighting between those representing different political and ideological trends was rife. The main discord was between the Zionists and the so-called Yiddishists, who were mainly socialists, non-religious and supported the cause of Jewish workers. There was even little uniformity within these two main groups. The Zionist movement was composed of a number of different factions such as the Revisionists, *Poalei Zion,* General Zionist, or *Mizrachi,* among others.

15

They were constantly squabbling about the future of the projected Jewish state, and about how the aim of building a national Jewish home was to be accomplished. Most Yiddishists belonged to the *Bund*, but some were members of the *Volkspartei*, the underground communist party, and other secular organizations.

Although Jewish cultural life in Vilno continued to be vigorous, yet, as in the previous centuries it remained insulated from outside influences. It drew its strength from within and from its connections and identification with other Jewish communities and organizations in Poland and all over the world. In 1919 the Jewish Historical and Ethnographic Society and Museum were founded in the city,[24] and in 1925 *YIVO*, or the Jewish Scientific Research Institute, was established in Vilno. The main purpose of *YIVO* was to assist in the revival of the Jewish national consciousness; the investigation of current Jewish cultural, national, and intellectual problems, as well as Yiddish linguistic studies. Albert Einstein and Sigmund Freud were honourary members of the *YIVO* presidium. In 1925 the Jewish Musical Institute commenced its activity in the city.

Between the two world wars the Jewish community of Vilno was served by several Jewish professional theatres, and many bands, choirs, and artistic lay groups sponsored by different Jewish institutions. Five publishing houses were active in the city, and three Jewish public libraries, as well as a number of smaller book lending institutions were in operation. Among them was the famous Strashun library, established in 1892, and named after the well known book collector Mathias Strashun (1817-1885) whose legacy, consisting of 7,000 rare volumes, formed the basis of the library's collection.[25] Six Yiddish and Hebrew newspapers, including *Undzer tog* (Our Day), *Ovent kurier* (Evening Courier), *Dos vort* (The Word), and *Vilner ekspres* (The Vilno Express) appeared in the city regularly.

Prior to the Second World War the Vilno community was served by more than a hundred orthodox synagogues and houses of worship of different sizes. Among them was the Great Synagogue, and the imposing Choral Synagogue on Zawalna (Pylimo, Komjaunimo) Street. Constructed in 1894 it was the only one to survive Nazi occupation and the onslaught of Soviet atheism. Synagogue facilities in Vilno were reserved for religious worship, study, and ritual functions only. Various social activities, instead, were centred at social, cultural, artistic, or sport organizations.

Since Polish state schools could hardly provide for the educational needs of Jewish children, an elaborate Jewish school network was set in operation. It reflected well the political split in the Jewish community. The few elementary state schools for Jewish children were supervised by Polish government authorities. Polish was the language of instruction and several hours each week were devoted to Jewish religious education. Most Jewish children, however, attended private elementary schools administered by various Jewish cultural, social, and religious institutions, or private individuals. In orthodox Talmud-Torahs religious instruction formed the core of the curriculum. In the religious schools of *Mizrachi* students were exposed to both Hebrew and Yiddish. In other Jewish elementary schools the language of instruction was Hebrew, Yiddish, or Polish respectively, depending on the political affiliation of the sponsors of a given school.

There were no state secondary schools for Jewish students in Vilno, and few Jews attended public high schools together with Polish students. Hence, most Jewish youngsters attended private secondary schools operated by Jewish institutions, or owned by Jewish business people.

Admission to state universities in Poland required a graduation diploma from a recognized secondary school. It was essential, therefore, that Jewish private secondary schools comply with the educational requirements of state authorities. Only graduates from schools granted full recognition by the state could be admitted to universities without special entrance examinations. Not all Jewish secondary schools, however, were granted full accreditation, and graduates of such schools were deprived of the possibility to attend university.

There were three basic secondary school varieties for Jewish students in the city. At the Vilno Real Gymnasium (1918-1941) the language of instruction was Yiddish. At the *Tarbut* (1916-1940) and *Tushiya* secondary schools it was Hebrew. In other schools, such as *Oswiata* or the one owned and administered by Epsztejn and Szpajzer, the language of instruction was Polish. Most of these schools followed official curricular requirements and adhered to the academic standards established by the government. Regardless of the language of instruction in a given school, subjects such as Polish language and literature, Polish history and geography were always taught in Polish. There were also in Vilno Jewish technical and vocational schools, catering to those who were seeking employment in trades and professions, a nursing training institute, Yiddish and Hebrew teachers seminaries, a school for mentally handicapped children, as well as ballet and music schools.

Most Jewish elementary schools were supported by the community at large, and education was free of charge. Some private elementary and most secondary schools charged tuition fees, and secondary education was accessible only to those who could afford it. Instructors for Jewish elementary schools were trained in appropriate Hebrew and Yiddish teachers seminaries, but those teaching at the secondary school level were usually university graduates. The academic level of instruction in Jewish secondary schools was relatively speaking very high, indeed. Since qualified Jewish educators, with graduate degrees from recognized universities, could seldom secure appropriate employment in educational institutions administered by the Polish government they were often forced to seek employment in Jewish schools.

Jewish sport clubs, such as *Maccabi*, *Jordan*, or *ZAKS* played an important role in tempering the bodies and spirit of Jewish young people. In addition to promoting fitness and competitive sports, these clubs served as gathering points for Jewish youths and as centres of social activity. It is interesting to note that the Vilno *Maccabi* sport club did not belong to the *Maccabi* World Union which advocated a Zionist approach to Jewish life and had branches all over the world. Instead, despite bearing a name with obvious historical connotations to the former Jewish state in Israel, Vilno *Maccabi* was controlled by Yiddishists and promoted anti-Zionist policies.

The Nazi invasion of Poland, in September 1939, transformed Jewish life in Vilno. Unexpectedly some 25,000 Jewish refugees arrived in Lithuania, of which 15,000 stayed in Vilno.[26] The Lithuanian government appeared to be tolerant to its national minorities, yet on 31 October 1939, several days after Vilno was transferred by the Soviets to Lithuanian jurisdiction, anti-Jewish riots were instigated by the anti-Semitic remnants of the former Polish regime.[27] Instead of helping to quell the disturbances the newly arrived Lithuanian police lent a helping hand to the culprits. The anti-Jewish riots were checked only by the arrival of Soviet tanks stationed at a nearby military base.

Soon the situation in the city stabilized and life assumed its natural course. The Lithuanian government in Kaunas treated the Jews of Vilnius with consideration and respect. It guaranteed them equality of rights and recognized the legal status of the Jewish municipal council. It prohibited, however, any political, business, or organizational activity of Jewish and other refugees from Poland. It appeared that, if only for a while, life in Vilnius was taking a turn for the better.

The incorporation of Lithuania into the USSR, in the summer of 1940, had far reaching consequences for the Jews of Vilnius. Many, in particular simple working people, were happy with their newly acquired ostensible freedom and equality and the alleged security provided by the virtue of becoming citizens of a powerful state such as the Soviet Union. But their hopes were short lived and they were able to enjoy these benefits only for a short while. Soon all forms of Jewish national, religious, and political expression were suppressed or banned all together. All Zionist societies were dissolved, and the activity of the *Bund* was prohibited. Jewish religious education and the teaching of Hebrew were forbidden. Moreover, in June 1941, a week before the Nazi invasion of the USSR, many Jewish community leaders were arrested. Soviet security units, assisted by local communists, rounded up successful business people, established professionals, and leaders of the local intelligentsia for deportation to Siberia. Trucks were roaming the streets of the city, evicting the so-called "enemies of the people," marked for banishment.

The German invasion of the USSR, on 22 June 1941, and the capture of Vilnius by Nazi troops two days later, stopped the purges, but it also changed the face of the city forever. It virtually wiped out part of its history. The Nazis, and their Lithuanian collaborators, poisoned the atmosphere and murdered the Jews. They tainted most of the population with the germ of hatred, xenophobia, and Jew baiting. Except for the few gentiles whose spirit remained pure, and who at the risk of personal life helped their haunted and downtrodden former neighbours, most resident of Vilnius were at best indifferent, while many cooperated with the oppressive regime.

NOTES

[1]. J. Jurginis,. V. Merkys, . A. Tautavicius, Vilniaus Miesto Istorija (Vilnius 1968), 58.

[2]. G. Agranovskii, and I. Guzenberg, Litovskii Ierusalim (Vilnius 1992), 4.

[3]. Ben-Zion Dinur, "The Jerusalem of Lithuania," inJerusalem of Lithuania, vol. 1, compiled by Leyzer Ran (New York 1974), XIX.

[4]. Jonas Zinkus, ed., Lithuania. An Encyclopedic Survey (Vilnius 1886), 43.

[5]. Israel Cohen, Vilna (Philadelphia 1992), 4

[6]. Ibid., 15.

[7]. Ibid., 30.

[8]. Masha Greenbaum, The Jews of Lithuania. A History of a Remarkable Community. 1316-1945 (Jerusalem 1995), 33-4.

[9]. Ibid., 29.

[10]. Howard Morley Sachar, The Course of Modern Jewish History (New York 1963), 86.

[11]. According to unofficial sources, in the middle of the seventeenth century, a delegation of rabbis from Vilnius presented the Rabbinical Council of Lithuania with a list of 333 scholars, residing in the city, who could recite the whole Talmud, including its commentaries, by heart. The senior rabbi of Lithuania was so impressed that he blessed Jewish Vilnius, and called it the Jerusalem of Lithuania. See Yerushalayim de'Lita, 1992, no. 4 (30), 2. According to another source "The expression [Jerusalem of Lithuania] is attributed to Napoleon who invoked it while [on a visit] to the capital of Lithuania." See Greenbaum, The Jews of Lithuania, 359.

[12]. Cohen, 99-100.

[13]. Jurginis, Merkys, Tautavicius, 304.

[14]. Sachar, 79-80.

[15]. Ibid., 207-8.

[16]. Encyclopaedia Judaica, vol. 16 (Jerusalem 1971), 147.

[17]. Greenbaum, 139-40.

[18]. Erich Haberer, Jews and Revolution in Nineteenth Century Russia (Cambridge 1995), 74-93.

[19]. Greenbaum, 150-1.

[20]. Sachar, 251-2.

[21]. Leyzer Ran, Jerusalem of Lithuania, 4.

[22]. Agranovskii, Guzenberg, 14.

[23]. Cohen, 391.

[24]. Encyclopaedia Judaica, vol. 16, 147.

[25]. Emanuelis Zingeris, "Knygu Hebraju ir Jidis Kalbomis Fondai Lietuvoje," Knygotyra (Vilnius 1987), no. 13 (20), 90-2.

[26]. Greenbaum, 289.

[27]. Algirdas Jakubcionis, "Lithuanian Attitudes Towards Jews, the Vilnius Ghetto, Its Inmates and Their Fate," in The Days of Memory, ed. by E. Zingeris (Vilnius 1995), 385.

C. THE CITY OF MY YOUTH

My personal life and that of my immediate family, composed of my parents and older sister, reflected well the general predicament of the Jewish community of Vilno. Born in 1894, my father Leo was a businessman. My mother Rose was two years younger. She was a housewife, helping father from time to time with his business affairs. My parents differed from each other in many ways. They had different tastes, attitudes, and views of life. I suspected that, as it was customary in those days, their marriage was arranged.

My father was a cosmopolitan modern worldly man. He liked to dress well, eat well, and always look his best. He went daily to the barber for a shave, wore a fashionable top hat, and carried a cane, not because he needed one, but because it was in vogue at that time. Having received his education in a Russian commercial school, father was considered a well educated man. He was a good provider, respected by his employees and associates in the business world, both Jewish and gentile. Father was always busy, preoccupied with business affairs and with himself. Except for providing for tuition in the private school which I attended, father seemed to have little interest in me or my education. That was mother's domain. Father never visited my school, nor did he ever speak to a teacher. The above notwithstanding, he was a dedicated son to his parents, and always concerned for the well being even of the extended family.

Mother was the opposite of my father. She spent most of her time at home. Family and the children were always at the centre of her attention. She was dedicated, hard working, persevering, but not very sentimental. The difference between my parents was apparently conditioned by their background and upbringing. My father represented the essence of refined city life, while mother hailed from the countryside.

My paternal grandparents, whose ancestors lived in Germany, were also business people. In their old age they moved in with us. That was the custom in those days. Children were supposed to look after their old and sick parents. The old age homes available then were only for the very poor and handicapped. Grandfather, an old man with a long grey beard, was a rabbinical scholar, always with a holy book in hand and preoccupied with study. Grandmother was the business woman who supported the family. She bore twelve children, nine of whom survived into adulthood.

The passing of my grandfather was my first close encounter with death. I was not even ten at that time. It brought home the devastating message that we were all mortal and that no one would last here forever. Both our paternal and maternal grandparents died in our home. We lived at that time in an apartment on Zawalna Street, just across the Jewish hospital and next to the Choral Synagogue. There were no Jewish funeral chapels in the city in those days and most funeral rites were usually performed in the private residence of the deceased. When grandfather died the table in our dining room was removed and his body was laid out on the floor and covered with a black sheet. Burning candles were placed around his head. The dining room was full of people, coming and going. Several men were hired to read from the book of Psalms, day and night.

It was the custom of Jews in those days that announcements about someone's death were placed in local Jewish newspapers and notices were posted on bill-boards all over the city. They informed the public, in Yiddish and Polish, of the name, age, and position, if any, of the deceased, and about the time and location from where the funeral procession was to follow. There were no special buses, or cars, for the transportation of the demised. The coffin was usually placed on a special funeral carriage and drawn by a single horse. The bereaved family and friends followed on foot to the outskirts of the city where the Jewish cemetery was located. There the corpse was washed, dressed in a white linen robe, and prepared for final internment. There were no speeches or sermons at the cemetery, just the traditional mourners prayer, the *Kadish*. According to tradition a small sack with sand, from the Holy Land, was placed in the grave to symbolize the unity of the Jews in the diaspora with the land of their forefathers in Israel. The simple wooden box was then lowered into the grave and family members covered it with earth. There were no excavating machines or mechanical shovels at the cemetery, in those days, and all work, summer or winter, was performed by hand. After my grandfather's funeral most family members returned to our apartment where they spent together a week of mourning, or the so-called *Shiva*.

John Steinbeck once said that "death is a personal matter, arousing sorrow, despair, fervour, a dry-hearted philosophy. Funerals, on the other hand, are social functions." When I compare the funerals of my grandparents with those I have attended in North America I have come to realize how much the world has changed, indeed. Grief caused by the loss of a loved one is always the same, but today social convention, influenced by technological progress, have affected, and even trivialized, the substance of ritual. Today beautiful funeral chapels cater to every whim of those attending. Highly paid professional clerics deliver impressive eulogies, hailing the achievements of individuals who they likely have never met while they were alive. A cortege of luxury limousines, even for people without adequate financial means, whisks away the demised with his or her family members to the cemetery, and in no time the ceremony is over. The social setting of this ceremony, however, which often invades the privacy of those bereaved, is not always conducive for the process of healing.

After grandfather's death our paternal grandmother continued to live with us. Shortly after she became afflicted by the total loss of memory. On some Friday nights, when everyone was ready for the festive dinner, she would calmly walk into the dining room wondering why everyone was ready to start the meal before grandfather returned from the synagogue. At other instances we, the children, would unearth, hidden under grandmother's bed, boxes with money printed by the Kerenski regime which ruled Russia between the February and October revolutions of 1917. The bank-notes were worthless and we liked to play with them. Yet grandmother believed that they were still good and she would chase us to get the new crisp notes back.

Grandmother died several years after her husband's death, and the funeral procedure changed little. After her death our large apartment seemed empty, but only for a while. In the late 1930s our family experienced directly the first effects of Nazi rule in Germany. In October 1938, 12,000 German Jews, with former Polish roots, were suddenly rounded up, packed into vans and trains, and dumped on the German-Polish border. The family of our grandmother's younger brother, who was born and lived all his life in Germany, was expelled to Poland. One day he, his wife, and daughter, turned up unexpectedly at our doorsteps in Vilno. We took them in, and cared for them. When the Germans captured Vilnius, in June 1941, the old couple perished in one of the early anti-Jewish actions. Their daughter, however, did manage to escape just before the arrival of the Nazis. Grandmother's brother belonged to the well known clan of the Frankfurter family, and relatives in America helped our cousin evade disaster by arranging for her entry visas to the Dutch colony Curacao and the USA. A transit visa through Japan was supplied by the Japanese Consulate in Lithuania. S.Ch. Sugihara, Japan's war time consul in Kaunas, disobeyed the orders of his own government and issued several thousand transit visas to Polish and Lithuanian Jews who tried to escape the impending Nazi invasion. Initially Sugihara was punished by the Japanese government for ignoring its orders. Only after Sugihara's death, in 1986, was an official apology offered to his widow for the maltreatment of her family. Israel honoured Sugihara in 1985, and in 1992 a street was named in Vilnius in honour of this Japanese diplomat.

The Frankfurters lived with us for three years. We looked at them with amazement. They represented a different civilization. To us being Jewish meant speaking Yiddish and being orthodox meant wearing traditional garb. The Frankfurters, instead, were observant orthodox Jews, but spoke only German. Their clothes were always modern and stylish, different from those worn by religious Jews in Vilno.

Our home was traditional, but not very religious. My father promised our grandfather, before the latter's death, that he will attend synagogue on Saturdays, and he kept his word. Most of the time he would take me along. We belonged to a small congregation of the Koidenov *Hasidim*. The prayer house was in the so-called *schul-hoif*, or the courtyard occupied by many small synagogues, located next to the Great Synagogue, on Niemecka, or German, Street. Mother maintained a kosher kitchen and all holidays were observed in proper tradition. For Passover there were special dishes and cutlery. On *Yom Kipur*, or day of atonement, everybody would fast. Adhering to tradition, and out of respect to the passing generation, my parents did the best to keep their Jewish heritage alive. Yet they refused to obey many strict orthodox laws which were part of the daily existence of our grandparents. My father, for example, was addicted to tobacco and could not abstain from smoking on the Sabbath.

Our mother's background differed greatly from that of our father's. Our maternal grandparents lived in the countryside. Even their surname, Chlavnovich, had a peasant ring. They lived in the small town of Taboryszki, some forty kilometres south-east of Vilno. The population of this town was composed of close to a dozen Jewish families. Their houses were located around the market place. The Catholic Church and the priest's household occupied a central position in town. The villages in the vicinity were inhabited by Polish and Belorussian peasants. Nearby there was an estate of the Polish nobleman, Wazynski, and a water mill. The Jewish inhabitants of Taboryszki were storekeepers, tradesmen, and farmers. They served the needs of those living in the adjoining villages.

Grandfather owned two houses. In one, the most imposing two storey wooden structure in town, lived my grandparents. The other was occupied by mother's sister, Fania, her husband Solomon, and their small daughter. Grandfather operated a general store, located in the bigger house. He also had a license to sell alcohol which was sold from another store in the smaller house. In Poland the state had a monopoly on the sale of liquor and only those with special permits could distribute and sell it. It was a lucrative business since only a limited number of licences were issued. The liquor store in Taboryszki was the only one selling alcoholic beverages in the vicinity. My grandfather was not only a businessman, but also a farmer. He owned land, horses, cows, and poultry. The farm produced wheat, fruit, and vegetables for the whole family, as well as for sale. I still could remember the taste of the freshly baked huge loafs of dark rye bread, the home made white cheese, or the sauerkraut delivered regularly to our house in Vilno.

Jewish life in Taboryszki had a peculiar flavour. Most Jews were not strictly observant. They were apparently not very educated nor were they preoccupied with study. Yet, on Saturdays, all stores were closed and everybody seemed to rest. There was no synagogue in town, because the community was too small to support one, but each Saturday all Jewish males would gather in a private house for prayers.

In our childhood, I, my sister, and my cousins would spend summers in Taboryszki. It was a happy, carefree time. Life was simple in the countryside. We even enjoyed the lack of city amenities. There was no electricity, no running water, and only one telephone in the local post office, but the fresh air was unpolluted and felt good. The food was wholesome, and we were free to roam the unobstructed stretches of land and forests. Life in Taboryszki moved slowly. People were never in a hurry, most were used to their monotonous life and were satisfied with their lot. My maternal grandparents lived a long life. In old age, when they were getting ill, they would come to Vilno for medical treatment and stay with us for long periods of time. Both died before the war. They were spared the torture and anguish which was soon to become the lot of most Jewish inhabitants of Taboryszki.

My childhood and youth were uneventful. I grew up surrounded and sheltered by family and friends, yet I had ample opportunity, prompted by my inquisitiveness, to explore the world around and learn first hand, early in life, about the intricacies of national and political interrelationships. I attended the *Tarbut* elementary and secondary schools. A high-school diploma in Poland usually required twelve years of study. The school year lasted close to ten months. We attended classes six days a week, from Sunday to Friday. Discipline at school was strict and the curriculum set. All subjects were compulsory and there were no elective courses. We studied four languages: Polish, Hebrew, English, and Latin. Mathematics, physics, and chemistry, as well as history and geography, were compulsory subjects. Labour and physical education were also part of the curriculum. Before entering grade eleven each student was supposed to determine the course of his future education. In the last two years of study classes were divided into two distinct streams, each with a different curriculum. In one stream the humanities and social sciences were emphasized. In the other one, the stress was on the study of mathematics and the sciences. The language of instruction at our school was Hebrew. By the time I was in grade six I spoke it fluently. The academic standards at our school were very high. Students were expected to work hard. There were six to seven forty-five minute class sessions daily, and several hours of homework in addition. Many of our teachers were advanced scholars with Ph.D. degrees from recognized universities. Upon my arrival to North America I was pleased to learn that Dr. Abraham Melezin, my former geography teacher from *Tarbut*, was a Professor at New York City University.

Religion was not a part of the curriculum at our school. Growing up in Vilno I came to realize that religious practice was not a subject that could, or should, be taught at school. The skills of prayer and ritual should be acquired by practical application, fostered by upbringing, rather than by theoretical deliberation at school. Moreover, if home and school promote different educational philosophies and values there is a danger that students may turn into hypocrites early in life. There were no prayer books in our school and no religious services were ever conducted there. Yet, every student understood the language of prayer, and could easily relate to its meaning. That was particularly important, because in those days there were no bilingual prayer books in Vilno, neither were there any conservative or reform congregations. Anything in a prayer book, written in a language other than Hebrew, was regarded as sacrilege.

At school we studied Jewish history, Hebrew literature, the Pentateuch, the Prophets and various commentaries as historical documents rather than holy texts. We did not wear any head covers at school, but were required to put on our caps when religious texts were studied. Our school was Zionist in spirit, but no single political ideology was promoted. Everyone was free to join any group of his or her political choice. Some students belonged to the leftist *Hashomer Hatsair*, others to the conservative *Betar* or *Masada*. The pupils at *Tarbut* were required to speak only Hebrew to each other. The biggest enemy of our Hebrew teachers was the Yiddish vernacular. An organization at school called *B'nei Yehuda*, or the sons of Judah, promoted the use of Hebrew. Its members were obligated to speak only Hebrew to any one who knew the language. The membership in that organization was voluntary, yet those who refused to join could expect little mercy from the teachers of Hebrew language and literature. Our teachers were highly idealistic individuals. Their main objective was to instill in us Jewish Zionist values by identifying with the land of Israel, and the language and culture of our forefathers. In fact, while I was a student of *Tarbut* several of our teachers, including our principal Dr. Shuster, departed for Palestine. In retrospect, I appreciate the efforts of our Hebrew teachers. I have come to realize that it is impossible to retain, for long, language skills learned but not practised. In those days, however, we detested the students who were snooping around and informing the teachers that we were talking Yiddish to each other, instead of Hebrew.

Most students attending our school belonged to the Jewish middle-class. Yet many had difficulty with coming up in time with the tuition fees which were relatively high and due monthly. In the beginning of each month the teacher of the early morning class would enter the class-room with a list of those who were behind with their payments. Rather crudely he would call out their names and send them to the school office. There they were asked to remind their parents about the outstanding debt and then given a note permitting to return to class. In case there was a long delay in settling an account a student was usually removed from class and sent home. Some pupils never returned to school, an indication that private education was beyond the means of a given family. This was a harsh and humiliating experience. Despite the fact that it was the responsibility of parents, rather than children, to make sure that tuition fees were paid in due time, children from poor families were approached directly to be reminded, in the beginning of each month, of their poverty. There was no intent to spare the students from an awareness of the harsh realities of life, and of the sacrifices their parents were making in order to provide them with a good education. Moreover, Jewish private schools operated on stringent budgets. School offices were poorly staffed, and there was little money to spare on non-academic expenditures such as administration, including mail and telephone expenses. Besides, few parents had telephones in those days to be contacted directly.

Secondary education at *Tarbut* was a privilege rather than a right. It was logically structured, consistent, and with a purpose. Discipline, personal responsibility, and respect for the teacher were important components of the learning process. The school was little interested in catering to the students' whims. Few parents questioned in those days whether the children were happy or depressed, whether they enjoyed study and the school environment or not. The objective of the school was to provide its pupils with a set of skills and values and it was the responsibility of the students to absorb as much as they could. The school was mainly concerned with the preparation of Jewish youngsters for a difficult and unpredictable future. It is worth mentioning that the institutions of guidance counsellor, or school psychologist, were non-existent in those days. Few students were prepared to seek outside help for their emotional or psychological problems anyway, because it could imply inadequacy and inferiority. Harsh life and experience were the real teacher.

It took many years before I could truly appreciate the level and value of education provided by the *Tarbut* school system. For close to twenty years, until 1958, living under Nazi and Soviet rule, I have not heard a spoken Hebrew word. Nor did I have any opportunity to read or write in Hebrew. Upon my arrival to Canada, however, I was surprised at the ease with which I soon recovered my forgotten language skills. It did not take long before my proficiency in Hebrew was adequate to become first a teacher and, later, a principal of a Hebrew school. We were taught in *Tarbut* the modern dialect of Sephardic Hebrew which was widely used in Israel. I recall how on my first visit to Israel in 1971 the stewardess, on an El-Al plane, refused to give me a tourist custom declaration form. Judging by my fluency in Hebrew she suspected that I was a former Israeli citizen presently living abroad.

The school was not the only source of my education. We lived in a multinational, cosmopolitan environment. The cultural atmosphere reigning in the city, with its historical past, characterized by a constant transition of rulers, made a great impact on most city inhabitants. Each generation, in the same family, was exposed to a variety of different cultural, social, and historical influences. Each generation benefitted from the education and experience of children and parents. The young generation inherited a mixture of old skills, values, and habits, from parents and grandparents. These, in turn, were combined with a new culture, language and history advanced by those currently in power. My father, myself, and my daughter Rose, were born in the same city, but in three different countries. My father was born in Russia when the city was called Vilna. I was born in Poland when its name was changed to Wilno (Vilno), while my daughter was born in the city of Vilnius, the capital of Soviet Lithuania. Each of us grew up in a different environment, and each attended a school with a different language of instruction. At home, however, the young absorbed parts of the cultural heritage of their parents and grandparents, combining it with the fruits of their own education and modern world view.

Historical circumstances have forced me to become a polyglot while still a child. I grew up speaking fluently half a dozen different languages. My parents were educated in Russia and they spoke to the children Russian. My grandparents preferred Yiddish, the language spoken by most Jewish people in town. Hebrew was the language I mastered at school. Yet Polish was the official language of the state. It was taught in all schools and everyone was required to know it. In the late 1930s, even before the Nazis had managed to occupy our city, I was impelled to learn German because that was the only language our relatives, exiled from Germany, could speak. Late in 1939, after Vilno was incorporated into Lithuania, Lithuanian has become the official language. It was taught in all schools and we were compelled to become fluent yet in another language.

Many Jewish youngsters in Vilno had accomplished, prior to the war, the difficult and enviable task of mastering half a dozen different languages without ever taking an advanced formal language study course. Before the

29

end of the war, in 1945, when I served as a soldier in the Soviet army, one senior officer suspected that I was a foreign spy. How otherwise, he wondered, could anyone be fluent in so many languages without having ever attended university. The officer in question was not the only one puzzled by our educational background and upbringing. Only those familiar with the history of Vilno could appreciate the breath of cultural, social, and religious knowledge to which we were exposed.

School and family provided us with emotional support and a sense of security. They could not protect us, however, from the alien world and hostile environment which we faced every time we ventured outside our sheltered surroundings. Jewish young people in Vilno were never a part of the general community at large. Even those who attended Polish state schools, and lived in districts inhabited mostly by gentiles, were ostracized and isolated. There were in Vilno assimilated Jews who regarded themselves as Poles of the faith of Moses. There were, however, few Jewish converts to Christianity and not many mixed marriages. Yet, even those who consciously decided to abandon their attachment to Judaism had difficulty in becoming integrated into the gentile community and were seldom accepted with open arms. It was not solely a matter of religion. Race, ethnic background, and mentality determined one's place in society. It was not easy for any Jew by birth to conceal his true identity. Non-Jewish inhabitants of Eastern Europe had an uncanny ability of recognizing a Jew even in disguise. The nineteenth century Russian genius, F. Dostoevsky, once suggested that a Jew could always be identified by the sight of eternal affliction in his eyes.

Jews lived in Poland for centuries, and were the only non-Slavic major national minority group in the country. They had a distinct appearance, not altered yet by the effects of inter-marriage. Their life, isolated from outside influences, fostered a peculiar mentality, and fomented a mark on their facial features. These were the reasons why Jews had a hard time in escaping Nazi persecution. It was almost impossible for a Jew to assume a different, non Jewish identity. Local gentiles could spot a Jew from a distance without difficulty and when they did, in many instances, they betrayed the Jew to the Nazis.

Before the war Jews were free to live in any part of the city, yet most inhabited an area in which there were few gentiles. Thus, for example, except for the janitor, not a single non-Jewish family lived in our apartment house. The same was true of most other houses in the same district. Jews occupied a well defined part of the city in which they felt safe. But as soon as a Jew ventured outside its limits he or she was vulnerable to taunts, insults, and even physical abuse.

30

There were instances of violence against Jews in Vilno, perpetrated by Polish youths and representatives of local nationalistic and fascist organizations. In some cases, such assaults assumed the form of pogroms. A boisterous mob would invade the Jewish district, break windows, destroy property, loot Jewish stores, and strike down anyone on its way. The Polish police seldom interfered and the attackers usually had a free hand in their pernicious endeavours. Sometimes Jewish youngsters, as well as the so-called Jewish "strong men," or fearless members of the criminal underground, would come out from hiding to face the attackers head on. In one such violent skirmish, on 10 November 1931, the Polish student St. Waclawski was stoned to death. It was a hint that fascist thugs could no longer victimize the Jewish community without endangering their own safety.

The dead student became a martyr. The annual commemoration of his death often gave cause to new pogroms and violent attacks on the Jewish people. Gangs of students and hooligans roamed the street in search of victims, destroying everything in sight. We lived in the 1930s on the second floor of a four-storey apartment building. During one of such pogroms some of our windows were shattered, and our balcony was littered with cobble-stones. My father had a hand gun which he kept hidden at home. I did not know whether he had an official permit to carry it, but I saw how during one of the pogroms he grabbed the gun and rushed to face the attackers. Mother entreated him to relent. Everybody knew that a new Waclawski would bring only new suffering to the Jews of Vilno.

Different segments of the Jewish population reacted to the realities of life in a hostile environment in different ways. Religious Jews tried to protect their spiritual and physical existence by total isolation. They avoided any contact with non-Jews. Assimilated Jews tried to escape their Jewish identity by pretending that they were little different from their Polish neighbours. Such claims, however, were usually resented by their gentile compatriots. Most Jews had no choice but to accept the realities of life as an alien minority in an unfriendly environment. The antagonism between the Jewish minority and the Polish majority was exacerbated by the fact that they lived in one city, and in one country, but in two different worlds. Except for limited economic interaction they had little contact, and even less in common with each other.

My first close exposure to non-Jewish youths dates back to 1938 when, at the age of thirteen, I became actively involved in sport competition. I learned early in childhood to skate, ski, swim, and ride a bicycle. I was skating and skiing, together with other youngsters, on the street, and on the playground in front of our house. The skates or skis were usually attached

31

to ordinary walking shoes and could be removed at any moment without difficulty. We had no special outfits for outdoor activity, but life hardened us, and we endured the bitter cold without a murmur. In the summer we would gather on Saturdays with friends and go to one of the beaches on the shore of the Vilja river to bathe, play, and swim. It was often difficult to avoid the attention of our fathers who expected us to join them in the Sabbath morning synagogue services. But Saturday was the only free day we had, since all Jewish schools were open six days a week. Physical activity and outdoor games were an important part of my life. It was a domain which not my parents, nor the parents of my friends, showed much interest in. Luckily neither did they bother to interfere. It was perhaps the only area of activity where Jewish youngsters were given so much freedom. It was of particular significance to us in the summer, since we had a lot of free time, and summer camps were not available to unaffiliated youths.

My involvement in a variety of sport activities affected negatively my school work, for I had little time for study and the preparation of my homework. My home room and Polish literature teacher, Ms. Winter, dubbed me "the May student," or one of those who began studying in May, just before the end of the school year. As a "May student" I was desperate to catch up with the backlog of work, and somehow pass into the next grade. My parents were not happy about the situation. Mother tried to pressure me and force me to work harder, but with little success. By the middle of 1938 I was a member of the school basketball team, and I joined the sport club *Jordan*.

In the spring of 1938 the *Jordan* junior basketball team managed to advance into the final round of the city championship competitions. The other team in the finals was *Ognisko*. It represented the local Polish railway workers. The first game was played at our home court and we won. The second final game, which was to decide the championship, was played at the *Ognisko* premises, located in an area seldom frequented by Jews. We arrived at the cite of competition in good time, but the place was already full of spectators. There was no one, however, to support our team. No Jewish youngster would venture into this lion's den. As soon as the game began shrieks, taunts, and intimidation followed. Young thugs with knives positioned themselves just behind the basket stand of our opponents and threatened us as soon as we tried to score a point. During the game neither the referees, nor the policemen present, tried to introduce some semblance of order in this "sport competition." After the game, however, when the *Ognisko* team and fans celebrated their victory, they escorted us into an area of relative safety.

The *Jordan* basketball team usually practised in our school gym, late in the evening, after the boxers of *Jordan* would complete their work-out. One evening all members of our basketball team decided to try their luck at boxing. It did not take long before most abandoned that sport. I decided to stay on. I was attracted to boxing by the sheer fact that I was more successful at it than my physically stronger friends and peers. My physical qualities were unimpressive. I was small. My height never reached above 1.70 m. or 5'8", and my weight at that time was just over 50 kg., or close to 120 lb., but I was agile and fast, and my reflexes were good.

My parents did not know that I became a boxer, actively participating in competition. When mother would ask what caused my black eye I would reply that I had a fight at school. Mother would go to school to complain to my teachers, but no culprit could ever be found. Once, one of my father's business associates, a fan of boxing, asked father whether he was proud of his son's accomplishments in the ring. My surprised father came home and relayed the "good" news to mother. After a long interrogation, and much pressure, they realized that there was no way of stopping me at that stage of the game. They decided that one day my opponents will punish me so badly that I will abandon the sport of my own free volition. They were mistaken. Boxing became a part of my life and a school that taught me many important survival skills.

Boxing may be dangerous and the sight of blood unappealing, yet the training process provides for excellent all-round physical and mental development of body and mind. A boxer in the ring is a lonely creature always left to himself, and defeat in the ring is always connected with physical pain and a sense of shame. Boxing tempered my body and strengthened my spirit. It taught me to muster, at times of need, all my hidden inner physical and mental resources in order to overcome adversity during the years of war and Nazi occupation.

My first appearance in formal competitions took place in 1938. I was then not even fourteen. I soon was paired with much older boxers. I won most of my early fights, but victory did not come easily. With speed, maneuverability, and good defence skills I had to make up for what I lacked in age, physical strength, and endurance. My success in the ring turned me into an instant hero in the Jewish community. I was nicknamed "Joe Louis," after the famous American heavy weight, who in a fight for the absolute world championship defeated, on 22 June 1938, the representative of Nazi Germany Max Schmelling.

Life at school became easier as well. My teacher of Latin, Mr. Spiro, for example, inquired one day whether I was related to the boxer Shneidman. When I told him that I was the fighter in question, he asked me for a ticket to the next boxing competition. I did not know whether he came to see me fighting, but from that day on he always gave me good marks — which I seldom deserved — without ever testing my knowledge of Latin in class. Years later I blamed Mr. Spiro for my inadequate proficiency in Latin.

Participation in competition with non-Jewish opponents exposed me directly to a new and hostile world about which I heard, but was not familiar with. Non-Jewish spectators at boxing matches often gave vent to their nationalistic and anti-Jewish sentiments, and it was difficult to ignore the loud and continuous shrieks "strike the Jew." Jewish viewers, on the other hand, kept a low profile, and seldom dared to support openly a Jewish athlete. They were careful not to enrage their Polish antagonists who were always ready to avenge the defeat of a Polish boxer, and take it out on those who backed his opponent. There were instances, during or after sport competitions, when Jewish boys were beaten up by Polish hoodlums, and the police would look the other way. By 1939 I was well known among the Polish sport fans. After I fought a draw with their hero, Lendzin, the best internationally acclaimed boxer in Vilno and one of the best bantam weights all over Poland, I gained their recognition. When I walked the streets of the city Polish youngsters recognized me instantly and showed respect.

The school year in Vilno started on 1 September. In August 1939, just before I reached the age of fifteen, I was invited to participate in a special training camp for promising boxers from all over Poland. It was to take place on the outskirts of the town Grandzicze, near the city of Grodno on the Nieman river, some 150 km from Vilno. I was the youngest participant and the only Jew in the camp. We lived in tents, worked hard, and I felt comfortable in this new environment. Late in August things began to change. Getting up in the morning we would notice that some older boxers were missing from our tents and we wondered about their disappearance. On 1 September 1939 everything became clear. Nazi Germany invaded Poland and, in anticipation of war, the Polish government began to mobilize its reserves. Those disappearing from our tents were young man of call-up age summoned to join their military units.

It took several days before I was able to leave the camp and move back in the direction of Vilno. Cities, bridges, and roads were bombed by the German air force, and travel in any direction was extremely dangerous. Wherever possible railway trains continued to move, but they were crowded, slow, and unreliable. On my way home I used different means of transportation and also walked for miles along the highway. My parents were in despair. There was no one who knew anything about my fate, or could tell them something about my whereabouts. War disrupted lines of communication and subverted the work of state and social institutions. It took days before I managed to return to Vilno. Upon my arrival I realized that things were changing swiftly. The city was exposed to several air attacks. Polish army detachments were abandoning the city in a hurry, moving away in an unknown direction. The front was approaching rapidly and the old system of government was disintegrating. The Jewish people were in a frenzy. Everyone desperately wanted to do something, or rush somewhere, which was both aimless and undefinable. Everyone was afraid of the Nazi onslaught, but no one knew what to do, or how to protect oneself. The actions of most were fostered by fear and lacked logic. Smart people, successful in life, appeared helpless in this new situation. I was surprised by this upheaval. I hardly recovered from my arduous trip home when the whole world around me seemed to be falling apart.

Most Jews greeted the appearance of Soviet troops on the streets of Vilno, in September 1939, with a sigh of relief. For all practical purposes the war was over for us. It was clear that, at least for a while, we were spared the calamity of Nazi occupation which faced the rest of Polish Jewry. The arrival of Soviet officials and the presence of the Red Army exposed us directly to communist rule. We were of course impressed by the Soviet tanks and by the alleged strength of the Soviet army, but we were amazed by the outlandish way Soviet officials and their families were dressed, and by the general ignorance of Soviet soldiers and officers. Many jokes sprung up in those days in the city, ridiculing the new arrivals. It was obvious that they were brainwashed. Their superiors prepared them appropriately for the task of facing the capitalist world. They were instructed to praise the Soviet state, and stress its superiority over other systems of government. It became, however, soon apparent that the living standards, to which we were accustomed in impoverished Poland, were much higher than those existing in the USSR.

Soviet soldiers exhibited a strange fascination with hand watches and everyone wanted to have one. The few watches in the possession of soldiers were huge in size and ugly. We called them "onions." Local kids spared no effort to unearth any available old or damaged watch and sell it to an eager Soviet buyer. In no time the soldier in question would find out that he was cheated. The old watches looked appealing, but they were seldom in good working order. When Soviet soldiers were asked about life in the Soviet Union, they were always ready with positive replies. To the question whether all people in the Soviet Union had watches, a soldier would usually reply that several new watch manufacturing plants had just been constructed and there were more watches in the country than required. To the question whether bananas were available in the USSR the same soldier would reply, without hesitation, that there was an abundance of bananas, because just recently a new banana factory had been set in operation.

Local youths had fun in their dealings with the Soviet soldiers. Our parents, instead, had difficulty in adopting to the new conditions of life. Local communists came out from hiding, infiltrated the new local administration and police and, with the support of the new Soviet officials, started to put political and economic pressure on local business people, storekeepers, and former political adversaries. Fortunately the Soviets did not stay long enough to do much damage. Several weeks after their arrival they departed, handing over the city and vicinity to the independent state of Lithuania. Many, in particular Jewish communists, preferred to live under Soviet rule, and they left the city together with the departing Soviet army. They moved eastward and most of them settled in Soviet Belorussia. On their way out from the city, the Soviets took possession of and moved to the USSR, anything of particular value to the Soviet state. Thus, for example, they disassembled the radio manufacturing plant "Elektrit," the largest and best known factory of that kind in Poland, and moved it together with its workers to the city of Minsk.

The arrival of the new Lithuanian administration did not bode well for the Jews of Vilno. It started with an anti-Jewish pogrom initiated by local anti-Semitic thugs. We looked at our new rulers with amazement. We did not know their language, nor did we know much about their customs or history. In Poland everything connected with the Lithuanian people, or their history, was taboo. Until then tiny Lithuania was usually pictured in the Polish press as an enemy of the Polish people. According to unofficial data some 5,000 Lithuanians lived in Vilno before the war. They usually kept a low profile. But there was one Lithuanian secondary school, named after Grand Duke Vytautas, a clear indication that there was in the city a sizeable Lithuanian community. It was evident to anyone that in Poland the Lithuanian minority was discriminated against. Once, in the late 1930s, an anti-Lithuanian demonstration was organized in the city. Students from all secondary schools, including Jewish and Lithuanian schools were to participate in this public display of political expression. It was a cruel joke on the part of the local Polish authorities. Young Lithuanians were forced to demonstrate against their own brethren and motherland.

It did not take long for the new Lithuanian administration to take charge of its newly acquired territories. The city was renamed to Vilnius, and the names of most streets were changed as well. Most street names, connected with Polish history and Polish personalities, were replaced by appropriate names of Lithuanian historical and cultural significance. Other names, without political meaning, were just translated into Lithuanian. The new names were difficult to pronounce, and for a while had little meaning for us.

The name of the main street in Vilnius reflected the changing political and geographic situation of the city over the years, and illustrated the effect of the transition of power on life in the city. Thus, under the rule of Russian tsars the main street was called Georgievskii Prospekt, or George Boulevard. The Polish rulers renamed it to Adam Mickewicz Street. In September 1939 the temporary Soviet Belorussian administration changed its name to Lenin Street. Several weeks later the Lithuanians renamed it in turn to Gedimino Street. In 1940, with the incorporation of Lithuania into the USSR, the name of the main street was changed again to Lenin Street. Under German rule it was called Gedimino again, and after the war it was renamed, first to Stalin Street, and later to Lenin Street. Today it is again Gedimino Street.

The transfer of the city to Lithuanian jurisdiction was connected with the arrival of Lithuanian police and military units, as well as with the influx of many civilians from Lithuania proper. Lithuanian policemen represented an impressive force. They were all strong and tall. We dubbed them the 1.80 met., or six feet, ones. The army units, on the other hand, failed to impress us. After the Polish cavalry and the huge Soviet tanks, Lithuanian mechanized vehicles looked like toy cars. The youngsters in the city joked that the crew of a Lithuanian tank was composed of seventy-one men: one was riding inside, while seventy others were pushing it from the outside. Life under Lithuanian rule soon settled into a peaceful routine, little different from life before the war. Lithuania was at that time a small, but well managed country. Its agriculture produced more than its population could consume, and for close to a year we lived in relative peace, away from both the Nazi menace, and our new Soviet "friends."

The 1939-40 school year exposed us to major changes in our course of study. Hebrew remained the language of instruction at our school, but Polish language, literature, and history were replaced by Lithuanian language and history. We were soon amazed to learn that the history of our city was allegedly different from what we were taught, over the years, by our Polish teachers. In fact the same teachers began telling us a different story.

In the summer of 1940 things began to change drastically again! Lithuania became a Soviet republic and the streets of Vilnius were again inundated by Soviet soldiers and officials. The names of the streets were changed again, and new social and state institutions replaced the old ones. It was again a time when it was good to be poor and downtrodden. Local communists came out from hiding again and assisted the new administration in nationalizing all property, and arresting representatives of opposing political parties. The irony of fate played a sad joke on many local

Jews. They were oppressed all their lives by the former regime, yet when the Soviets arrived many of them were looked down upon and tyrannized by the new rulers, only because they were not destitute and managed to make a meagre living. In practice national hatred, fuelled by animal instincts, is little different from class oppression, generated by ideological conviction. But the latter is more dangerous, because it is rationalized and sophisticated, and it is instigated and supported by the regime in power.

My last school year, 1940-1941, was different from all other years. I was already in grade eleven, but secondary education in Poland required twelve years of study. In the USSR, instead, secondary education was limited to ten years of schooling. The Soviets changed the old system abruptly. They shortened the time of study to eleven years and introduced a new curriculum. The designation *Tarbut* was removed from the name of our school and Yiddish replaced Hebrew as the language of instruction. All subjects connected with religion and the land of Israel were removed from the programme. The subject-matter of the social sciences and the interpretation of universal history were changed, as well. It suddenly appeared that much of our knowledge, acquired in long years of study, was useless if not totally harmful.

Usually the last year of secondary school is the time to contemplate and prepare for a future career. I planned, after graduation to continue study in an institution of higher learning. In Poland, admission of Jews to universities was restricted, but excellent marks and money to pay for tuition could help secure a place in some educational establishment. In the new Soviet conditions, ability and money were no longer the determining factors. Education was free of charge and having money was often a hindrance rather than an advantage. Universities were closed to those well-to-do and ability was no longer most important. Class and social background had become most significant and communist youth leaders, rather than professors, were deciding who was to be admitted to any institution of higher learning. My chances for admission were, indeed, very slim. My father was a successful businessman and one of those marked for deportation to Siberia. As a son of a bourgeois "enemy of the people" I was not entitled to make use of the "free" benefits provided by the Soviet state. Soon my dilemma was solved by the realities of life. After 22 June 1941 there was no need any more to worry about trivial things such as education. The unexpected course of history had taken care of our destiny and exposed us to the real school of life in which there was only one grade, namely pass or fail. In practical terms it meant the distinction between destruction and survival, between life and death. In times of social strife young people mature rapidly, even without formal schooling. Life takes its course and all one can do is try do the best under given circumstances. The Nazi invasion absolved me from the difficult task of planning my future. The occupiers had a readily available plan for me, for my family, and for my brethren. The immediate objective of my life became thus physical survival by any means. It was a task for which neither school nor parents could prepare me, because no one in his or her wildest dreams could imagine the barbarity and cruelty to which allegedly civilized people could subject their fellow humans.

CHAPTER TWO
THE NAZI OCCUPATION

A. THE FIRST SHOCK

22 June 1941. The first Sunday of the summer. It was a bright sunny day. Not a cloud in the sky. I ventured with a group of school friends into the nearby Zakret forest to enjoy the day and participate in a cross-country one kilometre race. My mood was elated. The school year was just over. The fresh air, old fir trees, and nearby river produced an air of tranquillity. I could hardly suspect that at this very moment the Hitler hordes were already in the process of carrying out their treacherous so-called Barbarossa plan, the aim of which was to destroy Soviet Russia, subjugate its people, and murder all the Jews in Eastern Europe.

The German invasion of the Soviet Union started early that morning, but I learned about it only at noon. Speeding on my bicycle, on the way home from the forest, I was mindful of the sounds of alarm in the city. I suspected that this was one of the false air defence exercises, conducted for the last several days by the local authorities. Little did I know that this time it was for real, that German planes were hovering over the city and dropping real bombs. The empty streets and the sight of people hurrying in a frenzy into hiding, shattered somewhat my confidence. I feared that something terrible was going to happen, but I refused to succumb to these evil premonitions. It did not take long, however, before I reached home and the horrible truth became reality. Mother opened the door. We looked at each other bewildered. One word uttered by her said it all: war.

A multitude of different ideas flooded my mind. Various emotions swept through my heart, but nothing definite. I was in a state of terrible shock. One thought, however, stood out among others. It was an awareness that a war between Nazi Germany and the Soviet Union was not for a day, a week, or a month. The battle between these two giants could last many years. I knew enough about the Nazi atrocities to recognize that tragedy was in store for us, that our lives were in danger, and that we could do little to help each other. Hence the struggle for survival would be intense, long, and difficult.

The first day of war passed in commotion and turmoil. Falling bombs deprived us of our freedom to move, and we could not go outside right away. We were forced to hide in shelters and were in the dark about the actual situation in the city. There was no one around who could give useful advice, or provide necessary information. Most people were paralysed by the unexpected shock of war. Logic impaired by fear degenerated into inertness. My friends, with whom I spent this memorable morning, rushed off to join their families. I never saw any of them again. They were all hunted down and murdered by Lithuanian collaborators of the Nazis in the first days of war. Next morning, Monday 23 June 1941, the situation became even more tense and confusing. Soviet military units abandoned the city in haste and disarray. The German army was already close and it was clear to everyone that Vilnius would soon be occupied by the advancing Nazi troops.

Life did not prepare me to make decisions where the distinction between right and wrong was equal to the extreme difference between life and death. It did not take long, however, before it became apparent to me that at times of war chance shaped the fate of individuals and even nations and that absolute freedom was a delusion. For the first time in my life I was forced to take charge of my destiny and I decided to leave town without delay.

I wanted to join a group and run away as far as possible from the advancing front line. I wanted to escape the Nazi onslaught. But I was young, naive, and inexperienced. I had no map or compass. I did not know the direction of the German advances and, most importantly, I had no older companion or guide. I did look for my older cousin, Boris, who was five years my senior, but I was late. I learned soon that he had left town already. It appeared that he moved eastward in the direction of Minsk, the capital of Soviet Belorussia. German mechanized units, however, were faster than the disorganized fugitives from Vilnius. Somewhat later we learned that my cousin and his friends did not manage to elude the Nazi assault and perished in unexplained circumstances.

By noon of 23 June 1941 Vilnius, still the capital of Soviet Lithuania, was on the verge of anarchy. It was in no man's land. The Soviet administration was fleeing while the Wehrmacht was still miles away. The situation demanded action. I could wait no longer. I took my bicycle and left town. I moved in the direction of Taboryszki, the small town where I spent, in my childhood, many memorable summers. It was still the home of my mother's sister and her family. And, besides, it was the only road out of town I was familiar with. I did not realize at that time that Taboryszki was located to the south-east of Vilnius, and that by going there I was actually moving in the direction of the advancing enemy. When I reached Taboryszki in the evening I was told that there was no need to rush anywhere, because the German army was already to the east of us. By now we were all trapped in the Nazi cage.

The German army entered Vilnius on Tuesday, 24 June 1941, but there were no Germans in Taboryszki , yet. They occupied first big cities and administrative centres, paying little attention to small towns, villages, and hamlets. My presence in Taboryszki was dangerous to myself, as well as to my relatives. I was a stranger there and as a fugitive I could easily be

44

suspected and denounced of collaboration with the Soviet regime. A week passed. There were still no Germans in sight. Life appeared to be normal, but there were endless rumours which did not augur well. Since I was ignorant about the situation in Vilnius and had no contact with my parents, I started to worry about them. Soon an opportunity presented itself to return to the city and I decided to make use of it. Unexpectedly Fima Mintz, a young man in his twenties, came to look for his friend, my cousin Boris. When he realized that Boris was not in Taboryszki, he suggested that I join him on his way back to Vilnius. I gathered my belongings and soon we were on our way. That was when I encountered for the first time German soldiers, face to face. A military unit was moving in the direction of Taboryszki. Deep in my heart I was happy that I will not be there when they arrive, yet I could hardly imagine what awaited me in my native city.

It was a hot summer day and I was getting tired. We covered already some thirty kilometres on foot. To my surprise some ten kilometres from Vilnius, near the small town of Rudomino, Fima announced that he was not going any further. Instead he was to join his family which had a hiding place in the vicinity. I was shocked, the more so since he refused to let me stay with them even over night. I was desperate. Evening was approaching rapidly and I was left all alone in the middle of the road. My entreaties did not help. When I tried to follow Fima he threatened to call the local police. Fima's cowardly action was vile and underhanded. He should have told me in Taboryszki that he did not intend to go to Vilnius. But he kept it secret. He used me for company for he feared to walk alone. He knew that I would have refused to join him had I known of his real intentions. The war just started but its effect on the behaviour of formerly respectable people was already clear. Common decency was replaced in most cases by fear and self-interest, fostered by the irrational instinct of self-preservation. I had no choice but to continue on my way to Vilnius, hoping to arrive home before the curfew of nine P.M.

Soon I was within the boundaries of the city. Vilnius was my native town. I lived there all my life. Every corner reminded me of my childhood and youth. Now I was walking there as a stranger. The streets were the same, but the atmosphere was different. German soldiers were all around and Nazi flags with swastikas all over. I was tired, my feet were swollen, I could not wait to get home. It was already late in the evening, almost nine P.M. The streets were empty. Jews were afraid to appear in public. Not far from home I was stopped by a Lithuanian policeman. He asked me in Lithuanian; "Zydas" - a Jew? I gave him an evading reply, showing my student identification card. He let me go. A block away from my home, a column of Jews was driven out from a courtyard across the street. Without asking any questions one of the policemen pushed me into the column and made me follow the others into the nearby police station.

The yard in the station was full of young and middle-aged Jews. It did not take long before we were ordered into column formation again and driven in the direction of the railway station. Night was approaching rapidly, but my exhausting long walk from Taboryszki did not come to an end yet. I could hardly stand on my injured feet. I wondered where we were moving to and what for. Terrible thoughts were crowding my head. The Jews, together with me, were fearful and alarmed. Some suggested that we will be transported somewhere in an unknown direction. Others were saying that we will be shot as soon as we get out of town. Such ideas did little to cheer me up, yet I was not ready to submit without a fight. At one point I began contemplating the possibility of escape. I soon realized that we were surrounded by armed guards and since I could hardly walk there was little chance of surviving a chase anyway.

It turned out, that fateful night, that we were still destined to live. By the time we arrived at the railway station it was already pitch-dark. We were split into working gangs and forced to unload a train full of bags with cement. It was hard work. I could barely lift the heavy bags. German guards and Lithuanian policemen were watching us and it was dangerous to stay idle. Early morning when the train was already empty they gave us back our personal identification cards and let us go. Barely alive I made my way home. There was no guarantee, however, that I would get there safely. There was always the possibility that another police gang could apprehend me and take me again somewhere else. I was lucky to get home. My parents knew that I had been detained that night and they were worried. All day I rested and nursed my sick feet in hiding. I tried hard to evade the possible incursion of the so-called "catchers" who were invading Jewish homes in search of young males.

Soon after the capture of the city by the Wehrmacht, the SS, the Gestapo, and the German civil administration made their appearance. 30 June 1941 the Lithuanian temporary government announced the formation of auxiliary police battalions, the main objective of which was to assist the Nazis in their anti-Jewish endeavours. Beginning early in July 1941 a number of decrees concerning the Jewish population were issued by the local German administration. They imposed numerous restrictions on the Jews of Vilnius. At first every Jew was required to wear a white band with a yellow circle and the letter "J", for Jude or Jew, on his or her right arm. Somewhat later all Jews were ordered to wear yellow stars of David on the left side of their chests and backs. Jews were ordered to turn in their telephones and radio sets and they were forbidden to use public transportation, parks, and recreational facilities. They were also required at all times to be ready to perform any job assigned to them by those in power. Henceforth they were forbidden to walk on the side walks and were required to march only in a single line on the right side of the road. All Jewish business and social activity was stopped and a curfew from dusk to dawn was established for all Jews. Thus the Nazis intended to intimidate and degrade the Jewish people, weaken their spirit, and dull the instinct of self-preservation. Moreover, by keeping them confused, and in the dark about their future, they wanted to turn them into easy prey for the Nazi death machine.

It was early July 1941, the second week of Nazi occupation, and most Jews still refused to believe that German soldiers and Lithuanian policemen would be capable of indiscriminate murder. Yet, at the very dawn of the war, the Paneriai (Ponary) forest, just outside the city boundaries, was already turned into a place of mass murder and a grave for thousands of Jews, who with many other innocent individuals were the first to fall prey to the insatiable murderous Nazi beast.

"The systematic extermination of the Jews of Vilna started... when *Einsatzkommand 9* arrived and began its activities."[1] It appeared in the city 2 July 1941 and its massacres began a few days later. But individual Jews were indiscriminately murdered by the SS and the Lithuanian auxiliary police even earlier. The arrest of Jews in Vilnius began on the second day after the city was occupied by the Nazis. 11 July 1941 was the day when the first Nazi victims were murdered in Ponary. 348 Jews and Soviet war prisoners, previously incarcerated in the Lukiszki prison were brought to Ponary for execution.[2]

At the same time, a special unit, composed of young armed Lithuanian thugs, called "Ypatingas Burys" or special squad, was organized by the local authorities. Its members, dubbed "the catchers," were roaming the streets, apprehending and leading away their Jewish victims. Those detained were never seen alive again. First they were taken to the Lukiszki prison and later transferred to Ponary for execution. Since most of those captured were young males it was believed, at first, that they were taken away somewhere for work. It did not take long, however, before rumours about Ponary began to spread and the horrid truth that all those detained by the "catchers" were murdered in cold blood became reality. The squad of the so-called "catchers" was initially composed of some 130 Lithuanian volunteers. In July and August 1941 they murdered in Ponary, on average, some 500 Jews daily.[3]

I was startled and shocked to learn about the fate of those apprehended by the "catchers", the more so since among the "catchers" were several young Lithuanians I knew. They were former students of the local Lithuanian high school, and members of a well known basketball club. I was astonished to learn how little time it took to unleash the evil instinct in those who were previously regarded as decent young men. Given unlimited power they were now ready to murder just for the fun of it.

After the war was over I was overwhelmed by the news that most "catchers" survived the war. Only twenty former members of the "Ypatingas Burys" were arrested, put on trial, and convicted by Soviet and Polish authorities.[4] Most others moved to North America and Australia where they were accepted with dignity as courageous fighters against communism and Soviet rule. In 1985 some twenty former "catchers" were still alive.[5] In fact, prior to June 1941, most of them collaborated with the Soviet regime. After the Nazis arrived they did nothing else but round up, rob, and murder defenceless Jews. Between 1 September and 25 November 1941 alone, members of the Ypatingas Burys, with the assistance of German soldiers and Lithuanian police, murdered in Ponary 18,898 individuals. In the towns and villages adjoining to Vilnius they killed another 13,501 people, the absolute majority of which were Jewish.[6]

My return from Taboryszki was arduous and dangerous, but when I arrived in Vilnius, early in July, I was instantly exposed to the hazardous realities of existence under Nazi rule. I kept thinking of the relative tranquillity in Taboryszki and thought that there life might be safer. I decided to leave town without delay. After a long walk, by evening, I was back in the country-side. There, life still appeared as peaceful as before my departure. Only from time to time would Lithuanian policemen arrive and cause some trouble. This external serenity, however, was deceptive. Rumours of atrocities committed by the occupiers and their local collaborators were spreading. It appeared that it was peace before a storm which no one could foresee or forestall.

On 10 July 1941, the third Thursday after the beginning of the war, Lithuanian policemen arrived in Taboryszki. They intended to arrest several Jewish youngsters, allegedly former members of the Young Communist League. Jewish youths who grew up in the country-side were usually tough and fearless and always ready to put up a fight before surrender. The police were out to apprehend two brothers, members of the large Kotler family. One of them was caught and placed under arrest. While the police were searching for the other one, a third brother managed to infiltrate unnoticed the place of incarceration and set free the arrested youngster. The policemen became enraged. They ransacked the houses of local Jews, shouting, shooting, and abusing their inhabitants. At one point a rumour was spread that a Jew had shot a hand-gun at one of the policemen. This was, of course, a provocation and deliberate malicious lie, but it had a purpose.

At the very time, when Lithuanian policemen were ravaging Jewish homes, a punitive German SS detachment arrived in Taboryszki. Incited by the local police, the Germans soon went into action. An order was circulated that at eight P.M. all Jews were to gather in the marketplace. I was frightened. As an outsider I was in greater danger than most others. I could be suspected of any possible transgression. I tried to escape, but wherever I turned there were German soldiers and policemen. I soon realized that the town was surrounded and I was trapped. At the appointed hour all Jews remaining in town huddled close to each other in the marketplace. From a house across the street, where the post office was located, several German officers moved in our direction. They approached us, separated the men from the others, and ordered all women and children into the nearby house of my relatives. Six Jewish males remained in the marketplace. Two were old, close to seventy. I was the youngest, sixteen at that time. The three remaining were middle-aged, between twenty and fifty. The most conspicuous was my uncle. He was a handsome man in his mid-thirties, tall, well built, and good looking.

While we were standing, clustered together, a squad of German soldiers, armed with rifles and fixed bayonets, approached in marching order. They stopped nearby in military formation. It suddenly dawned on me that they were here, fully armed, probably with the purpose of killing and we were apparently the intended victims. It was clear that something unexpected and terrible was going to occur. Everything was happening very fast. A German officer came forward and ordered us to form a straight line. Pushing and shoving each other we continuously changed places. No one knew in what order the imminent execution would proceed. No one wanted to be killed first. Most had hoped that perhaps a miracle might happen and some of us would be spared. Hence, instinctively, everyone tried to position himself as far as possible from the firing squad. Seeing this commotion the senior officer shrieked, making us freeze in place. It turned out that I was first in line, next to the firing squad. I feared that I will be executed first. Different ideas were crowding my head at that moment, yet one thought stood out most vividly. I was thinking of my mother's despair and devastation upon learning of my fate. I felt sorry for her, perhaps even more than for myself. It was an instinctive impulse, affirming the invisible natural bond between mother and child. I had no special relationship with my mother. She was a caring and dedicated woman, but also a rational, strict, and unsentimental disciplinarian. At this dark moment, however, she was nearer to me than anyone else.

We were standing dumbfounded, expecting our destiny. The senior officer stepped forward. I was the first approached by him. He came up to me, stopped, looked at me, noticed the badge attached to my jacket, and asked: "communist"? In halting German I replied something to the effect that it was a sport badge. The officer hesitated for a moment and moved on along the line. The few seconds seemed like eternity. He stopped again in front of my uncle. He looked at him, ordered him out from the line, and placed him in front of the firing squad. The murder was executed according to military rule. It could appear to the uninitiated spectator that it was committed in fulfilment of the verdict of a legitimate court of law. It all happened very quickly. An order was given and the squad, composed of six soldiers, shot the helpless and bewildered man. In the last seconds of his life he tried to say something in self-defence. He fell to the ground. A soldier with a red-cross arm band approached the victim and took his pulse. He motioned to the officer in charge that the victim was still showing signs of life. Another soldier came forth, aimed his rifle at the dying man's head and shot him from close range.

I was standing a few steps away and could witness the murder of an innocent man from close proximity. The sight of my uncle dying in agony had a shattering effect on me. Needless to say, I was never before exposed to such scenes of wanton violence and murder. The cruelty of this act was even more horrifying since my aunt and her little daughter were watching it all from the window of their house. After the execution the firing squad marched away. I realized that for the time being we were spared, but for how long? There was, however, no time to contemplate our predicament. We were immediately put to work. We were forced to dig a grave and bury the dead man then and there. After we finished our job the five of us who survived the initial massacre were led away by soldiers in the direction of the nearby estate. There we were locked up in a small dirty stable full of horse manure. On our way we were cursed by the soldiers who guarded us. One of them went into a long tirade relating a story of how Jews allegedly set on fire the Reichstag in Berlin.

When we were finally locked up I experienced a sense of temporary relief. On the one hand, it was the first time in my life that I lost my freedom to move and was under arrest. On the other, I was relieved that, at least for a while, there were no Germans among us and I could sit down to gather my thoughts. It took a while before I could make sense of all that happened that day. I realized that from now on fear, insecurity, and uncertainty will accompany me at all times. And yet, despite physical exhaustion and emotional devastation, or perhaps because of it, when night came I fell asleep on the dirty floor without a blanket or pillow.

The five of us, who were spared the fate of my uncle, spent thirteen horrid days together in the dingy little stable cell. It was a time when cruelty, torture, and murder were the order of the day. I was amazed by the malicious ingenuity of our captors and their eagerness to devise each day new means of torture. Their bestial, insatiable thirst for the blood of innocent victims was, indeed without limits. I came to realize, at that time, that humans belonged to the most cruel, living creatures; that the potential for evil lurked in everyone. Ivan Karamazov, the hero of F. Dostoevsky's novel *The Brothers Karamazov* said once that to "speak of man's 'bestial cruelty' .... is very unfair and insulting to the beast: a beast can never be so cruel as a man, so ingeniously, so artistically cruel." Indeed, the morality of the predatory animal is much higher than that of man. A predator will kill only when hungry and will seldom touch one of its own kind.

In captivity we were exposed to both physical and emotional torture. We were kept starving for four days. On the fifth day the door of our makeshift cell opened and we were driven to work. We were famished and weak and could hardly walk. Our first job assignment was a cruel joke. We were ordered to clean a field kitchen and permitted to eat all the food remaining in the big pot. It was, of course, a premeditated act of abuse. The Germans knew well that it was dangerous to eat much on an empty stomach, after several days of starvation. They enjoyed watching us eat eagerly, because they knew that we would pay dearly with our health for the food they gave us. Indeed, it did not take long before most of us got ill. We suffered terribly for this Nazi "generosity."

Soon we realized that our jailors belonged to a punitive detachment charged with the duty of apprehending all undesirable elements in the vicinity. Their main objective was to intimidate and instil fear in the simple peasant populace. Any individual suspected of supporting Soviet rule was viewed as a potential enemy. Any one denounced by a neighbour for the slightest grievance was tortured and murdered without mercy. They were killing local peasants indiscriminately. Executions were usually conducted in the same orderly manner as that of my uncle's. The victims were usually buried on the grounds of the estate, just behind the stable which became our home for the time being. Our job was to dig the graves and bury the dead. In some instances we were brought out after the execution. On other occasions we would witness the killing and then do our job.

Sometimes those condemned to die were kept over night in the basement under the stable. Once, a peasant apparently brought for execution and incarcerated in the basement, managed to escape in the darkness of the night. The next night another victim was placed in the same cell. This time, ready for any eventuality, the Germans placed a soldier with a machine gun just outside the small window frame of the basement. A barrage of machine gun fire woke us up in the middle of the night. It appeared that as soon as the new prisoner tried to make his escape, by climbing through the small opening in the wall, the soldier on guard opened fire. That was when the door of our stable cell was thrown wide open and we were driven outside. I suspected the worst. I was even ready to take the risk of trying to escape in the darkness of the night. But instead of being ordered to go outside, we were taken down into the basement. We were instructed to gather the remains of the murdered prisoner and take them outside. The upper part of the peasant's dead body stuck out from the window. The machine gun cut the body of the unfortunate man in half. We gathered all the scattered remains and buried them near the stable.

One morning we were hastily driven in the direction of the local mill, some half a mile away from the place of our incarceration. On our way we were accompanied by an officers and a firing squad. Upon arrival we were ordered to dig a grave. As soon as the grave was ready the door of a storage room at the mill opened and a prisoner was led in our direction. That was when we recognized one of the Kotler brothers who managed initially to escape from the Nazi clutches. When the soldiers brought him over for execution, just before the order was given to shoot, the young Kotler began to run, trying to reach the nearby bushes. At first the Germans chased him, but driven by the insatiable thirst for life the barefoot Kotler ran much faster that his oppressors, and in no time he was some fifty metres away from them. The Germans then stopped running, and began aiming at him from their rifles. They managed to hit him and the wounded boy slowed down. The soldiers hit him again, and he finally fell to the ground. Then the Germans caught up with him and killed him on the spot. After we buried the boy near the mill we were taken back to the stable. The fate of the young Kotler devastated us, but his courage and determination inspired us. He did not surrender without a battle and fought the enemy until his last breathe.

It appeared that by performing diligently our duties we were serving a useful purpose. Thus, we hoped that if there was nothing for us to do our jailors would leave us in peace. But that was not the case. They tortured us continuously with great ingenuity. On one occasion it was announced that we were going to be shot. We were ordered to dig our own graves. The firing squad arrived, we were lined up, and an order to fire was given. Our jailors performed a mock execution. The shots were aimed over our heads. To the great joy of our torturers one old man fainted. When he woke up he was pestered by the Germans that heaven was also occupied by the Wehrmacht. Soon other victims were brought and put to death. We buried them in the graves we prepared for ourselves.

The cruelty of mental and emotional torture was more difficult to bear than simple physical abuse. On the third day of our incarceration a record player was placed outside the little window of our stable room. A record, with a Hebrew religious tune, was set in slow motion and a soldier was winding the mechanism all day long. The distorted thick voice of the cantor and the warped religious tune, repeating itself endlessly, drove us mad. One old man could not take it any longer. He tried to hang himself. The Germans, however, were watching us. They made sure that we sat, facing the window, and listened. We saved the old man from suicide not only for his sake, but for our own sake as well, for we feared we would be punished for his death.

At dawn, on the thirteenth day of our incarceration, the doors of our makeshift prison were unexpectedly opened. We did not venture outside, but we could see the commotion. It took a while before we realized that the punitive detachment was getting ready to move. The soldiers were in a rush. They paid little attention to us, yet no one could be sure of what they had in store for us. As on numerous previous occasions, I experienced an impulsive urge to use the opportunity and make an attempt to flee. I looked, however, at the old men in the stable cell and I knew that I should not dare challenge the authority of those in power, for the old men would surely have to pay with their lives for my possible freedom. Luckily the Germans let us all go free. Given, apparently, an unexpected order to move, they were in haste to depart and evidently loath to bother with us. As we walked from the estate to town I looked timidly back to make sure that no one followed us, and that our "freedom" was not another cruel joke perpetrated by our captors. At the marketplace we split up and everyone went to join their family. I entered the house of my relatives and faced my widowed aunt and her orphaned little daughter. No words could express their grief. Hardly a month passed since the war started, but their lives were already shattered for good.

I did not stay in Taboryszki long. I realized that my presence there was dangerous for my relatives, as well as for myself. I left the same day on a hazardous journey that brought me back to Vilnius. The Jews remaining in Taboryszki were gratified by the alleged magnanimity of the Germans who set their relatives free. But their hopes were false and the reprieve was temporary. On 22-23 September 1941 close to 3,000 Jews inhabiting small towns and villages in the south-east vicinity of Vilnius, including that of Turgiele, Taboryszki, Mednik, and others, were rounded up and murdered in cold blood. Among them were also my recent cell mates from the Taboryszki stable prison. It did not take long before all Jewish communities in the Vilnius region were wiped out completely, and the country-side had become covered with mass graves of innocent Jewish victims.

I returned to Vilnius late in July 1941. My trip back home was full of danger. As I walked on foot along the highway I saw a truck loaded with milk cans on its way to the city. The driver stopped and offered a ride to a peasant woman. I decided to join her. After a while the truck stopped again to take on another group of peasants. Several women climbed onto the truck, but the truck was full and there was no room for all of them. When one of those left behind saw me in the truck she started to yell that there was room for a Jew, but not for her. A Lithuanian policeman, sitting in the cabin next to the driver, heard the screams. He jumped out from the cabin and, gun in hand, looked for the Jew in question. Before he could see me in the crowd I hopped over board and ran into the nearby forest. Soon I was out of his sight. He fired several shots and tried to pursue me, but to no avail.

My experiences in Taboryszki, and on my way home, prepared me for the worst. I was cognizant of the hazards of daily life under Nazi rule and suspicious of anyone or anything that could pose danger. When I arrived in Vilnius I felt more comfortable and secure than in the countryside. I was together with my immediate family and I knew well the surroundings. And besides, it was easier to hide and remain inconspicuous in the mass. Life, however, continued to be precarious. The "catchers" were relentless in their daily barbaric pursuit of new victims. Any German, or Lithuanian official, was free to enlist forcibly the services of any Jew free of charge. In fact, employment in a German military unit, or other important enterprise, was of great benefit to the downtrodden Jew. First of all it provided him with some security from the "catchers." In addition, it was easier to procure food for oneself and one's family. I was lucky. Soon after my arrival from Taboryszki I managed to secure a job at a military bakery, located on the outskirts of the city. All day I was unloading trains with sacks of flour, and loading them back with freshly baked bread. It was hard work. My young slender body often trembled under the weight of the heavy one hundred kilogram sacks. But I was never hungry. All day I ate as much as I could, and each day I was permitted to take home a loaf of bread. Nonetheless, the daily trips to work and back were always fraught with danger. My employers supplied me with a certificate which stated that I was employed by the Wehrmacht and that no one was supposed to touch me. The above notwithstanding, when the "catchers" were short of victims they paid little attention to such documents. They would seize unsuspecting Jewish men, on their way home from work, haul them away to prison, and from there to Ponary. I worked in the bakery for five weeks, until the day when all Jews, still remaining in the city, were forced into a ghetto.

The fate of East European Jewry was the subject of Nazi deliberations long before the beginning of the Second World War. As early as in the 1920s Adolf Hitler promulgated his racist "philosophy" according to which Germany was allegedly brought to ruin in the First World War not by the Allies, but rather by socialists, international bankers, and above all by the Jews. Hitler's determination to carve out so-called *Lebensraum*, or living space, for the Aryan race in Eastern Europe did not bode well either for the Slavs, or for the Jews. Until his assumption of power in Germany, however, Hitler did not have the necessary means to put his fascist and anti-Semitic policies into action. All that changed in 1933. With the help of back room intrigues, political manipulation, anti-communist and anti-Jewish provocations, as well as systematic terror, Hitler managed to gain power, and assume dictatorial control of the German state. Anti-Semitism became an important ingredient of his nationalistic programme, aimed at the destruction of all progressive, free-thinking, liberal, and non-Aryan. As opposed to the conventional, "theoretical," German anti-Semitism of the early century, Nazi anti-Semitism was characterized by unprecedented virulence, identified with Hitler's own fanatical hatred of Jews. According to Hitler, the Jew was not really a human being, but a mythical figure and an image which embodied all evil. Hitler's anti-Semitism was stimulated by emotional impulses which defied logic, but it was also nurtured by political considerations and cunning ambitions. Hitler projected into the image of the international Jew all he feared and detested within himself. The Jew was to Hitler a Freemason and supporter of clerical fundamentalism, as well as a Marxist and international banker, all at the same time.

Hitler's initial anti-Semitic programme and his racist policies had a two-fold objective. On the one hand, they were aimed at the physical and spiritual destruction of German Jewry. On the other, they were conducted with the purpose of re-educating and brainwashing the German people, and instilling in them the notion that they belonged to a superior race. In this respect the Jew was a convenient defenceless scapegoat the abuse of which was to illustrate Hitler's alleged notion of racial superiority. Hitler intended to turn Germans into a nation of racists and brutal Jew haters, capable of putting his vicious and murderous "final solution" into action.

Until 1938 the Nazi administration was occupied with the gradual and systematic eradication of Jewish life in Germany proper. In November 1938 the so-called *Kristallnacht*, or Crystal Night, the first anti-Jewish pogrom on German soil in generations was initiated and destructive physical attacks on individual Jews and Jewish institutions became the order of the day. After the *Anschluss* of Austria, in the spring of 1938, Austrian Jews shared the fate of their German brethren. In the fall of 1938 the Sudeten region of Eastern Czechoslovakia, inhabited by many Germans, was relinquished to Nazi rule. In March 1939 Czechoslovakia was invaded by the German army, and incorporated into the so-called "Great Reich." Soon the Jews of Czechoslovakia, the first Slavic country to be occupied by the Germans, began to experience the oppression and brutality of the Nazi regime. But in September 1939, when the Nazi troops invaded Poland, systematic mass murder was not official policy yet. Indeed, Jews were expelled, deported, and victimized in many ways, but not murdered en masse, yet.

Soon the Nazi attitude to their Jewish subjects began to change drastically. Prior to the invasion of the Soviet Union, in June 1941, Hitler entrusted Reinhard Heydrich, chief of the Gestapo and the Reich Main Security Office, with the preparation of the "final solution" of the Jewish question. It literally meant the physical destruction of all Jewish people under Nazi jurisdiction by all available means. On 20 January 1942 the Wannsee gathering, famous for its notoriety, was convened at the Office of the International Police Commission on Wannsee Street in Berlin. Among the fifteen people present were the SS and Gestapo heads of all territories occupied by the Nazis. Heydrich revealed at the meeting the "final solution" of the Jewish question to his top staff members. The physical extermination of the Jewish people was accepted then as the official policy of the German Nazi state. In fact, the assassination of innocent Jews in Eastern Europe did take place even prior to the official announcement made at the Wannsee gathering, but the methods and scope of murder were different.[7]

Beginning with June 1941 Jews in the Soviet territories occupied by the Nazis, were systematically killed by the *Einsatzgruppen*. These were special operational SS units, formed in May 1941, and charged with the duty of exterminating all Jews in the East.[8] Heydrich sent four units of *Einsatzgruppen* into the occupied Soviet regions. Each unit consisted of close to a thousand men, one for each military front in the East. These units followed on the heels of the invading Wehrmacht and, with the help of local non-German militias, composed mainly of Lithuanian, Latvian, Estonian, or Ukrainian hirelings, slaughtered as many Jews as possible. The extermination technique was simple. Jews in small towns and villages were rounded up, herded together, and driven into nearby forests or quarries where they were machine-gunned by SS soldiers and local thugs, directly in the burial pits prepared for them in advance.

The extermination of Jews in major urban centres posed a number of problems which the *Einsatzgruppen* could not solve single-handedly. Sheer numbers made it difficult to murder all Jews at once. Hence, just as in Vilnius, prior to herding them into ghettos Jews were at first killed selectively. The SS *Einsatzgruppen* completed their task in occupied Eastern Europe in 1943. By that time some 800,000 Jews were indiscriminately murdered by German Nazis and their local mercenaries.[9] Most of those who survived this initial onslaught died later from starvation and disease in the ghettos, or by direct execution in gas chambers, the construction of which followed the decisions announced at the Wannsee conference. In fact as early as late in 1941 the Nazis had already made use of makeshift gas chambers. At first the mentally defective, crippled, and inmates of psychiatric hospitals were killed there. By mid-1942 the monstrous Nazi death machinery was in place and the mass murder of Jews in the gas chambers and crematoria such as in Auschwitz-Birkenau, Majdanek, or Belzec was in full swing.

NOTES

[1]. Yitzhak Arad, Ghetto in Flames (Jerusalem 1980), 49-50.
[2]. Arunas Bubnys, "Special SD and German Security Police Squad in Vilnius (1941-1944)," in The Days of Memory, ed. by E. Zingeris (Vilnius 1995), 183.
[3]. Ibid., 185.
[4]. Ibid., 188.
[5]. Ibid., 496.
[6]. Ibid., 185.
[7]. Howard Morley Sachar, The Course of Modern Jewish History (New York 1963), 441-2.
[8]. Bubnys, 181.
[9]. Sachar, 443.

B. THE GHETTO IN VILNIUS

The early months of Nazi occupation were a time of anxiety, confusion, mental distress, and physical torture. No one expected, or could imagine, the degree of cruelty and ruthlessness exhibited by the occupiers and their local supporters. There was not a single Jewish family in town that had not already lost in these early months some of its members to the hungry Nazi beast. From the approximately 80,000, Jews residing in Vilnius before the war, about 35,000 were killed even before the ghetto was established.[1] The selective murder of Jews, conducted by the *Einsatzgruppen* and their local Lithuanian mercenaries, continued in Vilnius for close to two months, until the establishment of the ghetto. Most of those murdered then were able-bodied men, allegedly taken to work. Early in September 1941, in preparation to the formation of the ghetto, the indiscriminate mass slaughter began. Families, including women, children, and the elderly, were dragged away to Ponary and killed.

One day in the summer, on my way home from the bakery, I noticed a large column of Jews, men, women, and children marching under guard in my direction. I had no way of knowing of their destination, but I sensed something evil. I decided to get out of their way and keep out of sight. I entered a courtyard and continued on my way home by crossing backyards and climbing fences. I approached home, but decided to survey the situation before I entered. One of the four storey buildings next to our apartment house was half empty. It was damaged by a bomb. I climbed up to the roof, hid in the attic, and tried to observe the situation in the surrounding area. From the top I could see how across the street German soldiers and Lithuanian policemen were chasing out Jews from their houses. The victims were ordered into column formation and driven in the direction of the centre of the city. Being told, apparently, that they will be transferred to some other place of residence, the Jews tried to take along whatever they could. Caught by surprise, they were forced to leave their most valuable possessions behind. Little did they know, at that time, that it made no difference anyway. Hastened and beaten by their tormentors, and unable to carry off whatever they took, they shed most of their belongings and just held on to their children and relatives.

I was not sure, at that time, of the scope of the action and I feared that next the Nazis would evict the Jewish residents from our side of the street. I decided to wait and continued to hide in the attic. It soon turned out that after the area across the street was cleared, relative peace prevailed for a while. I then joined my family and awaited the inevitable.

On 31 August - 2 September 1941 thousands of Jews, who lived in the areas designated for the ghetto, were evicted from their places of residence and driven en masse first to Lukiszki prison, and then to the Ponary forest, where 1-3 September 1941 they were indiscriminately slaughtered by machine-gun fire and buried in the pits prepared for them in advance. After the Jewish district, located on both sides of Vokeciu (Niemiecka) Street, was emptied of its original Jewish inhabitants, the few gentile families residing there were moved to other parts of the city. On 6 September 1941 all Jews of Vilnius, who managed to survive this initial devastation, were driven into the narrow streets of what was to become the newly formed Vilnius ghetto. Our family did not have to go far, we lived just across the street, yet we could take along only the most indispensable things: some bedding, clothing, dishes. We left behind all that my parents had worked for, and saved over the years.

The creation of the ghetto exposed the cunning nature of the oppressor. In order to unnerve the victims and undermine their possible resolve to resist, all Jews were removed from the comfort of their own homes and resettled in the cramped inhuman ghetto conditions, hardly conducive for normal existence. Initially, there were two ghettos in Vilnius, one on each side of Vokeciu Street. This street was an important thoroughfare and it was kept open to regular city traffic. The large first ghetto, situated in the square between Vokeciu, Arkliu (Konska), Pylimo (Zawalna), and Lydos (Lidska) streets, was initially occupied by some 29,000 Jews. The smaller second ghetto, composed of Zydu (Zydowska), Stikliu (Szkliana), Antokolskio (Antokolskiego), and Gaono (Gaona) streets, was inhabited by some 11,000 Jews.[2] It included also the courtyard in which the Great Synagogue, and many small houses of worship were located.

The creation of two ghettos was another shrewd Nazi ploy. It splintered the Jewish community, broke off lines of communication, and made it easier to carry out the hideous Nazi plans. The second ghetto was doomed from the outset. In October 1941 a number of Nazi actions were conducted with the purpose of reducing the ghetto population. 1-2 October 1941, on the Day of Atonement, 2,200 Jews from the first ghetto, and 1,700 from the second, were taken to Ponary for extermination. The following two days another 2,000 Jews were removed from the second ghetto to Ponary. Two weeks later, 15-16 October 1941, 3,000 residents of the second ghetto were transferred to Ponary, and murdered the same day. By the last week of October 1941 the second ghetto was virtually empty.[3] For all practical purposes only one ghetto remained in the city. It appeared, however, that the Nazis still entertained some plans for the second ghetto and retained it for a while empty, but intact.

In October 1941 the Nazi administration issued, on behalf of appropriate German employers, some 3,000 special work permits, or the so-called life saving "yellow certificates," to selected residents of the first ghetto. According to Nazi intentions there were to remain in Vilnius no more than 12,000 Jews, just enough to serve the local military and economic needs of the occupiers. This number included those who were actually employed in German military units or other institutions, as well as their family members composed of a spouse and no more than two children under sixteen. 24 October 1941, those with yellow passes went to work together with their families. In their absence all those remaining in the ghetto were removed for execution. 3 November 1941, holders of yellow certificates and their families were transferred to the vacated premises of the second ghetto. The first ghetto was then searched again for those in hiding. Three days later those with yellow certificates and their families were permitted to return from the second ghetto to their initial residences in the first ghetto. In the two actions, connected with the yellow passes, 6,200 Jews were rounded up and moved to Ponary for destruction. After having served the treacherous purpose of the Nazis, the second ghetto was liquidated altogether.[4]

It was well known in the ghetto that the actual ghetto population still exceeded the number allowed by the occupiers by many thousands. Among the illegal ghetto residents were Jews without "yellow certificates" who managed to escape during the Nazi actions, into temporary hiding places in the city, only to return back to the ghetto when the danger was over. There were also those who were able to delude the vigilant eye of the oppressor by concealing their existence in elaborate bunkers constructed well in advance in the ghetto. By November 1941, when the destructive actions ceased temporarily, and some stability was established, the ghetto was inhabited by close to 20,000 Jews. By then more than two thirds of the pre-war Jewish population of Vilnius had been brutally killed and buried in mass graves on the outskirts of the city.

Ghettos were created by the Nazis not only with the purpose of dehumanizing, degrading, and oppressing their Jewish inhabitants, but also to exploit them as a source of cheap labour in the service of the German war machine. The Vilnius ghetto was not different. It operated on the same principles as did most other ghettos in major east European cities. It was extremely overcrowded. Several unrelated families were usually herded together in one small room. In order to isolate and separate the Jews from their gentile neighbours, walls were erected to cut off the streets which connected the ghetto with the rest of the city. The inhabitants of the ghetto were trapped within this large prison camp. To enter or exit from the ghetto was possible only through one gate, continuously guarded from the outside by German soldiers and Lithuanian policemen.

The first few months in the ghetto were the most difficult. Indeed, young males were no longer assaulted by the "catchers," but liquidation actions conducted by the Germans were numerous and they reduced the number of ghetto residents by thousands. The first victims were the sick, old, and feeble. Next was the turn of children, mainly orphans. And, finally, many of those without yellow certificates, or appropriate protection by their employers, were hunted down and destroyed. My father did have a proper job, and he managed to procure a yellow certificate which was supposed to provide his immediate family with the necessary protection. Unfortunately, only children under sixteen qualified as family members, and everyone older was regarded as an adult. Hence, since I was already seventeen, and my sister nineteen, we were adults and not entitled for the protection provided by our father's yellow certificate. Our parents were extremely worried. The lives of their children were hanging by a thread. I was also anxious, but tried to retain my composure, and hoped for the best. Luckily, when our documets were checked by the vigilant Gestapo control, we managed to pass for young teenagers.

We lived in the ghetto in a first floor apartment on 7 Strashun Street. There were three small rooms in the flat. They were extremely overcrowded. Three families, a total of ten people, lived in our room. Those residing in the other rooms were required to cross our room on the way to their rooms. We slept on the floor, or on makeshift bunks, which were removed during the day. Running water was available in the kitchen, but there was no toilet or bathroom in the apartment. There was a wood burning stove in the kitchen, but there was seldom any firewood to cook a meal. We had a hot plate to warm up the food, but the electric current was so weak that it would take hours to boil a cup of water.

One of the main concerns in the life of each family in the ghetto was the daily safe return from work of the bread-winner. It was of particular importance because without the food brought in daily by those who worked in the city many people, in particular those who always stayed within the perimeters of the ghetto, could hardly survive on the meagre food rations provided by the Nazi administration. People who had no access to the extra crumbs brought in by relatives who worked outside were doomed to a slow death by malnutrition and starvation. It was, however, forbidden by law to bring anything into the ghetto from the outside. Any attempt to smuggle in some food, or firewood, was regarded as a major crime.

My father and sister worked on a farm on the outskirts of the city. I worked for over a year for a German enterprise which dry-cleaned and repaired military garments for the German air force. Seven Jewish males were employed in the plant. Some were mechanics, others stalkers and labourers. The other workers were Polish, and the supervisors were Polish Germans, or *Volks-Deutsche* as they were called. The upper management was German, but seldom in attendance. Those in charge would arrive only from time to time to inspect the plant and its production. In the beginning, when the German Army was advancing, the *Volks-Deutsche* were loath to speak Polish and they claimed that they were Germans forced to live under Polish occupation. By the middle of 1943, when the withdrawal of the Wehrmacht from Soviet Russia became a fact, they were ready to acknowledge and reclaim their Polish roots. In general, as long as we performed our duties diligently, we were treated fairly. And, besides, it was better to work with local civilians in an ordinary industrial enterprise, then to labour under the watchful eye of German Nazis or SS men.

At first all Jews in the plant worked in the day shift. Somewhat later I was assigned to shift work. I was the only Jew to work in pair with a Pole, or *Volks-Deutsche*, for twelve hours at a time. On the one hand, my new position provided me with more independence and flexibility. But on the other, it was dangerous to walk the city streets, all alone, at irregular hours when few Jews walked to, or from work.

It was the task of the Jewish police to check whether Jews returning from work, tried to smuggle anything in. Usually, they turned a blind eye to those who tried to bring some food into the ghetto. Occasionally, Lithuanian policemen, standing at the ghetto gates, would search those entering and take away whatever they would find. In some instances, Gestapo officers would arrive unexpectedly, and conduct a brutal search of all those returning from work. Their searches were usually ferocious. Everything, including a piece of bread or a few potatoes, was taken away. In order to instill fear in the residents of the ghetto, the so-called "smugglers" were often beaten, arrested and taken away to the Lukiszki prison. From there they were usually transferred to Ponary for execution.

One day, in August 1942, Jews returning from work, were faced by the Gestapo at the ghetto gates. My father was among them. He carried a few vegetables hidden in his trousers. As soon as he saw that there was a search he tried to rid himself of his precious possessions, but it was already too late. He was too close to the gate to remain unnoticed. In fact father did manage to enter the ghetto safely. His hidden food was not discovered. The shock of his encounter with the dreaded Gestapo, however, was devastating. He collapsed soon after he entered the ghetto and died before any help could arrive. My father was not a strong man, but he was only forty-eight, and in normal circumstances could have lived with his medical condition for many years to come.

The death of a parent, especially a young father, is always perceived as a great family tragedy. In those days, however, when great numbers of Jews were brutally killed daily, and savage murder was as common to every Jew in the ghetto as life itself, many ghetto residents were envious of those who, rather than being slaughtered by raging Nazis and thrown into mass graves, died their own natural death and were taken for interment to the Vilnius Jewish cemetery. Those who died their own death in the ghetto were considered fortunate. They were looked upon as the ones chosen by God. The funeral procession, which followed the horse driven cart with the casket, could proceed only up to the gates of the ghetto. No one except for the coachman and a worker were permitted to follow to the graveyard. The graves of those who died in the ghetto and were buried at the Jewish cemetery were unmarked, but the Jewish religious community kept a record of the places and names of those who were buried there. After the war surviving family members could erect a monument and commemorate appropriately the death of their deceased relative.

To this day I recall my father's death and his funeral. I followed the cart with the casket up to the ghetto gates. I was shaken and distressed. It all happened so unexpectedly. On my way back to our crammed ghetto quarters it suddenly dawned on me that after father's death I was the only man in the family. I was only seventeen at that time, but my new responsibilities burdened my mind. There was, however, no time for contemplation or mourning. Life, as it was, continued, and the same day I had to go to work. My father's death was, in a sense, an act of defiance and his victory over the Nazi system of mass murder. The Nazis could oppress, torment, and kill those who were alive, but they had no power over the dead. After the war we erected a monument at the grave site where our father was buried. We paid him the last respects that we could not give him at the time of his demise.

After my father's death our mother and her older sister who lived together with us could subsist only with the help of whatever my sister and I could manage to smuggle in from the outside. Relatively speaking, our mother was still a young woman and, at the beginning of the war, was hardly forty-five. But in those days, in conditions of extreme oppression and suffering, people aged quickly. Any teenager was regarded as a mature individual and most who were over forty were considered elderly and decrepit.

Existence in the ghetto was usually conditioned by outside forces over which Jews had no control and individual life was moved by the natural impulse of self-preservation. Hence, no long range plans for any activity were possible and the main preoccupation of everyone was with practical matters of day-to-day survival. Well informed and intelligent people in the ghetto knew that all Jews under German rule were condemned to death and only the defeat of Nazi Germany could save the few not yet murdered by the Nazis. Hence, daily reality posed the brutal question which concerned everyone. It asked not who was to live and who was to die, but rather who will be killed first and who later. Deep in one's heart every ghetto Jew hoped for a miracle. Everyone believed that survival was possible and tried to do everything within his or her means to postpone imminent destruction for as long as possible.

This hope was nourished by the illusive and self-serving philosophy of so-called "work for life." The ghetto Jewish administration cultivated the notion that Jewish labour was indispensable and Jewish tradesmen irreplaceable and that as long as Jewish workers performed well in the service of the German war cause, the ghetto would remain intact. 1942 was the year when the notion of "work for life" prevailed in the ghetto. Its inhabitants lulled by the relative peace were able to conduct an illusory semi-normal existence in the shadows of the invisible and constantly lurking death. In spite of all odds, and perhaps just because of it, life in the ghetto was an expression of boundless hope for survival and an extreme example of the will to live.

The ghetto in Vilnius operated as an ostensible mini-state and it had its own internal Jewish administration. In July 1942, the Germans dissolved the Judenrat for alleged incompetence and appointed the police commissioner, Jacob Gens, to the position of head of the ghetto. The ghetto administration was composed of a number of departments, concerned with different aspect of daily life, such as health, food, housing, labour, industry, social welfare, and culture. It also formed a Jewish police, Jewish court, constructed a jail, and published a wall bulletin, *Geto yedies* (Ghetto News). In order to divert the attention of the Jews from impending danger, the Germans permitted the establishment in the ghetto of a number of cultural, social, and recreational institutions which helped to create a semblance of normal life in the ghetto. There were also in the ghetto a hospital, an outpatient clinic, a home for the aged, an orphanage, and a children's kitchen, as well as two general elementary schools, one secondary school, and a music school. The cultural and social needs of the ghetto population were served by a public library, a theatre, a symphony orchestra, two choirs, and a sport club. Three synagogues and a religious school functioned within the walls of the ghetto, and a number of political and youth organizations operated clandestinely.

Despite the external appearance of a normal life, which could satisfy the curiosity of a detached Red-Cross observer, the ghetto system of government was a devilish invention of the Nazis. It was created with the purpose of deceiving the Jews. By providing those herded together within the ghetto walls with a false sense of security, the Nazis were able to perpetrate and facilitate their next act of mass murder. In fact, the hospital, the home for the aged, and the orphanage were turned, by the occupiers, into gathering stations for all those they regarded as dispensable. From time to time the Gestapo would arrive unexpectedly and remove from the ghetto all the sick, homeless, and vulnerable for immediate destruction.

The intensity of existence in the ghetto was so high that there was little time to reflect on the past. All one's thoughts were concerned with the present. Furthermore, it was senseless to plan for the future. Social, cultural, or political activity was, in a sense, a form of mental and emotional escape. It was also a means of defiance, an affirmation of one's existence, and a refusal to accept the inevitable. It raised young people in the ghetto, even if only temporarily, to the level of ordinary human beings. Social activity provided them with an opportunity to make new friends. Human contacts were extremely important in the ghetto. Jews worked in different military and private enterprises in the city. Daily, they would come in touch with a variety of people and return home with an abundance of different kinds of information. This information, brought into the ghetto from the outside, circulated from mouth to mouth. The ghetto resembled a huge gossip mill. Jews were particularly interested in, and sensitive to, any news about the situation at the eastern front, as well as to information concerning the safety and future of the Jews in the Vilnius ghetto.

Social life alleviated, in some measure, the sensation of pervading doom and pessimism. Most ghetto Jews mastered a variety of survival skills. Some connected with physical existence, others with mental and emotional well-being. The grief of loss of the near ones was usually muffled by the continuous danger to oneself, and to those who were still alive.

Most Jews in the ghetto lived a double life. On the job, outside the ghetto, they kept a low profile, tried to remain inconspicuous, and bide their time. Most tried to perform their duties well in order to find favour with their employers and not incur the wrath of those in charge. In fact, a Jewish worker was never out of danger. Any German or Lithuanian could accuse him of sabotage with all the consequences to follow. When after a long day of work and a march on the road where horses and carts travel, the downtrodden Jew successfully passed the control at the gate and entered the ghetto, he or she felt, all of a sudden, a certain relief and sense of illusory freedom. This was, however, the freedom of degradation, the freedom of slavery. It was the freedom of an animal in a large cage, always at the mercy of his master. Once inside the ghetto it appeared to the Jew that, at least temporarily, he was free from the external pressures of an alien environment. In the ghetto, the Jew was an equal among his fallen brethren. He was not looked down upon, nor was he taunted by anyone. And above all he was with those who shared his destiny and wished him well. He was able to forget himself and, at least for a while, indulge in activities which provided him with an escape from his oppressive existence.

Since I was a well known athlete before the war, I joined the ghetto sport club located on 6 Strashun Street, next to the ghetto bath-house and jail. On one occasion special sport festivities were organized and I played in an exhibition basketball game in the presence of the Jewish ghetto leadership and some German officers. At another time I participated in a boxing match in the ghetto theatre hall. It was not easy to exert oneself and perform in depressing ghetto conditions. But I was young and my physical energies were not totally depleted yet. Besides, I hoped that as a good sportsman I might gain recognition and respect of the spectators, including the Jewish leaders of the ghetto. That was important, because the fate of any individual Jew was often determined by ghetto administrators who were forced by the Nazis to make the difficult choice between those who were to live, and those who were doomed to die. Moreover, the prizes awarded at sport competitions were of great importance. For the participation in the basketball game I received half a kilogram of sugar, and for the boxing match half a kilogram of butter. Malnutrition and starvation were rampant in those days and a pound of butter was no small thing. It could save a life. It is interesting to note that some older ghetto residents vehemently opposed the existence of recreational programmes and entertainment in the ghetto. They believed that the ghetto was a graveyard, and there was no place for fun at a cemetery. They spent their free time instead on reading, study, and talking.

The ghetto library, located on 6 Strashun Street, opened its doors on 19 September 1941, several days after the ghetto was created. It was always busy and short of books. Since there were no newspapers or radios in the ghetto, library books were in great demand. Reading fiction was a means of escaping into another, more beautiful, world. After every anti-Jewish action in the ghetto the number of readers would increase. The day after the 1 October 1941 action, when several thousand Jews were driven away from the ghetto and shot in Ponary, 300 books were lent out by the library. In fact, books were signed out from the library until the very last day of the ghetto's existence. On 13 October 1942 the ghetto library celebrated the lending of the 100,000th book. Out of the close to 17.000 ghetto inhabitants, 4,700 were library subscribers.[5]

That did not mean, of course, that the Nazis were indifferent to what the

Jews in the ghetto were reading. To the contrary, along with physical destruction they were also intent on annihilating the Jewish cultural and religious heritage and obliterating everything connected with Jewish intellectual and spiritual life. Since Vilnius was recognized as one of the most important centres of Jewish learning it received special attention from the Nazi authorities. In July 1941 Dr. Gothart, an adviser to Himmler, arrived in Vilnius. He assembled a group of Jewish scholars and ordered them to segregate and prepare lists of all Jewish books of any significance for transportation to Germany. In January 1942 Dr. Pohl, an adviser to Reichsleiter Alfred Rosenberg and the director of the Frankfurt Museum for the Study of East-European Peoples, appeared in the city. Delegated by the Nazis in 1933 for three years to Jerusalem to study Jewish literature and oriental studies, Dr. Pohl was consequently regarded by the Nazis as a leading specialist in Jewish affairs. Under his supervision the most important Jewish books from the Strashun and *YIVO* libraries were sent to Germany, while most other books were sold for pulp, or simply destroyed. Only a fraction of the Jewish books available in Vilnius before the war survived this ravage and only some of the rare books were saved by the few Jews employed by Dr. Pohl's organization. They risked their lives daily in order to save remnants of the Jewish cultural heritage.[6]

The ghetto theatre was located in the premises of the former so-called small city hall on 3 Konska (Arkliu) Street. Since Konska Street constituted one of the outside ghetto walls, the only available entrance to the theatre was through 6 Rudnicka (Rudninku) Street. The hall contained 315 seats. The theatre began its activity early in 1942. During the first year of operation it gave 111 performances, and sold 34,804 tickets.[7] The ghetto symphony orchestra, conducted by Mr. Durmashkin, as well as Jewish choirs and soloists performed, from time to time, in the same hall.

There were in the ghetto a number of industrial enterprises producing goods for internal consumption, as well as for the use of the German administration. People working there were spared the inevitability of facing hostile Nazis on a daily basis. They were, however, deprived of the opportunity to venture outside the ghetto and procure some additional food. Those employed outside the ghetto marched to and from work in groups. An appointed Jewish foreman, or brigadier as he was then called, was in charge of the group. He was responsible for the performance of the gang, and for any transgression of its members.

The issue of policing and ghetto administration is invariably complex. Any generalization on the role of the Judenrats and the Jewish ghetto police is dangerous. The actions and motivation of each Jewish policeman or administrator merit separate judgement. It is a well known fact that many

Jewish policemen in the Vilnius ghetto were active members of the underground resistance movement. They informed the underground about possible Nazi actions; they assisted members of the underground in trouble with the ghetto administration, and, most importantly, they helped to smuggle arms into the ghetto. On the other hand, there were also the few who fulfilled the brutal orders of their German bosses with extraordinary zeal. Many members of the ghetto administration and the police were people with no roots in the city. They were born and lived before the war somewhere else. Many were refugees from the western regions of Poland who came to Vilnius in September 1939. They had few friends or relatives in town and no ties with the local Jewish community. That made it easier for them to overstep the moral bounds that separated common decency from unacceptable behaviour. Most, however, were in the main decent young people who accepted their jobs in good faith.

The Jewish ghetto police was charged with the responsibility of keeping law and order within the bounds of the ghetto. It was required to uncover any illegal anti-Nazi activity within the ghetto and it was also called upon, from time to time, to assist the Nazis in their deportation actions. In such cases, the ethical dilemma faced by each policeman was indeed immense. Each had to decide for himself whether he was to save his own skin by sacrificing the lives of his neighbours, friends, and relatives, or he was to protect his dignity by refusing to acquiesce to the demands of the Nazis. The choice was not an easy one, and often impulsive. German suspicion that a Jewish policeman tried to assist those targeted for deportation and murder was fraught with dangerous consequences, and it could imperil the life of the policeman in question. The behaviour of each policeman was determined by his character traits, by the social environment which helped form his personality, as well as by the balance between good and evil in each individual. It was also influenced by the complex and personal relationship between the natural instinct of self-preservation and the moral principles inherited and acquired by each individual from his family, friends, and teachers. In the beginning, police service seemed to most conscripted young and inexperienced Jewish boys as a positive, valiant, and daring occupation. They did not realize yet then that some of them would be turned into passive tools of a manipulative, murderous regime.

There were some Jewish leaders and policemen who were drunk with power and abused their subjects. Most, however, were appointed to positions they were forced to accept, and walked a tight-rope attempting to maintain a balance between the needs to serve the hated regime, and provide a service to the ghetto population.

Today, some regard former Jewish ghetto leaders as traitors to the Jewish cause and as conscious collaborators with the Nazi regime. Others view them as sorry victims. Indeed, many Jewish ghetto leaders were entangled in a web of lies and deceit and were often carried away by their delusions of grandeur, believing that they had a mission to fulfil. They assumed that by acquiescing to the demands of the Nazis they were saving themselves, helping at the same time the ghetto survive.

Jacob Gens, the head of the ghetto in Vilnius, was in a sense a self-righteous dictator who believed in himself and in his mission. According to some historians he ruled with an iron hand and was as "hated among many Jews as the Nazi rulers themselves."[8] Indeed, Gens was a controversial figure, and his attitudes were often contradictory, but he was not a traitor. For all his weaknesses and wrongdoings he did not share any common goals and aspirations with the Germans. He was coerced by Nazi terror to submit and comply and he tried to protect his Jewish subjects to the best of his limited possibilities. Gens adhered to the philosophy of "work for life," and he sincerely believed that by surrendering the weak and the old to the thirsty-for-blood Nazi extermination machine he was buying time and saving the young and able-bodied. He was of course wrong. The Germans used and abused him and when his services were no longer required they killed him, on 14 September 1943, without much ado, just a week before the final liquidation of the Vilnius ghetto. Gens could have, perhaps, saved himself. After all he was a former captain in the Lithuanian Army, his wife was not Jewish, and he had many useful contacts in the local Lithuanian community. He was even warned by some German officials that he was summoned to the Gestapo for the last time. But it was below his dignity to try escape danger and cowardly to abandon those from whom he constantly demanded trust.

Gens was one of the major tragic figures of the ghetto in Vilnius. Basically an upright man, of dignified bearing, he believed in justice and common decency. Life forced him to serve a base cause, but till the last moment he believed that his activity would yield positive results. His straightforward and truthful military approach to life, however, was no match to the perfidious nature of Nazi politics and diplomacy. He failed not for lack of faith or dedication, but because his cause was doomed from the outset. No individual was permitted to slow the operation of the Nazi extermination machine and interfere with the course of the "final solution."

The fate of the ghettos in Nazi occupied Eastern Europe was determined on 21 June 1943 when Heinrich Himmler, the Chief of the SS, issued an order according to which all ghettos in Eastern Europe were to be liquidated and the surviving Jews transferred to concentration camps. The ghetto in Vilnius survived for two years. Its final liquidation began on 23 September 1943. The young and able-bodied men and women were transferred to concentration camps, mainly in Estonia and Latvia, while all others were transported to death camps. My mother and sister survived for two years in the ghetto. When the ghetto was liquidated they were separated, and my sister was shipped to a concentration labour camp in Kaizerwald, Latvia. Mother, instead, was sent together with other women, children, and elderly men to one of the death camps for extermination.

Several thousand Jewish specialists escaped execution for another eight months. These were the workers who lived all the time in two special blocks outside the perimeters of the ghetto. One group was employed in the fur and leather manufacturing plant, *Kailis*. Another group, consisting of mechanics and engineers, was employed by the German company *Herres Kraft Park* (*H.K.P.*), and was engaged in the repair of military vehicles and other combat equipment. Most residents of *Kailis* and *H.K.P.*, however, did not survive the war. A week before the liberation of Vilnius these special blocks were transferred from the Wehrmacht to the SS, and their residents were taken to Ponary for execution. Those who tried to resist, or escape, were killed on the spot. Except for the few who managed to evade detection in hiding, the Germans killed all others just several days before the Soviet Army entered Vilnius.

Late in 1943, in anticipation of the possible withdrawal from Vilnius, the Nazis devised a plan the intention of which was to cover up all traces of their crimes. With that purpose they brought eighty Jews and Soviet war prisoners to Ponary, and keeping them literally in chains, the Nazis forced them to exhume the corpses of the victims murdered there and cremate them on the spot. According to different accounts, between December 1943 and 15 April 1944, between 56,000 and 68,000 corpses were exhumed and burned in Ponary. In the night of 15 April 1944 thirteen of the slave labourers managed to escape from their dungeon in Ponary. Eleven of them joined the partisans in the Rudninku forest.[9]

NOTES

[1]. Encyclopaedia Judaica, vol. 16 (Jerusalem 1971), 148.

[2]. G. Agranovskii, and I. Guzenberg, Litovskii Ierusalim (Vilnius 1992), 24.

[3]. Ibid., 26.

[4]. Yitzhak Arad, Ghetto in Flames, (Jerusalem, 1980),139.

[5]. Joshua Sobol, "The Passion of Life in the Ghetto," in The Days of Memory, (Vilinus, 1995), 250.

[6]. A. Sutskever, Fun Vilner geto (Moscow 1946), 114-21.

[7]. Sobol, 48-9.

[8]. Randolph L. Braham, ed., Contemporary Views of the Holocaust (Boston 1983), 10.

[9]. Arunas Bubnys, "Special SD and German Security Police Squad in Vilinus "(1941-1944), in The Days of Memory, (Vilinus 1995),186-7

C. RESISTANCE AND SURVIVAL

The fate of world Jewry in 1939-1945 was inseparably linked to the final outcome of the Second World War. So was the physical survival of each individual Jew. The sheer notion of the hypothetical possibility of a Nazi victory in the war, and its repercussions for the future of the Jewish people, is frightening indeed. All Jews under Nazi rule were summarily convicted to death not as individuals, but en masse; not for individual crimes or transgressions, but for no other reason than xenophobia, chauvinism, hatred, and an ideology which proclaimed the superiority of one race over all other. As opposed to the common criminal, locked up and convicted to die on a certain day and hour, all Jews were condemned to death, but no one knew exactly when one's final hour will come. It is true that Jews were not the only Nazi victims. Members of other nations were murdered as well. But, as opposed to most others, all Jews were victims. In ordinary circumstances a criminal convicted to death by a court of law has recourse to a legal system of justice. He can appeal his conviction. He may use all possible legal means to postpone execution, hoping that eventually his sentence will be commuted. Nazi Germany, however, was no democratic society, and the Jew was placed outside the law. Anyone could kill a Jew anytime, any place, without having to face any charges.

Jews, residing in areas occupied by Germany, experienced Nazi atrocities in shock and disbelief. They were, however, ill prepared by their life experience to cope successfully with this new reality. Jews were isolated in ghettos, incarcerated in camps, or jailed in prisons, but regardless of circumstances they were always kept in the dark about their future destiny. In order to turn Jews into subjects of easy prey and render them helpless in the face of a surprise attack, at the least probable time, the Nazis applied different means of disinformation and psychological distraction. In order to divert the attention of their victims from possible danger, the Nazi occupiers placed Jews in conditions of extreme tension and tremendous physical and mental stress. By subjugating the Jews to constant humiliation and degradation, by limiting their mobility and access to information, by continuous physical exploitation and deprivation the Nazis intended to strip each Jew of his or her self-esteem and destroy one's internal adaptive and defensive mechanism. Physical and mental torture were a means of breaking resistance and turning Jews into docile, submissive victims.

In these conditions of extreme hardship the first step to survival was recognition of the imminent danger of physical annihilation. The denial of reality is usually a primitive psychological mechanism and, in a sense, an expression of readiness to submit. In fact the first to perish, under Nazi occupation, were those who had little faith in themselves, but believed that it was someone else's duty to save them. Among the first victims were members of two diverse, extreme groups. Their behaviour was largely conditioned by their past, their education, and upbringing. The assimilated Jews belonged to one group who refused to recognize the danger. They expected to be treated no differently from other uncommitted Poles or Lithuanians. Ultra-Orthodox Jews formed the other group. They believed that their destiny was God's will and, except for prayer, there was little they could do to alleviate the situation.

It is suggested that the actions of people are often determined by two polar and contradictory traits of nature. On the one hand, they are driven by the natural instinct of self-preservation, while on the other, their actions are often induced by the irrational impulse of self-destruction. According to Arthur Schopenhauer the will to live "is incapable of further explanation, but is the basis for every explanation... it is the most real thing we know, in fact the kernel of reality itself."[1] In a paper written in 1916 the Russian psycho-physiologist Ivan Pavlov declared that "all life is the fulfilment of a single aim, namely the preservation of life; it is the unceasing activity of what is commonly called the life instinct."[2] According to Pavlov this instinct takes the form of the goal reflex which motivates the activity of humans.

It is an accepted reality that love nurtures life and that a positive meaning of life nourishes the irrational instinct of self-preservation. It is also well known that many kill themselves when the terror of death becomes less horrifying than the horror of life; that inclinations to suicide appear when the complete exhaustion of love of life sets in. Man is ready to kill himself when life loses its meaning to him, when all illusions are gone, and when he is unable to bridge the gap between himself and his own life. Logically, life makes no sense in a world in which man is an outcast. Paradoxically, in times of war, famine, or natural calamity few people commit suicide. In 1941-1942 Jews in the Nazi occupied territories were reduced to walking skeletons, and yet the suicide rate among them actually declined by 65 per cent from the pre-war level.[3] These facts may seem puzzling, but it appears that in the austere and cruel circumstances of Nazi tyranny, life acquired new meaning. Life itself, expressed in the miracle of existence which is beyond ordinary human comprehension, gave meaning to suffering, and energy to cope and hope. In conditions of complete degradation and constant danger of destruction, physical survival became the meaning of life. The instinct of self-preservation brought to the fore all dormant physical, mental, and emotional resources of the human body and stimulated the actions aimed at survival, even by those who for all practical purposes were already half dead. The instinct of self-preservation and a realization that survival did have meaning was nurtured by the hope that the allied forces would be victorious, and that the destructive Nazi war machine would soon be vanquished. This hope for a brighter future and the desire to see the enemy subdued gave strength to the oppressed and stimulated their actions aimed at self-defense and survival. Hope, of course, is a force which can nurture the human spirit and help muster one's hidden emotional and mental resources. Unless it is supported, however, by positive action it can turn into a disarming and often dangerous delusion.

Resistance to Nazi intimidation, cruelty, and tyranny was an important component of the struggle for survival and a practical expression of hope. The main objective of any form of resistance was survival. Death with dignity was the second choice. Even in the most hopeless situations, and without illusions, there were always those who chose to resist. Resistance could be passive or active; as well as individual or collective. In fact, existence itself was in a sense an expression of resistance. Every Jew under Nazi rule resisted death. By learning to cope with tribulations, to which few ordinary mortals were ever exposed in our modern times, he or she struggled against the overwhelming odds of daily existence. In order to overcome the initial shock of degradation, and begin the process of adaptation to the new, and always fraught with danger, conditions of life, passive resistance often took the form of ostensible submission. It was reinforced by the victim's concealed efforts to retain clarity of mind, protect his or her personality from disintegration, and preserve one's identity. On another level, passive resistance could take the form of hiding, adopting a false identity, or simply learning to ignore the world around, and accept reality at its face value. Apathy is a mechanism of self-defense, and indifference could serve as a protective shield from the indignities suffered on a daily basis. It could also serve as a mental escape from the gruelling conditions of life; help retain clarity of vision, physical stamina, and the nervous energy required to perform the duties assigned to each captive by his jailors. As it is, life is a continuous process of adaptation. Under Nazi rule most Jews were in the constant process of trying to escape one trap, only to be ensnared into another one.

Active resistance to Nazi oppression took a variety of different forms. In most instances it was connected with the use of force and it was conditioned by the kind of weapon the victim was able to procure. Individual armed resistance to Nazi occupation was in most cases doomed to failure. The most one could do was kill or wound one's oppressor, with the help of a gun or a knife, only to be murdered on the spot by another Nazi.

74

Exhausted from malnutrition and tormented by physical and mental abuse, the Jew seldom had the opportunity to escape. Only in rare instances could one delude the vigilant eye of the well fed and armed Nazis, and escape their pursuit which inevitably followed. But even then only those with good connections in the non-Jewish community and a place to hide outside the ghetto or camp had a chance to survive. Most others had nowhere to go. Danger lurked all over.

Individual armed resistance was in most cases an act of desperation and a sign of moral strength. It was an open challenge to the Nazi oppressive machine and an expression of defiance to a society which sanctified mass murder and ignored the value of human life. Moreover, by refusing to accept the verdict of the torturer and punishing the tyrant instead, the victim was asserting one's personal dignity and reaffirming that, regardless of what the oppressor might claim, his or her life, as the life of any other human being, had absolute and independent value. Despite one's inescapable destruction, and the use of violence which the Jew abhorred, his or her actions were justified. They raised the victim to a new level of spiritual fortitude and defied a system which legalized the mass murder of innocent people.

Organized armed resistance of a group was another matter. Yet it could give no guarantee of survival. In fact, the opposite was often the case. But the group provided spiritual and emotional support, and a sense of belonging. The sheer notion of resisting the enemy's vile and pernicious racist ideology and the determination not to submit to his overwhelming military force, provided members of the organized resistance with a sense of self-esteem and a realization that they served a worthwhile cause. In practical terms, well organized armed resistance groups had a possibility to procure arms, make contact with non-Jewish underground resistance organizations, and seek out useful intelligence information.

In most instances, Jewish organized armed resistance included activities such as sabotage; armed opposition to the enemy within the walls of the ghetto or camp; or the escape to the forest with the purpose of joining the anti-Nazi partisan movement. In different circumstances the tactical moves of anti-Nazi ghetto fighters varied, but the policy of no surrender, even when there was little chance of escaping, was in most instances their ultimate strategy.

Survival, which was the main objective of each Jew under Nazi occupation, was often subject to the whims and changing moods of the Nazi oppressor. Nonetheless, in many instances the attempt to resist or escape could pose an important ethical test. There was often a price to be paid for the sheer hope of survival. Thus, for example, in some cases Jews in ghettos or camps were forced to perform tasks which were contrary to the moral standards and values to which they adhered prior to their enslavement. The refusal to obey the oppressor's orders, however, was tantamount to death. In other cases, active resistance, or failed attempts of escape, precipitated harsh punishment. When armed Jews, trying to escape from the ghetto, were apprehended or killed in battle by the Nazis, their family members and associates were usually rounded up and summarily executed. Thus, armed resistance and attempts to escape raised the spirit of those concerned and provided them with hope for survival, but posed a grave danger to the very existence of many others. Consequently, the passive submission of many was not only the result of Nazi intimidation and repression. Instead, it was often an ethical choice of those who did not want to abandon their families, or try to save themselves by endangering the lives of others.

The vicious racist policies, promulgated by the Nazi regime, condemned to death all Jews within their domain. In the final analysis, only the destruction of the Nazi state could save the remnants of European Jewry from imminent danger. Indeed, most Jews hoped for and expected a speedy victory of the allies which would set open the doors of concentration camps and save those who were still alive.

The possibility of survival was thus a race with time. However, the nearer the end of the war came and with it the downfall of the Nazi regime, the more intense and vicious became the Nazi atrocities. The Nazis wanted to kill as many witnesses of their crimes as possible, trying to cover up all traces of their evil.

Surviving Nazi occupation was in most instances determined by chance. Nonetheless, physical strength and conditioning, as well as personal character traits of each individual were important factors. Of no less significance was will power and emotional stamina. There were many instances when weak emaciated individuals, but who were strong in spirit, could cope better with the dehumanizing conditions of slave labour than those of great physical strength, but who lacked mental fortitude and the determination to live.

The relationship between armed resistance and survival was tentative at best. Just as in the case of a plague, or natural disaster, no one could predict who will survive. In the final analysis those who were lucky survived. The above notwithstanding, most of those who joined the underground resistance movement managed to save themselves, and those who perished in battle with the Nazi enemy did not die in vain.

It is the right of every citizen to resist oppression in a lawless society and fight those in power. Under Nazi occupation a young Jew, who managed to procure a gun, all of a sudden became free. The intended victim could now take the law into his or her own hands and mete out justice to one's tormentor. Regardless, whether the armed Jew survived or was killed by the oppressor, the gun turned one from a downtrodden and despised insect into a human being again. Only a gun could give back the Jew his or her dignity. Only force could provide the Jew with relative and often, only symbolic, freedom. It was the only viable means for turning the oppressor and victim into relative equals.

NOTES

[1]. Arthur Schopenhauer, The World as Will and Representation, tr. from the German by E.F.J. Payne, vol. 2 (New York 1966), 351.
[2]. Jaques Choron, Suicide (New York 1972), 31.
[3]. Howard Morley Sachar, The Course of Modern Jewish History, (New York, 1963) 445.

D. THE JEWISH UNDERGROUND

Clandestine Jewish anti-Nazi activity started the day the Wehrmacht entered Vilnius. It was conditioned by the sheer fact that people had only one choice: to submit or to resist, and many chose the latter. At the forefront of Jewish organized resistance were members of a variety of political and youth organizations.

In the summer of 1940, after the incorporation of Lithuania into the Soviet Union, Zionist organizations and the *Bund* were outlawed and their political activity forbidden. Members of these groups who remained conscious of their political identity and intended to remain active were driven by the Soviets underground. Members of the communist party, instead, who were previously victimized and imprisoned by Polish authorities came out into the open and became politically operative. German occupation equalized, in a sense, the status of all Jewish political groups, and the ghetto walls shielded them all, up to a point, from outside interference. In 1941 the Nazis were still not adequately familiar with the political fragmentation within the Jewish community and did not make any distinction between Jewish adherents of different political ideologies. Hence, members of different youth organizations had relative freedom to resume political activity.

In the early days of occupation, Jewish political activists sought to re-establish their former social and political ties. A variety of Zionist groups, such as the leftist *Poalei Zion* and *Hashomer Hatsair*, the far right revisionist *Betar*, as well as *Hechaluts*, the general Zionists, and the religious *Mizrachi*, among others, became active. The anti-Zionist *Bund* and members of the communist party also organized and got ready to operate in the underground. Most groups were small, depleted by the loss of many young males to the pre-ghetto "catchers," or the early surprise extermination actions within the ghetto. These groups were loosely organized, not homogeneous, and most members lacked any experience in underground activity. They were ill equipped to operate in conditions of extreme secrecy and in circumstances demanding persistence, determination, physical strength, and military training. Besides, except for the communists, most other groups were just coming out from their former Soviet underground.

It was clear to everyone in the Jewish underground that, in the given situation, no single group could wage successful battle against the oppressor. It was apparent that the cause of resistance to the Nazi extermination machine and the objective of saving as many Jewish lives as possible could be advanced only by unified action with the participation of all political and ideological youth groups in the ghetto. Only well planned, motivated, and supervised activity, conducted by a force which was united in aim and spirit, could have any chance of success. Unfortunately, the ideological doctrines of different underground groups were so distinct that no ideological compromise was possible, and no organization with a single theoretical agenda could be formed.

The above notwithstanding, and despite political and ideological disparity, members of various Jewish political groups tried to establish contact with each other, and explore jointly problems of adaptation, survival, physical and emotional support, as well as issues of resistance and organizational unity. The pragmatic approach to life, necessitated by ghetto conditions, forced the leaders of the Jewish political underground to accept the reality that a time had come when ideological and political differences were secondary to matters of ethnic and racial identity, and that issues of national unity were to be placed above ideological or class interests. The enemy paid little attention to the political views of different Jews. In a sense they were all equal to the Nazis. The Nazis envisaged a common destiny for all of them. They were all doomed.

Thus, confronted by the same enemy, out to destroy all Jews, Jewish political leaders were compelled to disregard, at least temporarily, their ideological differences, and began negotiations with the purpose of creating a single fighting organization in the ghetto. It was obvious to everyone that it was preferable to fight and try to survive together, rather than wage struggle in small groups, and face inevitable extinction apart. Nevertheless, even after having decided to form a single unified underground combat organization, the leaders of different political parties could not agree on the general strategy and tactical moves of this proposed new fighting body. The communists recognized the futility of combat within the walls of the ghetto and favoured joining forces with the pro-Soviet underground outside the ghetto. Their highest priority was to inflict as much damage as possible on the Nazi war machine and, at the first opportunity, leave the ghetto in order to join the pro-Soviet partisans in the nearby forests. Zionists, on the other hand, showed, at first, little enthusiasm to the idea of uniting with those to whom the very notion of a Jewish homeland in Israel was heresy and who, just a few months earlier, outlawed their activity and deprived them of their freedom. Ideologically, Nazi fascism and Soviet communism were equally repugnant to the Zionists. In the end, however, common sense prevailed and representatives of different political groups in the ghetto managed to reconcile their programmatic differences and arrive at an agreement to form a single unified combat organization.

Formally, 21 January 1942 is regarded as the day that denotes the beginning of Jewish armed resistance to Nazi occupation in the Vilnius ghetto. On that day, representatives of a number of different political groups gathered to assert their resolve not to submit any longer to Nazi tyranny and to prepare for battle with the oppressor. Among the participants of that fateful meeting were representatives of the Communists (Y. Wittenberg and Ch. Borovska), *Hashomer Hatsair* (A. Kovner), *Betar* (J. Glazman), *Hanoar Hatsioni* (N. Reznik), and some others.

The gathering adopted a resolution which proclaimed the establishment of the so-called *Fareinikte Partisaner Organizatsie* (F.P.O.), or United Partisan Organization, and outlined its basic tenets and mode of operation. The resolution stated, among others, that the aim of this new armed combat underground organization was to operate in the Vilnius ghetto with the purpose of unifying all forces able and willing to assist in the resistance to the Nazi occupiers. The main objective of F.P.O. was to prepare people in the ghetto for mass armed resistance, in case the Nazis intended to liquidate the ghetto. The organization asserted its readiness to carry out acts of sabotage in Nazi occupied territory and it declared its support for the Red Army in its struggle against the Nazi invader. The F.P.O. asserted also its support to pro-Soviet partisans fighting against Nazi occupation and expressed readiness to join their ranks when conditions would warrant it. Y. Wittenberg was elected commander-in-chief of the F.P.O. and J. Glazman and A. Kovner were appointed to its command staff.[1]

The agreement of the Zionists and, in particular of the *Betar*, to cooperate with the communists was an act of desperation and a sign of the times. The initial resolution of the newly formed F.P.O. was the result of programmatic, organizational compromise. It combined Jewish national and communist political objectives. The Zionists maintained that armed resistance was the only honourable resort available to the ghetto Jew. The communists contended that armed struggle within the ghetto walls was futile and, therefore, only by merging forces with the pro-Soviet underground outside the ghetto, and by joining the Soviet partisans in the forest, could Jews successfully oppose Nazi tyranny. The communists contended that their plan was pragmatic. It offered, at least to the young and brave, a chance for survival. The Zionist approach, they claimed, was suicidal and doomed to failure.

Future events in the ghetto have proven that neither scheme was foolproof. On the one hand, armed resistance and combat within the ghetto reduced the possibility of survival to a minimum. On the other hand, the non-Jewish communist underground outside the ghetto was initially very small and vulnerable and could provide little assistance to those confined in the cramped ghetto quarters. Furthermore, it was under continuous surveillance of the Gestapo and Lithuanian police and in constant danger of being uncovered. Events in the summer of 1943 illustrated clearly that the failure of the communist underground in the city was fraught with dangerous consequences not only to the Jewish communists, but to all residents of the ghetto as well. When the communist underground in the city was uncovered the very existence of the Jewish resistance movement in the ghetto was compromised and the lives of its leaders were imperilled.

Early in 1942 the discord between the Zionist and communist approaches to the application of the resistance strategy in the ghetto was still academic. Members of the F.P.O. were not ready yet, at that time, to mount any armed action within the ghetto, neither was there any possibility to join the ranks of Soviet partisans simply because there were no partisans in the vicinity of Vilnius, at that time, anyway. Hence, 1942, the year of relative stability in the ghetto, was also the year of growth, development, and maturing of the ghetto underground movement.

The resolve to form an underground organization in the ghetto required determination, steadfastness, and strong leadership. The leaders of the groups that initially joined the F.P.O. were strong individuals, experienced in clandestine political ventures. They devised the framework for the organization's operation and formed the nucleus of its command structure. However, the political groups that joined the F.P.O. represented only a fraction of the ghetto youth. Some political groups were not approached by the organizers of the F.P.O., while others refused to accept its initial programme and modus operandi. Moreover, most young people in the ghetto lacked political affiliation, and were thus left out of any involvement in organized underground activity. In the spring of 1942, after protracted negotiations, representatives of *Bund* agreed to join the F.P.O., and, A. Chvoinik, one of their members, was co-opted to the command of the organization. Similarly, N. Reznik, one of the original founding members of the F.P.O., joined the command staff.

The F.P.O. grew steadily, and by the summer of 1943, its active membership was close to three hundred. In absolute terms, three hundred was a ridiculously small number, hardly adequate to confront the overwhelming forces of the enemy. However, when one considered the conditions of extreme oppression and the dangers of mounting any organized anti-Nazi activity in the ghetto, one could certainly appreciate this figure. The F.P.O. was composed of several battalions, divided into platoons, and small cells of three to five people in each. There were also staff and intelligence units, attached to the command. It was clear that as a fighting organization the F.P.O. needed arms. Hence, its first objective was to procure as many weapons and ammunition as possible. By the summer of 1943 the F.P.O. was in possession of a considerable amount of ammunition, including many hand-guns, grenades, and several machine-guns. Separate weapon components, smuggled in from the city by F.P.O. members, were assembled, and made combat ready, in the ghetto. Production of Molotov cocktails and hand grenades was also established in the ghetto. The F.P.O. launched a secret military combat training programme for its members, and organized the operation of a clandestine printing press. It established contacts with the communist underground in the city, with Jews in other ghettos, as well as with representatives of Soviet partisan units in the Belorussian forests.

The F.P.O. was not the only underground resistance group operating in the ghetto. There were also other groups, of different sizes and various political stripes, the members of which, however, were not motivated by immediate ideological or political considerations. Members of these groups discarded the notion of confrontation with the enemy inside the ghetto as futile and preferred the only military option they considered viable at that time. Their main objective was to leave the ghetto as soon as possible and, at the first opportunity, join pro-Soviet partisans in the Lithuanian and Belorussian forests. Only in extreme circumstances, when there could be no way out from the ghetto, were they prepared to face the Nazis and join the resistance within the ghetto walls. Their first and only choice was survival, and if that was impossible then, at least, death with dignity.

One of the largest and best known such groups, composed of some members of Zionist youth, was organized early in 1942. Its leader was Yechiel Sheinbaum, a mature man of close to thirty with former army service experience. At one point this group wanted to join the F.P.O., but negotiations conducted in the summer of 1942 produced no compromise. The F.P.O. was prepared to admit members of the Yechiel group as individuals, while Yechiel insisted on retaining his group's identity within the general F.P.O. framework. He wanted his group to become an affiliate of the F.P.O. with a separate membership. Another underground unit, the *Kamfsgruppe* - Battle Group, or as some called it the Second Organization, was formed by mature individuals, former soldiers, some members of the revisionist *Betar*, as well as ghetto policemen. Membership in these two groups was not constrained by conditions of former party affiliation and it grew rather rapidly. Late in 1942, Yechiel and the Battle Group agreed to merge, forming one fighting organization under the leadership of Yechiel. Thus, early in 1943 there were, in fact, in the ghetto two independent major resistance organizations.

Attempts to unify all underground resistance activity, with the purpose of forming a single fighting organization, with a joined command, continued well into 1943. The Yechiel unit, merged now with the Battle Group, and some other unaffiliated youth groups, represented a significant force. Negotiations between the F.P.O. and Yechiel resumed in the spring of 1943, and an agreement was apparently reached. But there are conflicting reports as to the success of these negotiations. Some suggest that late in the summer of 1943, when the danger of ghetto liquidation was already imminent, "an almost complete coalition was effected between the F.P.O. and the Yechiel organization."[2] Others assert that in May 1943 an agreement was reached according to which the Yechiel group became an affiliate of the F.P.O. retaining, however, its distinctness as a separate unit with autonomous rights. It continued to exercise control over the arms in possession of its members, and it was free to admit to its group new members, by-passing the scrutiny of the F.P.O. leadership. Yechiel Sheinbaum was co-opted to the F.P.O. staff command as a representative of his group. It was apparent that the priorities of the Yechiel group were different from those established by the F.P.O. command. The Yechiel fighters, however, agreed to take part in combat activity within the ghetto, if the situation, at a given time, warranted such action, and there was no other choice. It appeared thus that despite the agreement to cooperate and coordinate action, the alleged union between the F.P.O. and the Yechiel group "did not lead to the fusion and unification of the two organizations."[3]

Whatever the organizational status of these two combat units, their joint membership, by the summer of 1943, reached close to 500. However, few youths in the ghetto outside these groups knew much about them. That did not mean that unaffiliated young people in the ghetto were passive or apathetic. Rumours circulating in the ghetto about planned armed resistance infused them with determination. Young people arriving from the nearby forests and telling stories about increasing partisan activity in the region inspired them with hope. And news about the success of the Red Army, in particular after its Stalingrad victory, fostered the anticipation of possible liberation. With increasing vigour unaffiliated young people in the ghetto sought means to organize, procure weapons, and initiate whatever activity possible in self-defence.

I belonged to a group composed of such individuals. We started to organize in the summer of 1942 and, by the spring of 1943, we were ready to act. Our group consisted of close to fifteen young men, most seventeen - nineteen years old. We were friends from before the war, previously actively involved in sporting endeavours, but without ideological commitments or any political party affiliation. One of our leaders was Chaim Rubanowicz, a former boxer and a young man strong in body and spirit. Our main objective was to acquire weapons and leave the ghetto for the forest as soon as possible. In case that would become impossible, a hand- gun could help escape incarceration, or at least kill some Nazis before being driven by them to death.

The acquisition of arms was an expensive and dangerous undertaking. Daily risking our lives, we stole from our German employers whatever it was possible to sell. We bartered it for flour, lard, or other food products, and smuggled it into the ghetto. We used the money acquired from selling the food for the purpose of buying weapons. My shift work at the air force dry-cleaning plant enabled me to steal military garments and remove them from the premises in the darkness of the night, when no one was around. I sold the garments to peasants arriving from the country-side, or exchanged them for food, contributing the proceeds to our weapons' fund. We procured hand-guns and grenades in many different ways. We purchased guns from local civilians and, even in rare instances, from German soldiers. Some of us, who worked in German military units, would steal weapons from our employers. Others would bring into the ghetto discarded or abandoned weapon components, which were later fixed, assembled, and put into service. By the summer of 1943, each member of our group had a hand-gun and at least one grenade.

The possession of a reliable grenade was of utmost importance. We knew that in case of direct armed confrontation with the Nazis a situation might arise when there would be no chance to use a gun. The danger of being caught alive, and then interrogated, tortured, and executed was real. Since death was inevitable anyway, a grenade was a sure means of immediate self-destruction. It could save one from unnecessary torture and suffering, inflicting, at the same time, some pain on the enemy, as well.

In our group there were no men with previous army service experience. We were all too young for that. Hence, we knew nothing about the handling or maintenance of military equipment. We approached a former Jewish soldier in the Polish army and with his help learned to use our weapons. At the same time we managed to make contact with several Jewish youngsters from the country-side who were in touch with Soviet partisans in the Belorussian forests. Our intention was to leave the ghetto as soon as possible, and, with the help of our new guides, move to the forests at Lake Narocz, some 150 kilometres from Vilnius.

Life in the ghetto, however, was complex and full of unexpected surprises, not of the best kind. Making plans for the future was usually a futile endeavour. In the spring of 1943 the situation in the ghetto began to change drastically. The increasing number of illicit contacts between Jews in the ghetto and the outside world, as well as the traffic between the ghetto and the forest alerted the Germans. They became suspicious of secret

Jewish activity and believed that weapons were concealed in the ghetto. Their conjecture was corroborated by several unexpected and unrelated events. On 21 April 1943 a group of armed young people, members of the Battle Group, left the ghetto and moved in the direction of the Rudninkai forests (Rudnicka puszcza). On their way they unexpectedly encountered a German military detachment. A fierce battle ensued and most Jewish fighters perished. J. Gens, the head of the ghetto, was incensed. The revelation that armed young people were hiding in the ghetto undermined his credibility with the Germans and endangered the very existence of the ghetto. That did not mean that Gens was unaware of the existence of an organized resistance movement in the ghetto. In fact, he was even in touch with some of its members and gave money for the purchase of guns to the Battle Group. He donated also some cash, from Judenrat funds, to the F.P.O. But Gens considered the behaviour of some F.P.O. leaders arrogant and he resented what he regarded as their reckless activity. In his view, such action endangered the very existence of the ghetto and the safety of its residents.

Internal ghetto politics and squabbles between the F.P.O., Gens, and the police affected little the attitude of the German administration. Early in July 1943, their suspicion that there were, indeed armed Jews in the ghetto was reinforced. The Nazis uncovered communist underground activity in Vilnius and arrested the secretary of the city underground communist party organization, J. Vitas, as well as another member of this committee, V. Kozlowski. Tortured by his interrogators, Kozlowski broke down and named Wittenberg as one of the members of the city underground communist party committee.

B. Kittel, the German security police officer in charge of Jewish affairs in Vilnius, appeared soon in the ghetto demanding that the Jewish ghetto authorities arrest and hand over Wittenberg to the Gestapo. He threatened that if his request was not complied with, the Germans would proceed with the immediate liquidation of the ghetto. As soon as Wittenberg found out about the menace to his safety he went into hiding and the Jewish police failed to apprehend him. On 15 July 1943, Gens invited members of the F.P.O. command to his office for an ostensible information session. That was when the Jewish police appeared on the scene and arrested Wittenberg. According to Ruzka Korchak, Wittenberg was then handed over to several Gestapo men and Lithuanian policemen who accompanied him to the gates of the ghetto. When on his way Wittenberg heard loud calls from his F.P.O. friends that "Wittenberg is arrested, everyone to the gate in order to set him free," he eluded the vigilant eyes of his jailers and disappeared in the darkness of the night. The Germans gave chase in an attempt to recapture him, but to no avail.[4] In no time Wittenberg was whisked away by his comrades to a new hiding place. The German authorities did not relent. "At dawn on 16 July the ghetto was faced with an ultimatum. Wittenberg had to surrender before 6 P.M., or aircraft summoned from Kaunas would set the ghetto on fire and destroy it together with its inhabitants."[5]

16 July 1943 was a day of extreme tension in the ghetto. By stressing continuously that only the surrender of Wittenberg could save the remaining Jews of Vilnius, Jewish authorities manipulated the public mood in the ghetto and orchestrated a confrontation between the general ghetto population and the underground ghetto resistance movement. It was impossible to know, at that time, whether the German threat to bomb the ghetto was real or just a bluff; whether it was a serious intention of collective punishment, or just a means to intimidate the ghetto population. However, since the barbarity and ruthlessness of the Nazis was well known, no one wanted to challenge them and put their real intentions to a test.

Under pressure of the ghetto Jewish authorities, who were supported by the general anti-F.P.O. mood in the ghetto, the F.P.O. relented. Its command decided to leave the final decision to Wittenberg himself. After all, not only the destiny of the ghetto was in jeopardy, but his personal fate was also at stake. At first Wittenberg was prepared to commit suicide, but the Germans demanded his surrender alive. After consulting with his closest friends in the F.P.O., members of the communist party, Wittenberg agreed to give himself up.

Kittel was expecting him at the ghetto gates. I remember how Wittenberg walked erect, his head up, on Rudnicka Street, towards the gates of the ghetto. He looked straight ahead. His face was that of a proud and courageous man. It was a tragic sight. Everyone in the ghetto knew that they saw Wittenberg for the last time. There would be no return for him from German prison. Yet most ghetto residents felt relief. They were made to believe that once Wittenberg was gone, the danger would pass and life would continue as before. That was, of course, another illusion. Next morning Wittenberg was found dead in prison. Some suggested that he was murdered by the Nazis.[6] According to other accounts he apparently committed suicide, with the help of poison given to him by Gens before the Nazis could interrogate and torture him. [7]

The Wittenberg affair unsettled the relative tranquillity in the ghetto. It placed the relationship of the F.P.O. with the ghetto population in a new perspective and it heightened the tension between the Jewish underground and the ghetto administration. It strained also the relationship between Gens and the F.P.O. leadership to the extreme. It also accelerated contacts with the partisans in the forest and provided those who intended to join the partisans with a new sense of urgency.

In the summer of 1943 increasing activity, connected with the contemplated departure of young people from the ghetto into the forest, was fostered by the arrival of young Jewish guides from the countryside. One of them, M. Shutan, was a native of the town of Swienciany, some eighty kilometres from Vilnius. He had established contacts with the Soviet partisan leadership in Western Belorussia and was ready to lead Jewish fighters into the forest. He appeared in the ghetto on several occasions. He was in touch with the F.P.O., as well as with other smaller independent youth groups. On one occasion he was arrested by the Jewish police and brought to see Gens. After an interview, Gens set Shutan free and permitted him to lead a group of young people from the ghetto to the forest. At their meeting, on 12 June 1943, Gens told Shutan: "I know of the existence of F.P.O., and all its arms caches. I know a time will come I will need them.... When the time for destruction of the ghetto comes, we shall need all the armed boys. We'll all fight then."[8]

After the Wittenberg affair, Shutan appeared in the ghetto again. He came on behalf of Colonel F. Markov, a former teacher in Western Belorussia, and presently the commander of the Soviet partisan brigade, named after Marshal K. Voroshilov. Shutan approached the F.P.O. leaders, suggesting that the time was ripe to leave the ghetto and join the partisans in the forest. The F.P.O. leadership was not ready to move yet, and refused Shutan's offer to lead them into the forest. Then Shutan went to see Gens. When he arrived at Gens' office the latter was already informed about Shutan's presence in the ghetto, as well as of his meeting with the F.P.O. command.

According to Shutan, his discussion with Gens was straightforward and candid. Gens said that he did not deceive Wittenberg, but he could not sacrifice the existence of the ghetto for the latter's safety. Gens expected the F.P.O. to fight for its leader. Instead, he claimed, his communist friends had abandoned and betrayed him in his time of need. Gens spoke of the F.P.O. leadership with disdain. Their handling of the Wittenberg affair undermined his faith in the combat readiness of this organization. He asserted that he knew all along that "they were, cowards... writers, poets, dreamers... who imagined themselves to be... the main power and spirit of the ghetto. They wanted to advise, dictate, and rule." Gens claimed that Glazman, who was, at that time, the deputy chief of police, as well as a members of the F.P.O. command, "wanted to give him [Gens] orders." Gens suggested that if that was the case "Glazman should have become the head of the ghetto administration and enforce any policy he desired." That would require, however, dealing directly with the Gestapo which Glazman obviously did not relish. Glazman "preferred that Gens would negotiate with the Gestapo, so that he could act and give orders from behind his back."[9] Gens stated that he knew that the partisans were ready to accept into their ranks only those who were young, able-bodied, and armed, while his responsibility was to protect and try to save all those who had no means of arming themselves, or possibility of escape.

The availability of guides to lead those who were armed, able, and willing to join the partisans hastened the departure of a number of groups and individuals who had been, until recently, indecisive. On 24 July 1943 the first group, composed of F.P.O. members, under the leadership of J. Glazman, moved to the Narocz forest. This unit was confronted on its way by a German ambush, and nine of its twenty-five members perished. The rest reached their initial destination. Glazman's unit was followed by several others, and by August 1943 a total of close to 150 young men and women managed to leave the ghetto and join various partisan detachments in the Belorussian and Lithuanian forests.

In the summer of 1943 the F.P.O. was still the best organized and armed resistance body in the ghetto. Its indecisiveness and lack of experience, however, hindered its ability to make quick decisions, or change its course of action on short notice. Furthermore, the operation of the F.P.O. was often constrained by previously adopted resolutions. On 4 April 1943 the F.P.O. promulgated and circulated among its members the newly adopted, so-called, Combat Regulations. According to this document the F.P.O. was to "rise in revolt and fight within the ghetto, if, in its estimation, a general liquidation of the ghetto and not a limited Aktion was being launched; and the initial site of combat would be the ghetto, not the forest."[10] A few weeks later a supplement to the Combat Regulations, entitled Explanations to the Regulations, was published. It clarified, up to a point, the intended course of action, but introduced also some confusion. The Explanation asserted that "the F.P.O. will begin to fight when danger threatens the ghetto in its entirety... it will not undertake action in the defense of the life of each individual Jew.... The F.P.O. will begin to fight at the time of an Aktion that they deem to be the beginning of the end.... when danger threatens the general existence of the ghetto.... The purpose of the F.P.O. is resistance and rescue.... Immediate withdrawal into the forest at this juncture would be interpreted as seeking personal refuge and rescue.... We shall go into the forest only in the afternoon of battle. After having carried out our mission we shall take with us as large a number of Jews as possible and forge our way into the forests."[11]

The intentions of the F.P.O. were certainly sincere and ethical, but also impractical and short-sighted. First of all, most ghetto residents opposed armed resistance to the Nazis, because they believed that it meant unavoidable death. Moreover, there was little likelihood that after an uprising in the ghetto many Jews would still be alive and able to move into the forest.

The outcome of the Wittenberg affair was ominous. It damaged the image and credibility of the F.P.O. and it paralysed, to a degree, the effectiveness of its actions. Furthermore, its maneuverability was handicapped by its cumbersome organizational structure. The F.P.O. was a closely knit organization with some characteristic features which hampered its activity. Most members of the organization were admitted on the basis of political and party affiliation rather than by the natural selection of those who were most fit for military combat duty. Thus, the general level of physical preparedness was below the one expected in a military unit, readying for battle. Moreover, personal contacts and political connections, rather than life experience, military training, and combat usefulness determined the hierarchical structure of this combat body. In addition, the percentage of female members in the organization was high. That did not mean in the least that women did not contribute to the anti-Nazi war effort in the ghetto. Indeed, they successfully performed important tasks of reconnaissance, sabotage, and smuggling weapons. Some perished heroically, facing head-on the Nazi enemy, and yet physical limitations restricted their role in direct military confrontation. These shortcomings hampered the combat readiness of the F.P.O. which could only partially be rectified by dedication, will power, and spiritual strength.

The multi-party compositin of the F.P.O. leadership impeded its decision-making process and limited its prospects of growth. The F.P.O. failed to assume the general leadership of all young people in the ghetto who were ready to fight, denying them the chance of getting involved in anti-Nazi activity. In 1942, at the early stages of operation, secrecy was of the utmost importance and the detachment of the F.P.O. from the masses was justified. But even in the summer of 1943, when the existence of an armed resistance movement in the ghetto was no longer a secret to any Jew, the F.P.O. continued its policy of isolation. The events early in September 1943, which were a prelude to the final liquidation of the ghetto, proved that the F.P.O. was unable to assess the situation objectively and incapable or unwilling either to open the gates and move into the forest, or put its Combat Regulations into practice.

After the Wittenberg affair the underground forces regrouped, and the Jewish police continued its efforts to keep those who were armed in check. But instead of seeking confrontation with the F.P.O., the police aimed at apprehending and disarming unaffiliated youths. One day, late in July, upon my return home, from work, I was confronted by several Jewish policemen. They searched our flat, arrested me, and took me to the ghetto jail on Lidska Street. I did have a hand gun, but it was well hidden in the ceiling of our kitchen and the policemen failed to find it. In prison I recognized several youngsters from our group. I realized then that someone informed the police about our existence.

The ghetto jail was neither a comfortable nor secure place to stay. It was not a location where convicted criminals served time. It was rather a temporary detention point and a transfer station to the city jail at Lukiszki from where there was no return. It was well known in the ghetto that, from time to time, German security police would unexpectedly arrive, enter the prison through a special gate directly from the city and empty its premises. In many instances what might have appeared, at first, as a temporary detention turned into a death sentence, since all those removed to Lukiszki were soon transferred to Ponary for execution. Luckily we did not stay long in jail. Since no arms were discovered and the jail premises were crowded, next day, after interrogation, we were set free. I later learned that some unidentified influential individuals interceded with the ghetto authorities on our behalf.

The month of August 1943 was perceived in the ghetto as a time before an impending storm; the tension was high. Events were evolving haphazardly and no one could foresee or predict the future intentions of the Nazis. Early in the month, hundreds of Jews were abducted from their work place, at the local airport in Porubanek, and transported to a concentration camp in Estonia. The Nazis demanded that 3,000 Jewish workers be made available for deportation. However, only 1,400 were apprehended and removed from the ghetto in an action which ended on 22 August 1943. It was becoming clear, even to the uninitiated, simple ghetto resident, that something ominous was in the air, that the days of the ghetto were apparently numbered, yet neither the F.P.O. nor Gens were ready to face reality. The F.P.O. did not regard the transports to Estonia as the beginning of the liquidation of the ghetto, and, therefore, did not intend to go into action. Gens, on the other hand, deluded himself as well. In a speech to the Jews in the ghetto he tried to calm their fears by raising hopes for a speedy liberation of Vilnius by the Red Army.[12] As it turned out both, Gens and the F.P.O., were wrong. Both paid a high price for their serious mistakes.

NOTES

[1]. For the history of the F.P.O. see, among others, Yitzhak Arad, Ghetto in Flames (Jerusalem 1980); Dov Levin Fighting Back. Lithuanian Jewry's Armed Resistance to the Nazis 1941-1945 (New York ,1985); Chaim Lazar, Destruction and Resistance (New York, 1985); Lester E. Eckman and Chaim Lazar, The Jewish Resistance. A History of the Jewish Partisans in Lithuania and White Russia During the Nazi Occupation 1940-1945 (New York, 1977); Reizel Korchak, Lehavot be'efer (Merhaviya 1946).

[2]. Dov Levin, 114.

[3]. Arad, 375.

[4]. Korchak, 162.

[5]. Vasilii Grossman and Il'ia Erenburg, eds. Chernaia kniga (Vilnius 1993), 254.

[6]. Masha Greenbaum, The Jews of Lithuania. A History of a Remarkable Community, 1316-1945 (Jerusalem 1995), 331.

[7]. Arad, 393.

[8]. Ibid., 383.

[9]. Moshe Shutan, Geto un vald (Tel-Aviv 1971), 150.

[10]. Arad, 242.

[11]. Ibid., 478-9.

[12]. Lazar, 93.

E. 12 strashun street

Wednesday, 1 September 1943, marked the beginning of the end of the Vilnius ghetto. It was a bloody day. The fate of the remaining Jews in the ghetto was sealed. At dawn the ghetto was surrounded by Nazi troops. The ghetto gates were closed, and no one was permitted to go to work outside the ghetto any more. Early in the morning Estonian SS-men entered the ghetto and began abducting people on the streets. It soon became clear that they intended to round up some 5,000 man and women for deportation to concentration camps in Estonia. The streets soon became empty. Most ghetto residents went into hiding.

When the F.P.O. command realized that the ghetto was surrounded it decided to fight back and issued a mobilization order. But even before the F.P.O. managed to gather its members and distribute the concealed weapons, most still unarmed fighters of one battalion were surrounded by German and Estonian soldiers and were removed with no resistance from the ghetto for transportation to Estonia. The F.P.O. leadership was shocked but could do little to alleviate the situation. This circumstance not only reduced the combat capability of the F.P.O., but also exposed the inadequate state of its intelligence service and the lack of communication between the command and fighting units.

The headquarters of the F.P.O. were located at 6 Strashun (currently 4 Zemaitijos) Street, on the premises of the ghetto bath-house. The three-storey structure was situated at the dead end of a street which was separated from the city by a high brick wall. Most F.P.O. forces, under the command of its leader, A. Kovner, were assembled there. It appeared that the F.P.O. was ready to act. According to Ruzka Korchak, one of the F.P.O. insiders, the initial plan stipulated that F.P.O. members were supposed to open fire at the Nazis entering the ghetto from a position near the ghetto gate, at 11 Rudnicka Street.[1] By six A.M., however, the ghetto was full of Germans who entered the ghetto unhindered. Then, the F.P.O. leadership devised a new plan according to which the position at 6 Strashun Street was to be the main centre of defence. In order to guard the approaches to 6 Strashun Street, two outposts were to be placed at 7 and 8 Strashun Street, and two front positions were to be located at 12 and 15 of the same street. The main objective of the fighters, placed at 12 Strashun Street, was to block the entrance of Nazis into the street and to protect the F.P.O. headquarters from any unexpected attack. For additional security a machine-gun was placed on the balcony of 7 Strashun Street which overlooked and exposed to fire the entrance into the street.

The F.P.O. envisaged that after the initial resistance of its fighters, the whole ghetto population would become involved in battle. If it transpired, however, that it would be impossible to defend the position at 6 Strashun Street, the F.P.O. command would order the ghetto wall to be blown up and open the road for escape into the city.[2]

The new challenge to the safety of the ghetto engendered a tacit agreement between the chief of the Jewish police and the F.P.O. according to which the F.P.O. was not to undertake any resistance activity unless the Germans approached its fighting positions.[3] Hence, the Jewish police tried hard to divert the attention of the Nazis and make sure that they did not enter Strashun Street. Gens still hoped that the ghetto might survive this deportation action and he was afraid that a chance confrontation between the Nazis and representatives of the Jewish resistance could lead to bloodshed which would inevitably end in mass slaughter and the immediate liquidation of the ghetto.

It took a while before J. Gens managed to persuade the leaders of the Gestapo to remove most Estonian and German soldiers from the ghetto, promising that the Jewish police would make a concentrated effort to deliver the required number of people. However, "when only 600 men had been arrested by the Jewish police by evening, the Germans and Estonians again entered the ghetto."[4] The assurances of the Jewish police notwithstanding that no Germans would enter Strashun Street and despite the presence of a machine-gun overlooking the whole Street, it was the responsibility of the fighters at the premises of the school at 12 Strashun Street to secure the approaches to the F.P.O. headquarters by blocking the entrance of the Nazis to Strashun Street from the adjacent Shavelska (Sauliu) Street.

The history of the outpost on 12 Strashun Street is a special case. That was the only place where the Nazis were greeted with fire, and, in that sense, the only expression of armed resistance in the ghetto. There are today many conflicting reports describing these events. Some are realistic, truthful, and to the point. Others are in the realm of documentary fiction. The well known Yiddish poet A. Sutskever, or I. Kowalski, for example, portray the affair in the language of heroic epos. Others do it in more restrained tones. In a book, published immediately after the war in Moscow, Sutskever wrote that "when the Germans approached [12 Strashun Street]... a fire was opened from the barricade.... The Germans called for reinforcements, and hundreds of murderers arrived in the ghetto. They opened heavy fire at 12 Strashun Street. The commander, Sheinbaum, who stood at the window, firing at the Germans, was the first to fall dead into the arms of his comrades. The fighter Reizel Korchak took over the command. The Germans, who were faced with strong resistance, blew up the building. Close to a hundred people perished under the rubble."[5]

Isaac Kowalski, an apparent members of the F.P.O., who claims to have been on 1 September 1943 at 12 Strashun Street, describes his alleged valiant exploits and takes credit for recovering the gun and ammunition of Sheinbaum who has been shot dead by the Germans. Kowalski asserts that "the partisan [F.P.O.] headquarters had abandoned the idea of resistance in the ghetto itself and decided to retreat to the woods and wage battle from there.... [but] if the Germans attacked partisan units, we were, as a last resort, to fight on the spot as well." Kowalski declares further that he was assigned, with twelve or thirteen other fighters, to the post on 12 Strashun Street. When the Germans blew up the house across the street, at 15 Strashun Street, the commander Sheinbaum ordered

"to fire at the Gestapo demolition men in the street as they stood admiring the results of their work. Ilya [Yechiel] Scheinbaum... threw a grenade into the group of Nazis outside. It was a direct hit. Those who were able to escape ran, but not for long. We saw them take dynamite sticks and run to our side of the building. We fired at them, but soon lost them from sight, for they took up positions at the walls of the building, where they could not be seen. For a while it was quiet. Then we heard commands to mine and blow up the entire house. We tried to find positions from which we would be able to fire at them and prevent their action. Ilya Scheinbaum leaned slightly out of a window to see where the Gestapo men were. At that moment there was a shot from below. I... saw Ilya falling. I... could see no injuries.... but I saw he was dead.... Ruszka Korczak gave orders to jump from the back windows.... I was the last to jump.... I barely had time to recover from the shock of falling when I heard the tremendous explosion that turned the entire building into a smoking heap of rubble."[6]

According to another account of the same events by Masha Greenbaum "when German units entered the Vilna ghetto on 1 September 1943 members of the underground engaged them in an armed clash in which Yehiel Sheinbaum, leader of an underground group that had joined the F.P.O., and other fighters were killed. The underground attack succeeded in killing or wounding several guards....Fearing that further hostilities between the underground and the German troops would lead to the immediate destruction of the ghetto, Gens negotiated a withdrawal of German soldiers by promising to meet the required quota of workers for the Estonian and Latvian camps."[7]

In books published in 1977 and 1985 respectively, Ch. Lazar, a member of the F.P.O., provides two conflicting accounts of the same events. In the first, written jointly with L. Eckman, he suggests that

"The front position on Straszuna 12 was commanded by Yehiel Sheinbaum.... When the Germans were seen approaching, Sheinbaum fired the first shot. The Germans called in reserves, and soon hundreds of armed men streamed into the ghetto to attack the barricade. It was a bloody battle, and the Germans were repulsed in several frontal assaults. Then, at the crucial moment, Sheinbaum fell, his body riddled with bullets. Chaim Napoleon and Reizel Korczak then took over the defense. The Germans soon received their reinforcements but could still make no headway. Failing to gain a foothold in frontal attacks, the Germans decided on a change of tactics. German troopers with loads of dynamite stole behind the Jewish position and mined the barricade and its foundations.... Many fighters whom the Germans could not subdue in open combat were struck down in the explosion."[8]

In another version of the same events Ch. Lazar asserts that

"the front position was in the school auditorium on 12 Straszun Street. A company of fighters was sent there, made up mainly of members of the Second organization.... Ilya Scheinbaum, a leader of the Second Organization and a former officer in the Polish Army, was chosen as commander of the position....The F.P.O. commander was upset by the appointment. He wanted members of his own movement in command. At the last minute, he appointed as commander of the position Rozka Korczak despite her lack of military knowledge, and made Scheinbaum her second-in-command.... At dusk several Gestapo men and Estonian soldiers came to the ghetto, and together with Gens and a number of Jewish policemen, approached the house on 12 Straszun Street to conduct a search, having heard that a lot of Jews were hiding in the yard. Ilya Scheinbaum stood at the window and saw the Germans approaching the building. According to plan, he fired shots and threw a grenade. But the grenade did not explode. The Germans retreated momentarily but then opened heavy fire on the position. A bullet struck Scheinbaum, killing him. Rozka, the commander of the position, gave no order to the fighters. She ran to the Headquarters and said that everything was in order at the position and did not relate what had happened. The fighters at the position were confused. They waited for instructions which did not come. Though they saw that the building was about to be blown up, they did not leave it. Chaim Napoleon was killed in the explosion and several other fighters were seriously wounded.... Dozens of Jewish tenants were buried under the rubble.[9] "

R. Korchak was one of the few members of the F.P.O. present that ominous day at 12 Strashun Street. In a book, originally published in 1946, she declared that Sheinbaum was appointed head of the position at 12 Strashun Street. He ordered that the fighters should open fire after him. When the Germans approached, Sheinbaum

"gives an order and shoots first. We open intense fire. We throw grenades from the windows in the direction of the approaching enemy. The enemy answers immediately with heavy fire. The first falls Sheinbaum, the commander of the position. The Germans move away fast, and there is no one to shoot at any more. Suddenly news arrive that the Germans intend to blow up the house. The group of fighters receives an order to withdraw and unite with the main forces on 6 Strashun Street.... All the block, where our position was located, was blown up. We soon learned that the Germans removed their wounded from Strashun Street, and withdrew from the ghetto.[10]"

Another version, provided by Y. Arad, gives the most sober, succinct, albeit incomplete, account of the events described. At noon on 1 September 1943

"the F.P.O. issued a proclamation to all ghetto inhabitants calling for armed resistance to deportation.... With the exception of a party of youngsters, who joined the F.P.O. positions on Straszuna Street, the inhabitants [of the ghetto] did not respond to the call for an uprising.... The F.P.O.fighters, under the command of Scheinbaum, who were in the forward position at 12 Straszuna opened fire at the Germans. They returned fire with automatic weapons. Scheinbaum was killed instantly, and the other combatants retreated to the main post at 6 Straszuna. The Germans blew up the house at no. 12 and left the ghetto at nightfall. [11]"

I was at 12 Strashun Street that fateful 1 September 1943, and witnessed the events described above closely. I lived in the ghetto on 7 Strashun Street. The leader of our group, Chaim Rubanovich, lived in the next house, at 5 Strashun Street. Since the base of our group was near the F.P.O. headquarters, allegdly protected by the Jewish police, most members of our group managed to escape the initial kidnapping assault by the Estonians, as well as the subsequent search by Jewish policemen who were ordered to take over from the Nazis the job of rounding up Jews for deportation to Estonia. At the first opportunity members of our group got together to contemplate our future course of action. We had no reliable information about the situation in the ghetto and we did not believe that those abducted were indeed taken to labour camps in Estonia. We knew that the Nazis could not be trusted and that a transport to Estonia could easily be diverted to any other destination. But we were trapped and there was no way out from the ghetto.

We knew that the F.P.O. headquarters were in the bath-house and we decided to get in touch with them and, if possible, join their ranks. We were resolved not to surrender without a struggle and we knew that it would be easier to fight together. By noon we were admitted to the front chamber of the F.P.O. headquarters where we were met by some of its leaders. Our proposition to join the F.P.O. was received coolly. We were offered admission to the F.P.O. as individuals, rather than as a group, on condition that we give up our weapons. We were told that once we were accepted and became members of the organization, the arms would be redistributed among the most deserving members of the F.P.O. It was even possible, we were told, that some of us might get our guns back.

It was obvious to us that the price of admission to the F.P.O. was too high, by far. We were offended by this arrogant treatment and suspected that the F.P.O. officials wanted to get our arms, in order to give them to their political associates and cronies. They surely knew how difficult it was to procure arms in the ghetto and that without a gun membership in their organization was meaningless, particularly to those who had no former political ties, or ideological connection, with the F.P.O. leadership. We turned down their proposition and were ready to leave. But then, before our departure from the F.P.O. headquarters, we were offered a chance to take part in the forthcoming battle. We were told of the alleged fortifications on 12 Strashun Street and it was suggested to us that we go there and join some other fighters. We were told that when the Germans enter the street, we should open fire and repulse the intruders. If Nazi reinforcements would arrive, the machine-gun, stationed on a balcony on 7 Strashun Street, will open fire, and repel the Nazi attackers. The battle plan seemed logical and, rather than surrender, we were eager to join in the struggle.

We arrived at 12 Strashun Street early in the afternoon. The lower floor of the building was cramped with ordinary ghetto dwellers. The school premises were located on the upper floor. Some of the rooms were still cluttered with school benches. A gate in front of the house led into a big yard. Some rooms in the school faced the street, others the yard. There was no barricade or any other fortifications at this front position. When we entered the school premises, on the second floor, we realized that some fighters were already there. We did not know any of them, nor did we know

97

of any battle plan. We could see, however, that some of those present were armed and knew each other. It appeared also that one of the men, older than the rest, was in charge. After a brief consultation it was agreed that we position ourselves near the windows and watch whether the Nazis would enter Strashun Street. In case the Nazis appeared on the street and approached our building, we were to open fire.

I was in a room facing the street. There were four windows in the room. At each window, hiding behind the wall, stood one fighter observing the street. I stood at one of the windows. Next to me was a member of our group, Samuel Shapiro. At the other two windows were two men from the other group. Somewhat later I learned about the identity of the one who stood at the forward position, at the window nearest to the possible German approach. It was Yechiel Sheinbaum, the leader of the so-called Combat Group, or Second Organization, apparently affiliated with the F.P.O. For quite a while the street was empty and there was no one in sight. We took turns standing on guard at the windows of the room. All of a sudden, late in the afternoon, Germans entered Strashun Street from behind the corner of Shavelska. Events unfolded very quickly. Yechiel fired first and we followed suit. Shapiro tossed a grenade which did not explode. I did not see whether any of the Germans were hit, but in seconds I saw Sheinbaum fall, struck down by a single bullet to his neck. While we were trying to pull away his body from the window the Germans on the street opened heavy fire with automatic weapons. Most bullets hit the ceiling which began to crumble. Pieces of plaster and brick fell on our heads. During that commotion a young woman rushed into the school-room, shouting: "Chaim [Rubanovich], take over the command," and she disappeared from sight just as fast. I was amazed at her appearance. I had never seen her before, and I wondered who she was. Much later I learned that this was Ruzka Korchak, a prominent member of the F.P.O., who, according to some accounts, was to lead the fighters in battle.

Everything was happening on 12 Strashun Street very quickly. There was no time for contemplation. While we were trying to retreat into the school corridor, facing the yard, the Germans continued to fire without stop. I was hardly out of the room, looking for my friends, when the part of the building which faced the street was blown up and levelled by dynamite. It was difficult to know exactly how many people perished under the rubble, but several members of our group were never seen again. And, of course, most occupants of the building who lived on the lower floor were surely killed.

In that turmoil I wondered what happened to the machine-gun on the balcony of 7 Strashun Street. Those on the balcony could certainly see the

Germans spraying us with submachine-gun fire, and by firing at them, they could delay their attack and help us retreat. But the F.P.O. position on 7 Strashun Street was silent. The F.P.O. fighters with the machine-gun failed to provide cover. They were probably more concerned with protecting their own headquarters, on 6 Strashun Street, than with our destiny. It was difficult to know at that time whether the gunners' refusal to pull the trigger was an impulsive reaction of fear and concern for their own safety, or the F.P.O. command failed to issue the necessary orders to act.

Many years later, in the early 1960s, I had an opportunity to meet Mr. S. Kowarsky in New York. He had been an active member of the F.P.O. and he admitted that he was one of those stationed with the machine-gun on the second floor balcony of 7 Strashun Street, that fateful afternoon. When I asked him whether they saw the Germans spraying us with fire, he replied that they surely did. The answer to my next question was more problematic. I asked him point-blank: why did he not pull the trigger then? First, he replied, there was no order to shoot and, besides, he continued had he then opened fire on the Nazis we would probably not be walking today peacefully here in New York. We would certainly all be dead. I could not help, but agree with him. Indeed, there was no chance of defeating the Nazis. Of course, we could inflict some casualties upon the enemy, but in the end, except for the few lucky ones who would manage to escape, most others would perish in the uneven battle with superior forces. The above notwithstanding, the question which bothered me most remained unanswered: why did the leaders of the F.P.O. mislead us? Why did they use us as fodder for the Nazi war machine with the sole purpose of protecting themselves?

Originally the intentions of the F.P.O. leaders were probably sincere. But they apparently panicked and concerned with their own survival decided to wait rather than fight. The fact that there were few original members of the F.P.O. on 12 Strashun Street was instructive. They preferred to place strangers in positions of danger, rather than risk the safety of their own political friends. That was why Sheinbaum and his people, as well as members of our group, were sent to 12 Strashun Street while the leadership of the F.P.O., with all their heavy weapons hid in the bath-house at 6 Strashun Street.

At the very moment when, accompanied by frightful tremors and noise, the school structure on 12 Strashun Street was collapsing, I was in the air jumping from a second floor window in the school corridor. It was difficult to know how I managed to land on the ground of the school yard unharmed. A young fellow next to me was not as fortunate. He carried a Molotov cocktail in the upper pocket of his shirt and when he landed on the ground the home made grenade exploded. I found out later that the young man was blinded. In ghetto conditions it was equal to a death sentence.

The rubble of the demolished building covered Strashun Street and blocked the passage to the F.P.O. headquarters. Unaware of what was happening on the street, I got together with a few of my friends who survived the 12 Strashun Street debacle and tried to get away from the scene of disaster as soon as possible. No one knew what the intentions of the Germans were, nor could one see whether they were trying to blow up the remaining part of the building. Concerned with our own safety, we did not venture onto the street. Instead, we climbed onto the roof and crawling stealthily reached the F.P.O. headquarters at 6 Strashun Street. But we were not welcome there. We were refused shelter and were left on the street. We were good enough to man their front position and protect them from a Nazi assault, but as soon as our task was accomplished we became redundant. Only established members of the organization were admitted to the barricade. We had no choice, but to seek shelter somewhere else. We gathered our men and sought counsel. We realized that we would have to ward for ourselves and that there was no one around we could rely on, or ask for help.

2 September 1943 in the morning. The ghetto was relatively calm, but the deportation action continued. We soon learned that most Germans and Estonians had withdrawn from the ghetto, leaving the job of rounding up Jewish men and women to the Jewish police. The action lasted for another four days. Lulled by the assurances of the Germans that those abducted were, indeed, deported to labour camps, many Jews, tired of hiding in bunkers, and afraid of being discovered there anyway, volunteered to join their family members apprehended before. They were inspired by rumours, circulating in the ghetto, that whole families, particularly husbands and wives, would be placed in camps together. Little did they know at that time that, in fact, men and women were sent to different destinations and that the notion of family unification was another sham by the German administration. The Jewish police was eager to produce the required number of inmates regardless, because Gens was assured by the Germans that as soon as the quota was fulfilled peace would reign in the ghetto, at least, for the next six months. The remaining Jews would be employed in factories and workshops to be established within the ghetto.

As long as the deportation action was in process members of our group did not venture outside. We were hiding on Strashun Street not far from the F.P.O. headquarters. We knew that the access to this area was blocked by the rubble of 12 Strashun Street, and assumed that a challenge to the F.P.O. position on 6 Strashun Street was unlikely.

On 5 September 1943, the deportation action was completed and temporary calm set in. Life assumed a peculiar semblance of normalcy. People were free to move around and communicate with each other, but no one was permitted to go outside the ghetto. The Jewish quarters were no longer surrounded by German soldiers, and, as in the "good old days," only Lithuanian policemen guarded the entrance gates to the ghetto from the outside. However, the atmosphere in the ghetto was extremely tense. There were still some 10,000 Jews remaining in the ghetto, and a sensation of imminent change for the worse was in the air.

On 6 September 1943, the F.P.O. came out with a new plan of action. Its main goal was now to leave the ghetto and move into the woods. However, if instead of rounding up the people for transportation to working camps, the Nazis decided to liquidate the ghetto completely, members of the F.P.O. would stop their escape to the forest, and, if necessary, fight the aggressor.[12]

The new situation in the ghetto, after 5 September 1943, created appropriate conditions for attempts to escape from the ghetto unnoticed. Indeed, between 5 and 15 September 1943, a hundred and fifty F.P.O. members left the ghetto for the Narocz and Rudnicki forests. After the death of Sheinbaum, the loose bond between the "Yechiel Combat Group" and the F.P.O. was severed, and some seventy members of this group left the ghetto without consulting the F.P.O. command as well.[13]

The fate of armed youths who did not belong to the F.P.O. and had no other political connections was more complicated. Our group's first priority was to join the partisans in the forest and we were ready and willing to abandon the ghetto immediately. However, without the cooperation of the F.P.O. and the assistance of the Jewish police, it was almost impossible to locate a secure exit from the ghetto. The temporary calm in the ghetto did not delude us. We did not trust the Germans, nor could we expect much from our Jewish leaders. They were confused, helpless, and concerned with their own survival. No wonder they could do little to help us.

As soon as the iron hoop around the ghetto loosened, several armed Jewish youths arrived from the forest. Risking their lives, they offered to lead unaffiliated young people into the woods to join the Soviet partisans. Our group was in contact with one such guide who was ready to lead us into the Narocz forest. We started to make preparations for departure without delay. We planned to exit through a gate on Bosaczkova-Karmelitu Street which was originally used for the removal of garbage and refuse from the ghetto premises. The keys to this gate were in the office of the Jewish police precinct. Everything seemed simple. Get the keys, open the gate, and move. But despite the fact that from the outside the iron grip on the ghetto was temporarily loosened, there were new immense obstacles within the ghetto. The ghetto police guarded all possible secret exits in order to preclude any abortive attempt to escape from the ghetto. They feared that once Jews were caught by the Germans on their way out, the ghetto might again be surrounded by soldiers. Moreover, their own intended escape could then be imperilled. The F.P.O. was also of little help. It was primarily concerned with the impending departure of its own members and it wanted to keep all possible exists secure.

Tuesday, 7 September 1943, two days after the deportation action was over, most members of our group were ready to move. At dusk, I took leave of my mother, sister, and other members of the family. The parting was swift, but heart-wrenching. I doubted whether I would ever see them again. My mother knew that I belonged to an underground resistance group and that I intended to join the partisans, but she never questioned my actions. I was free to make my own choices, but this burden of freedom was not easy to bear. Of course, mother would prefer me to stay with the family, but she also wanted me to stay alive, and no one knew where the chances for survival were better.

I took my gun and went to our gathering point. But to everyone's surprise, late in the evening, I was back home. We failed to leave the ghetto and were not permitted even to approach our intended point of departure. The following day, Wednesday, 8 September 1943, I again took leave of my relatives, and proceeded again to the intended exit gate. But nothing had changed. We were intimidated, verbally abused, but not permitted to leave. I returned home again.

Next evening, Thursday, 9 September 1943, I left home in a hurry without saying goodbye to anyone. No one believed any more that we would manage to get out from the ghetto. At the secret exit gate we were again faced by the Jewish police, and some other individuals, apparently members of the Jewish underground, who intended to block our departure. I recorded my experiences of that fateful night sometimes in the winter of 1943-44, while I was a member of a Soviet partisan detachment in the Belorussian forests. In the next few pages I quote from my memoirs, translated from the Russian original verbatim, without changes, deletions, or corrections. I was than eighteen years old, young, inexperienced, and impressionable. Some of my remarks might seem today naive, but they were sincere, unembellished, and based on first hand observations.

"9 September 1943. Night approaches. We were still standing at the gates of 5 Bosaczkova-Karmelitu Street not knowing what to do. Those in charge at the gate of Karmelitu Street tried to intimidate us and, in all probability, force us to remain in the ghetto. It was clear that their actions were wrong, and amounted to betrayal. The more so since among them was the Jewish police commissar N. Dreizin, a well known agents of the Gestapo. It was obvious that something vile and despicable was going on behind our backs. We found ourselves, that fateful night of 9 September 1943, in a situation from which there was no apparent way out. We were young, armed, and firmly believed in the possibility of escape, and we were ready to fight to protect our dignity. We were desperate and if denied the possibility to leave the ghetto we were ready for anything.

At one point, after long bickering, our group was split into several small formations, and we were promised by those in charge that these small groups will be permitted to exit at certain intervals. After several members of our group were allowed to depart, it was announced that no one would be granted permission to leave the ghetto this night any more. Consequently we were ordered to disperse. But since the gate on Karmelitu Street was the only exit from the ghetto available to us, and since that was the route which was supposed to lead us to our initial meeting point outside the city, we decided not to budge. We realized that we were cheated again, and that the politicians, who joined ranks with the police, had a hidden agenda. We decided to act immediately, and leave the ghetto this very night at any cost. Many members of our group were already outside the ghetto, while the rest was trapped and open to blackmail. We suspected that the politicians, with the help of the police, wanted to corner us, and get hold of our guns. After all, we remembered that they put us already in jail once before.

There was no time for contemplation. We had to act without delay. At eleven P.M. a curfew in the city came into effect, all movement stopped, and it was impossible to cross a street without being noticed by Lithuanian policemen or a German patrol. With the help of our secret contact man at the Jewish police precinct on Rudninku Street, we managed to get hold of a duplicate key to the gate at Karmelitu Street, avoiding thus the scrutiny of senior police officers. We opened the gate which led to a square, outside the ghetto wall, when no one was around. Unexpectedly something happened. Someone, apparently a passer by, flashed a light into the semi-opened gate. We moved back into the dark. We thought that this was a Lithuanian policeman or German soldier, guarding the ghetto from the outside. Fortunately, it turned out that this was not the case. A few minutes later, we approached the gate again. We opened it, looked outside, and could see no one around. We decided then to move.

Through the semi-opened gate we were leaving in pairs. Arm in arm, usually a man and a woman, pretending that they were a pair of lovers in the night. There were many people, that night, at this clandestine exit gate

103

from the ghetto. We did not know any of them, but were sure that they looked for a chance to escape. Some had apparently hiding places in the city; others wanted to join those moving into the forest. Despite the fact that the presence of unarmed strangers in our midst could endanger our passage, we did not prevent anyone from trying his or her luck. We knew that this might be their only chance for a new beginning. Pairs were leaving the ghetto in intervals of a few minutes. When one pair was already hardly visible, some fifty meters away, another couple would follow. I left the ghetto in pair with the wife of one of our group members. Her husband had left the ghetto in another pair a while ago. Our route was through little travelled city streets in the direction of the suburb of Zarzecze (Uzupiai), not far from the old Jewish cemetery. It was agreed that all our group members will meet at a certain point in the forest, just outside the city."

After our departure the situation in the ghetto was relaxed for another week, and F.P.O. fighters continued to leave the ghetto for the nearby forests. However, any one who did not belong to that organization was harassed and kept away from the hidden exits that were no longer secret to any one. This situation did not change even on 23 September 1943 - the day of the ghetto liquidation. The F.P.O. command, together with its remaining fighters, in total some eighty men and women, escaped from the ghetto through the city sewer system. This route was kept secret not only from unaffiliated ghetto youths, but even from the general F.P.O. membership, as well. When unorganized young people sensed that the end of the ghetto was near, many were desperate to leave, but the F.P.O. command remained true to itself to the very end. Orders were issued that no one, who did not belong to that organization, should be permitted to join the fighter groups on their way to the forest.[14]

My exit from the ghetto closed a chapter in my life. I left my family, many friends, and the oppressive past behind. I knew, however, little of what the future held in store for me. Neither did I know where I would get my next meal. Danger continued to lurk behind each corner. Still hiding from any one in sight I took off my yellow badges and started to act as a free man in open conflict with the Nazi regime. Together with my friends I was ready now to face my adversaries in open battle. Moreover, there was no need any longer to depend on the ostensible security provided by the ghetto walls. My departure from the ghetto severed also my relationship with, and dependence on, the Jewish police, the ghetto politicians, and the F.P.O. No longer did my struggle with the occupier and possible survival interfere with their plans or intentions, and I was glad.

Today, over fifty-four years after the events described, the story about the Jewish underground and the alleged uprising in the Vilnius ghetto is still incomplete. Most accounts are provided by former members of the underground movement who relate events from a personal perspective limited in scope. The views expressed in many recent studies rather than render an all-embracing and objective picture of the harrowing past often reflect the current political and social aims of their authors. Thus, for example, studies of the resistance movement in the Vilnius ghetto written by citizens of the former Soviet Union, and published in the USSR, place particular emphasis on the contribution of the Communist Party to the resistance under Nazi occupation. They do not mention that most participants of the underground movement in the Vilnius ghetto belonged to other political parties and that among the underground leaders were many Zionists. Other authors, mainly those who have settled after the Second World War in Israel, go to other extremes. They often minimize the significance of Soviet involvement in the underground war, failing to stress that without Soviet participation and the proximity of the front line, any resistance to Nazi occupation would be meaningless, and doomed to failure.

The otherwise informative books by Chaim Lazar may serve as an example of another kind of political prejudice. It may appear from his books that the author's main purpose is to identify and exalt the heroism and dedication of every single member of the resistance or partisan movements who was a member of the Zionist-revisionist organization *Betar*.[15] At a conference on Manifestations of Jewish Resistance, which took place in April 1968 in Jerusalem, Shimon Wiesenthal /Vienna/ urged the participants not to "avoid topics which may be unpleasant." He asserted that historical truth required that we "explain that the lack of unity among Jews during the holocaust period contributed to the magnitude of the calamity."[16]

Indeed, the lack of unity precluded the participation of many young able-bodied men in the ghetto underground movement. It also prevents , today, many scholars, politicians, and holocaust survivors from providing future generations with a complete and objective picture of the horrid past. In fact, even today there is no agreement among different authors as to whether there was indeed an uprising in the Vilnius ghetto. According to Ruzka Korchak "the underground did indeed go into action... freed the shackled Wittenberg from the Germans.... and laid down their arms only out of fear of slaughter of the Jews in the ghetto."[17] That was, of course, true. Most ghetto inhabitants were hostile to the F.P.O. and disapproved of their belligerent intentions. People in the ghetto supported the surrender of Wittenberg because they did not want to risk their safety by hiding Wittenberg in the ghetto. And, besides, it appeared that the leaders of the F.P.O. took the German threats seriously as well, fearing Nazi retaliation.

It was clear to everyone, including the F.P.O. leadership, that any armed anti-Nazi activity, connected with the resolve to protect Wittenberg, was fraught with terrible consequences to all ghetto residents, and no one wanted to risk unnecessary destruction.

Y. Gutman, another speaker at the Jerusalem conference in 1968, suggested that "there were uprisings in Bialystok, in Vilna, in Czestochowa, in Zaglebie. A handful of men fought. The masses did not join them."[18] Both, Korchak and Gutman are correct, but only up to a point. On 15 July 1943 the F.P.O. went into action to defend its commander, rather that the Jews in the ghetto. When, on 1 September 1943, the real trial began, the F.P.O. did not act. It ran for cover. In the Warsaw ghetto, for example, the masses participated in the uprising because the underground organization was a fighting formation. It led the masses and provided examples of heroism and dedication. In the Vilnius ghetto instead, the F.P.O. was indecisive, hesitant, always waiting. Even after its call to arms and the proclamation of 1 September 1943, it remained apathetic.

Indeed, as Gutman suggests, the masses "did not join the handful of men who fought" in the Vilnius ghetto. In fact, the F.P.O. did not join them either. The experience of 12 Strashun Street was an isolated incident which corroborates this proposition convincingly. What could the masses do with their bare hands? With no recourse to arms, and no connections to the outside world. Moreover, an uprising by the masses would certainly be suicidal. It would mean immediate destruction, instead of at least some vague hope of survival in a concentration camp.

Today, one might question whether armed resistance within the walls of the Vilnius ghetto was, indeed, the best course of action. In 1943, however, it was clear to anyone familiar with the underground movement that an uprising could have been staged indeed. There were caches of weapons and many young people ready to fight. But there was no one able and willing to organize and lead the ghetto youth in battle. The F.P.O. failed in its self-assumed mission. One might even surmise that it was not a fighting formation, but rather a coalition of different political groups. Instead of United Partisan Organization it should have, perhaps, been called United Political Organization. The initials are the same, but the meaning is different. The main objective of any partisan organization is to fight in support of a cause. In the case of the F.P.O., the initial objective of armed confrontation with the enemy degenerated into a struggle for personal survival. In normal circumstances political decisions are made by politicians, but the implementation of particular policies, involving military activity and warfare, are left to professionals with military training. The F.P.O. was able to deal with political issues, but it was totally unqualified to handle military matters. The initial military strategy of the F.P.O. which envisaged, as late as in the summer of 1943, the possibility of armed resistance within the ghetto was short-sighted. First, the ghetto population opposed it, and, besides, the F.P.O. lacked the resolve to act.

In an account written in March 1944, just before the capture of Vilnius by Soviet troops, N. Reznik, one of the members of the F.P.O. command staff, summarized the situation in a dispassionate and self-critical manner. He asserted that

"on 1 September 1943 when the Germans and Estonian police entered the Vilna ghetto, the shrunken FPO, taken by surprise, tried to mobilize for defence, but half the units could not reach their arsenal and others simply fled. Some resisters waited at their preselected bit of ghetto terrain for Germans to arrive, but no armed encounter of significance took place. The FPO did not impede the Germans in their work of rounding up some eight thousand Jews - about two thirds of the ghetto - for deportation. That FPO failure convinced the members that their most prudent course would be to leave the remnant ghetto. Within days about two hundred young people succeeded in joining the partisans in the woods."[19]

Despite its failure one should not blame the F.P.O. for its reluctance to join a losing battle. Its members were inexperienced, idealistic, and perhaps even a little naive. They were carried away by the idealistic notion of the importance of their mission. It took time before they were able to assess the situation realistically and replace their high sounding phraseology with a pragmatic approach to life, in which, in the end, their own survival became their main objective. Y. Arad summarized the dilemma of the F.P.O. succinctly and to the point. To the question "Why the Uprising Did not Take Place?" he replied "The F.P.O. blames the Jews for not joining their call for resistance when in fact they alone, and only they, could precipitate the bloody confrontation which no one wanted, not the Jews in the ghetto nor the F.P.O., everyone wanted to live and hoped for survival."[20]

The story of the F.P.O. is, nevertheless, an important part of the history of Jewish resistance to Nazi oppression. It illustrates both the strengths and weaknesses of underground movements in extreme situations. The F.P.O. failed to live up to its proclaimed objectives, but it gave hope and dignity to many otherwise downtrodden people in the ghetto. It challenged the Nazi rulers. It organized acts of sabotage, procured arms, and, in the end, helped its members escape to the forest. Perhaps, they could have done much more, but like all of us in the ghetto, they were ordinary mortals faced with insurmountable odds.

NOTES

[1]. Reizel Korchak, Lehavot be'efer (Merhaviya, 1965), 183.

[2]. Ibid., 184.

[3]. Chaim Lazar, Destruction and Resistance (New York 1985), 95.

[4]. Yehuda Bauer, A History of the Holocaust (New York 1982), 268.

[5]. A. Sutskever, Fun Vilner Geto (Moscow 1946),199.

[6]. Isaac Kowalski, A Secret Press in Nazi Europe. The Story of a Jewish United Partisan Organization (New York 1969), 203-4.

[7]. Masha Greenbaum, The Jews of Lithuania (Jerusalem 1995), 331.

[8]. L.E. Eckman and Chaim Lazar, Jewish Resistance, 35.

[9]. Lazar, 94-6.

[10]. Korchak, 186.

[11]. Y. Arad, Ghetto in Flames (Jerusalem 1980), 411-3.

[12]. Korchak, 191.

[13]. Dov Levin, Fighting Back (New York 1985), 114.

[14]. Arad, 433.

[15]. See, for example, Lazar, Destruction and Resistance.

[16]. Jewish Resistance During the Holocaust. Proceedings of the Conference on Manifestations of Jewish Resistance, Jerusalem, April 7-11, 1968 (Jerusalem 1971), 97.

[17]. Ibid., 256.

[18]. Ibid., 276.

[19]. Nisl Reznik, "Geshikhte fun FPO," March 12 1944, typescript, pp. 9-11. Quoted in Lucy S. Dawidowicz, The War Against the Jews 1933-1945 (New York 1986), 327.

[20]. Arad, 417.

F. IN THE FOREST

My timely escape from the ghetto was one of the small miracles which made surviving Nazi oppression possible. It was, however, only the first hurdle on the difficult path to safety. I was like a bird, just out of a cage, for the first time in years exposed to a natural environment which was alien to me.

Our group left the ghetto the night of 9 September 1943 in the dark, around ten P.M. We were supposed to cross the city inconspicuously and meet at the edge of a forest on the outskirts of the city. From there we were to move, all together, in the required direction. Our passage through the city was uneventful. Walking stealthily we managed to avoid any contact with people. It was sheer good luck that we did not come across anyone who could have caused trouble. Upon arrival at the agreed meeting point we were faced with the first surprise. Some members of our group were missing. They failed to reach our gathering spot in due time. Since no shots, however, were heard in the vicinity we presumed that they were safe. They had probably lost their way and had taken a different route out from the city.

Our situation was further complicated by the fact that on our way from the ghetto our group was unexpectedly joined by a number of strangers. We did not even know their names. All we knew was that these were desperate Jews who decided to try escape from the ghetto at any price. They attached themselves to our group by following us after our exit from the ghetto. Most were unarmed and could hardly cope with the difficulties of the trip. Yet, in good conscience, we could not abandon them to the mercy of the Nazis and were compelled to take them along. We waited until midnight for our missing friends, and then started our journey in the direction of Narocz.

It took almost a week to reach our final destination. We walked mostly during the night to avoid confrontation with the enemy, and hid in the forest during the day. Approximately half way to Narocz, we stopped for the day in a forest, not far from the river crossing of Oszmianka, near the town of Michaliszki. Most members of our group were young, bold, and full of hope. Yet we lacked discipline, vigilance, and military experience. Due to our negligence Germans were able to discover our encampment. They pursued and attacked us. Our group of close to twenty was dispersed. We tried to save ourselves by running in different directions deep into the forest. Confrontation with the enemy made no sense. Our hand-guns were no match for the automatic weapons in the hands of the German soldiers. By the time we eluded the Germans and the assault was over, it was already dark. We realized that one woman had been killed and a man wounded. Some others disappeared without trace. We searched the forest for survivors, but to no avail. Six members of our basic group managed to stay together.

Our first unexpected encounter as "free" men with the Nazis had a sobering effect. It shattered our false sense of security and reminded us of the possibility of meeting the enemy, who was constantly searching for new victims. We became more vigilant and suspicious of the slightest noise, or even the shadows in the dark forest. At night we crossed the river Oszmianka and continued on our way. This crossing was, in a sense, our first military operation. The bridge was guarded by Germans and the waters were too deep to cross on foot. Hence, a boat was necessary. We approached a peasant and asked him to take us across in return for money. He was frightened and refused. We then produced our guns and ordered him to follow. We warned him that if he were to betray us to the Germans, he and his family would be the first to be killed in retaliation.

We marched for another two nights before we approached the region of Narocz. On our way we encountered a group of Soviet partisans returning to their base in the forest and followed them to our destination. Not far from Narocz, we suddenly came under fire by a German ambush. We ran for cover into the nearby swamp and were forced to take a different route, putting on some extra twenty kilometres on our way to the final destination. Not far from the partisan bases we stopped walking during the night and continued on our way during the day. To our surprise, in an area controlled by the partisans, we uncovered another ambush. We managed to avoid it only to find out later that it was a partisan ambush waiting for Germans to pass. The following morning, exhausted but happy, we finally reached the dense forest where the partisan bases were located. We stopped at the base of the Jewish partisan detachment *Mest* (Vengeance) and joined its ranks. We also learned there that all members of our group, who survived the onslaught at Michaliszki, as well as those who lost their way at the outskirts of Vilnius, did manage to reach Narocz safely. We also encountered many Jewish and non-Jewish partisans, as well as other unarmed Jews who were roaming the forests in search of a place to hide.

By the summer of 1943 most of the interior of the Belorussian Soviet republic was controlled by Soviet partisans. Only the main highways, railway tracks and supply routes, from the hinterland to the front line, as well as major administrative centres were in the hands of the Germans. Several hundred partisan brigades operated in the Nazi occupied territories of the former Soviet Union. They were composed of run away Soviet war prisoners, former Soviet functionaries, young men who wanted to avoid conscription into German military or labour battalions, as well as paratroopers sent from behind the front line.

Statistics about the number of anti-Nazi Soviet partisans in Belorussia vary. Similarly, there are different accounts of Jewish participation in this war episode. According to one source between 50,000 and 55,000 Jews participated actively in anti-Nazi combat.[1] According to another source, the total number of partisans in Belorussia reached 370,000, including 30,000 Jews.[2] Y. Arad suggests that the number of Jewish partisans was somewhere between 25,000 and 30,000.[3] There are several reasons for these conflicting numbers. First of all, some figures refer to the number of Jewish partisans in Belorussia only, while other include those active in other areas occupied by the Nazis. And, besides, many Jews in Soviet partisan detachments, in particular soldiers and officers who managed to escape from German captivity, hid their true national identity in order to avoid the atmosphere of anti-Semitism prevalent in some partisan units. In addition, some Jewish historians include in the number of partisans unarmed Jews, hiding in the forests in the vicinity of partisan bases. Moreover, official Soviet statistics are far from reliable, particularly those compiled during the war during conditions of conspiracy and instability.

The Voroshilov brigade was one of several located in the forests and marshes of the lake Narocz partisan zone, in Western Belorussia. Prior to September 1939, this region was under Polish sovereignty. According to one Soviet history of the partisan movement in the region of Vileika, where lake Narocz was located, Jews comprised 4.5 per cent of the total number of partisans in the region.[4] It is suggested that "the Voroshilov brigade consisted, in 1944, of twelve separate units, with a total of 1,704 partisans.... including 105 Jews."[5] It is obvious that the author of this study, the former secretary of the underground communist party committee of this region, I. Klimov, who was instrumental in the dissolution of the Jewish partisan unit *Mest*, manipulates facts in order to minimize the Jewish contribution to the Soviet war effort. The existence of *Mest* was indeed short-lived, but Klimov avoids even mentioning its name in his book. Neither does he refer to the First Mounted Komsomol detachment which incorporated many Jews, former members of *Mest*. It is evident that in the summer of 1943 the number of Jews in the Voroshilov brigade was much higher than the 105 quoted in Klimov's study, allegedly from official Soviet archival documents. In my estimation, based on personal observations, the number of Jewish partisans in the Voroshilov brigade was well over 300.

Similarly different historians produce conflicting figures about the membership of Jews in Lithuanian partisan detachments. According to official figures, provided in November 1945 by the Lithuanian Partisan Headquarters in Moscow, there were altogether 3,904 anti-Nazi partisans in

Lithuania, among them 676 Jews. It is suspected, however, that the official figures minimize Jewish participation in underground activity in order to present a picture in which the number of members of a certain nationality, participating in the resistance movement, be proportionate to the number of inhabitants of this nationality in Lithuania in general.[6]

My first impressions of the partisan movement were overwhelming. I could never have imagined before that the partisans were so well organized and armed. They controlled the whole area around lake Narocz, including most towns and villages. They had their own reconnaissance, supply, staff, and combat units, and they formed, in a sense, a state within a state. Upon my arrival in the forest, I was overcome by a feeling of joy that instead of becoming a helpless victim of the murderous Nazis I might become an active member of the partisan forces and join the struggle against the oppressor. I felt sorry for the young Jews left behind in the ghetto who were deprived of this opportunity. By the end of the day all members of our group, who left the ghetto that memorable night, gathered. It was a happy reunion. We related to each other stories about our baptism of fire and made plans for the future. We travelled from the ghetto along different paths, but we all managed to find our way and reach the intended destination.

Mest was a partisan unit formed early in August 1943. Initially it was composed of close to seventy, mostly Jewish fighters. Some were former F.P.O. members, who arrived from the Vilnius ghetto under the leadership of J. Glazman, a member of the F.P.O. command. The commander of "Mest'" was Z. Ragovski (Butenas), a Jewish paratrooper originally from Kaunas. Glazman was appointed chief of staff. The Jewish partisan detachment was part of the Voroshilov Brigade, commanded at that time by Colonel F. Markov. Markov established contacts with the ghetto underground and sent emissaries to the ghetto to encourage young armed Jews to join the partisan movement. By the middle of September 1943, the membership of *Mest* was close to 230. It accepted into its ranks new arrivals from the Vilnius ghetto, as well as Jews from the Belorussian countryside.[7]

The camp of *Mest* was composed of bunkers, dug-outs, a field kitchen, bathhouse, and other makeshift facilities. It was different from other partisan bases because in addition to armed men and horse-riders, women, children, and elderly people moved around freely on the camp grounds. In order to avoid Nazi persecution some Jewish partisans who joined *Mest*, mostly former residents of nearby towns and villages, brought along into the forest their family members. These family members, along with other unarmed Jews who managed to escape from the Nazis, were biding their time in so-called family camps, located not far from partisan bases. According to M. Shteinberg, close to 23,000 Jews inhabited these family camps. V. Levin, on the other hand, suggests, that no more than 3,000 Jews resided in these encampments.[8]

The partisan leadership in Belorussia resented the presence of women and children near partisan bases. It was clear to everyone that the proximity of family members handicapped the fighting ability of Jewish partisans. Unlike most single run-away youngsters from the ghetto, a partisan with a family was always concerned with the survival of his loved ones. Moreover, he was supposed to provide them with food, clothing, and a safe environment, and he was seldom willing to move far from his wife and children.

From the first days of its existence, Jewish members of *Mest* participated actively in different combat missions. Risking their lives, they fulfilled the tasks assigned to them with honour and dignity. The above notwithstanding, the future of *Mest*, and most of its Jewish members was, at all times, uncertain. Early in September 1943 the Narocz partisan region was inspected by some high Soviet officials. The commander of the Voroshilov brigade was upbraided for having permitted the existence of a partisan detachment, established on the principle of nationality, and an order was given to disband *Mest*. It was claimed that the existence of such units was against Soviet class ideology and contrary to its internationalist principles.

Just a few weeks prior to the disbandment of *Mest*, the Belorussian Soviet partisan leadership disarmed and disbanded a detachment of the so-called A.K. (Armja Krajowa), or the Polish Home Army. The A.K. regarded the Polish government in exile, in London, England, as its superior and it opposed both Nazi occupation and Soviet rule. Most A.K. members were highly anti-Semitic, and many Soviet partisans, as well as Jews hiding in the forests, were killed by them. None the less, the A.K. unit, which operated in the Narocz region, had good relations and cooperated with the Voroshilov brigade partisans. Being afraid, however, of treachery Soviet partisan leaders abused the trust of the Poles, lured them cunningly into a trap, and killed their leaders.[9]

The process of the dissolution and reorganization of *Mest* was a shocking affair, rich in anti-Semitic overtones. It showed little concern for the emotions and safety of those who had just escaped from the Nazi clutches. The anti-Semitic sentiments of many Soviet partisans were motivated by a number of unrelated factors. First of all, many were former inhabitants of local towns and villages presently occupied by the Wehrmacht. Hence, they were exposed to Nazi anti-Jewish propaganda even before joining the partisan movement. Moreover, many such partisans collaborated earlier with the Nazi regime, served in the police, or worked in the local Nazi administration. The recent advances of the Soviet Army alerted them to the fact that the Germans might soon be forced to withdraw and many thought that by joining the Soviet partisans they would atone for their collaboration with the Nazis and would be forgiven for their betrayal of the Soviet motherland. No wonder many were anti-Semites. After all, former Belorussian policemen, who became members of Soviet partisan units, helped the Nazis murder their defenceless Jewish neighbours in towns and villages across Belorussia.

Anti-Jewish sentiments among Soviet partisans were further augmented by the fact that Jews, hiding in family camps in the nearby forests, had to eat and Jewish partisans helped them to procure food by confiscating it from local peasants. The peasants had no choice but share their provisions with the Jewish partisans, but they resented it and complained to partisan commanders that Jews robbed them and appropriated their food free of charge.

It did not take long before I realized that the initial euphoria connected with joining the partisan movement was short lived. On 23 September 1943, the day when the liquidation of the Vilnius ghetto began, *Mest* was finally disbanded, less than two months after its establishment. Some of its well armed Jewish members were transferred to the newly formed multinational unit called the First Mounted Komsomol Detachment. Most others were to form a so-called maintenance and supply unit which was to serve the needs of the whole Voroshilov brigade. I was lucky to be assigned to the new *Komsomol* detachment, but I was poorly armed. I had no rifle or any other automatic firearm. The only weapon in my possession was the small pistol which I had brought from the ghetto. And they wanted to take it away from me. Having a hand-gun was considered a mark of superiority among the partisans and every partisan commander wanted to have one, in addition to his automatic submachine-gun. Yet for all practical purposes a partisan without a good rifle was unarmed and vulnerable.

The dissolution of *Mest* was indeed an appalling affair. Many of those who managed, with great difficulty, to obtain small arms in the ghetto were disarmed. Some Jews who refused to relinquish their weapons were roughed up. They were told that their arms could be put to better use in the hands of more experienced Belorussian fighters. It was, of course a lame excuse, and a great injustice. Everybody knew that a small hand-gun was no match for an assault rifle, yet it was better than nothing. It could be used for the purpose of self-defence and help to procure food.

It did not take long before the new arrivals into the Narocz forest learned that their future would be hazardous and unpredictable, nor was their escape from the ghetto an assured ticket to survival. It was just a new opportunity to continue the same struggle in different circumstances. The dire experiences of the members of *Mest* notwithstanding, it is necessary to note that officially sanctioned anti-Semitism in Soviet partisan brigades was limited to isolated incidents. Moreover, it was not of the virulent destructive kind, perpetrated by the Nazi occupiers. Hundreds of Jewish partisans, scattered in the numerous units and brigades all over Belorussia, were given an opportunity to fight against the common enemy, regain their dignity, and survive.

A few days after *Mest* was disbanded the situation of Jewish fighters, as well as of those hiding in the family camps in the Narocz woods, was complicated further. The Germans initiated a large-scale blockade of the Narocz partisan zone and fighter detachments made a desperate attempt to retreat from the forest before the Nazi onslaught. The *Komsomol* unit left the forest in good time, taking along only those Jewish fighters who were accepted into this newly formed detachment. All others remained in the forest to ward for themselves.

By sheer chance, I was not among the *Komsomol* members who left the forest at the outset of the blockade. Several days earlier I was sent together with three other Jewish partisans, former residents of small towns in the region, to a village outside the woods to procure food and forage for the partisans. We got a horse and a peasant cart and proceeded to fulfil the assigned task. We procured even a bottle of the so-called *samogon*, or home made booze, to mark our new relative freedom. For me this celebration would be symbolic anyway, because the taste of the booze was terrible and I was not fond of alcohol. I was still under the sway of my former coaches who admonished me that if I wanted to become a champion I should avoid alcohol, sex, and cigarettes. It was, however, not our good fortune to be able to celebrate. Upon arrival at our camp we were surprised to find it empty and abandoned. We soon learned that German armoured divisions were invading the region and most partisan units left the forest in expectation of the impending blockade and its unavoidable ramifications.

My first month as a partisan in the Narocz forests was not an easy one. I faced new people and a new world full of unexpected surprises. All of a sudden I was alone in the forest. My friends from Vilnius, members of our ghetto underground group, were gone. They left the base before my return. The few people around, including my new colleagues who were on assignment with me, were as desperate as I was. Time was running out and the German blockade was approaching. My situation was dreadful, indeed. I had no notion of what to do, or how to escape this new Nazi onslaught. But then, as I was exploring the deserted partisan camp for signs of life, I came across a well armed young Jewish man, approximately my age.

Our eyes met and a conversation ensued. I soon learned that his name was Max Begun. He was the son of a pharmacist in the small Belorussian town of Parafianovo and a member of a special partisan unit, *Boevoi* (Fighting), which had its base in the vicinity of the former Jewish detachment. Max was a local man who new well the surroundings, the people, and the language. I asked him for advise and possible help. I did not expect much, but to my surprise he introduced me and my three new partisan colleagues to the commander of the *Boevoi* group, Nikolai Semenov. Against the advise of some other members of the group, Semenov decided to let us, at least for the time being, join his group.

The *Boevoi* group consisted of ten well armed fighters, and one woman - a radio operator. They had no spare rifles for us, but they gave us hand grenades for self-defence and explosives to carry. Next morning the group started getting ready to break through the Nazi cordon. Semenov contacted a trusted local resident who sent his son, a young boy, to guide us through the marsh and keep us informed of any unexpected danger. It was not easy to avoid being noticed by the advancing German soldiers. The concern for safety required continuous motion and maneuvering. A close familiarity with the terrain was necessary for survival. In this respect, the peasant boy's help was invaluable. Without him we could have hardly found our way.

German soldiers were combing the forest and the marsh. In order to live it was essential to avoid confrontation with the enemy. During the day we we hid in the swamps. The Germans were so near that in order to avoid detection it was necessary, at times, to lie under the water and breathe through a straw. Temporary salvation and respite would come at night. That was when we tried to move. We were hungry, thirsty, soaked in water, but most of all we were afraid of the daylight. The smallest rustle of the branches of a tree would alert us to the possible danger. We were hungry, yet food was the last thing on our minds. We survived by eating wild berries, growing in the marsh, and drinking the water of the swamp. We were ready to put up a fight, but there was no chance of survival against the superior forces of the enemy.

The siege of the forest lasted more than a week. Regular Wehrmacht divisions and SS battalions, supported by the air force, combed the forests and marshes of the region, destroying everything in sight. They ravaged and set on fire all villages in the surrounding area. They dismantled and razed to the ground all partisan bases and killed anyone encountered on their way. All those who did not escape in time, before the forest was encircled, and among them were several hundred Jews, including women and children, were in grave danger. They withdrew into the swamps at the lake shore, to which access was very difficult. Nonetheless, half of them perished. Many disorganized and inexperienced Jewish partisan groups, seeking to break through the blockade on their own, faced a similar fate. A group of some thirty-five partisans from Vilnius, under the leadership of J. Glazman, tried to evade the siege at Narocz by moving to another partisan region in the Kazan' forests, some one hundred kilometres to the north-east. Initially they succeeded in reaching their destination, but were later hunted down by Nazi troops and almost completely wiped out.[10]

Early in October, after the Germans completed, albeit not very successfully, their task, and withdrew from the forest, partisan units began the return to their former camps. All they found was total devastation. It did not take long, however, before the bases were again in operation, and partisans were again at their job of obstructing the Nazi war effort.

It took almost a week before our group managed to shake off the enemy and evade the siege. Our main objective, at this point, was to move several hundred kilometres eastward to the location of *Boevoi* headquarters in the Begomel district, on the Berezina river, in Eastern Belorussia. Our long trip eastward was difficult and arduous. We had to cross the well guarded railway tracks connecting central Europe with the north-eastern sector of the frontline, as well as the former border between Poland and the USSR which was still fortified and controlled by the Germans. On our way we were engaged in several skirmishes with German military units. We organized an ambush on the highway, killed several Germans, and took their weapons and documents. At another instance when I was searching a peasant's barn for concealed provisions, I discovered several hidden rifles. Thus, we acquired arms to equip all newcomers to the group. At last, I was equal with all others and I suddenly felt as a real partisan.

In one such confrontation with the enemy, Nikolai Semenov was killed. I was next to him at that time. He faced the enemy bravely, fought courageously, and died stoically. I was greatly affected by his death. He was the one who, against the advice of others, accepted me into his group, at a most difficult time and gave me a chance to fight and live.

From my short association with members of the *Boevoi* detachment I learned that this unit belonged to the "cream" of the partisan movement and that Semenov was the head of its advance reconnaissance group. Most of its members were parachutists, dropped from Soviet planes. Some were volunteers, students of institutes for physical culture, and leading sportsmen. Others were intelligence officers and military professionals. Only a small fraction of the detachment consisted of run away Soviet war prisoners and only several local youngsters were accepted. Max Begun was one of them. He was smart, disciplined, brave, but humble. He was respected and appreciated by most of his fellow partisans.

The *Boevoi* was an independent partisan detachment reporting directly to headquarters in Moscow. It was composed of some 180 members, armed with most modern weapons. It had its own medical staff, ammunition and weapon specialists, radio operators, as well as intelligence and military reconnaissance professionals. The detachment's headquarters were usually located in a safe partisan region, while small groups composed of some 15-20 partisans, were dispersed within a radius of some 150-200 kilometres from the centre, and usually located near the objects of their operation. Most groups were involved in military diversion such as blowing up bridges, trains, and other military installations, as well as in intelligence work. The aim was to gather information about the enemy, facilitate terrorist acts against the occupiers, destabilize the local administration, and infiltrate the local police, and non-German Nazi military units, composed mainly of Russians, Ukrainians, or Slovaks.

We arrived at the *Boevoi* headquarters in the second half of October. As a rule, *Boevoi* did not recruit any new partisans from the local population. Temporarily accepted newcomers were usually transferred to large combat brigades. I knew that my fate would be decided by the *Boevoi* leadership. The commander, Major Nekliudov, who was later awarded the golden star of a Hero of the Soviet Union, the highest military decoration in the USSR, was an ascetic man of thirty-three, but looked more like fifty years old. He was smart, intelligent, and fair. He abstained from drinking and forbade the partisans to do so. He was absolutely against plunder and the abuse of the local population. When we arrived I gathered that he was already briefed about the four former members of *Mest*, and he knew more about me than I expected. I was the only one of the four Jewish partisans to become a member of *Boevoi*. The others, including some non-Jewish fighters, were soon transferred to the *Kalinin* brigade.

The partisan zone near the Berezina river was well protected from all sides by forests, marshes, and old Soviet fortifications. An airfield was located within the zone and Soviet planes with weapons, ammunition, and food were landing there regularly. They were also removing the sick and the wounded. Most German divisions were engaged, at that time, at the front and no small Nazi army detachment would risk penetrating deep into the forest. The Nazis bombed this area, from time to time, but most partisan bases were invisible from the air.

In November 1943 the headquarters of *Boevoi* moved to a new location further west, and away from the approaching frontline. Its final destination was a village some ten kilometres from a German garrison and twenty kilometres from the old base of *Mest,* at Narocz. I was assigned to a reconnaissance unit, attached to the headquarters, and I started my new partisan life without delay. One of my first tasks was to help organize the defection of members of a Slovak military detachment, incorporated into the Nazi forces. After protracted negotiations and undercover work, half a dozen armed Slovaks deserted their military unit and joined the partisans.

Members of *Boevoi* were constantly on the move. They were mining railway tracks, blowing up bridges, organizing subversive activity among the local population, and gathering information about the location, movement, and disposition of German military units. This information was required for our own safety, but it was also useful to the leadership of the Soviet army. Most of our activity concentrated in the area of the Warsaw-Grodno-Vilnius-Daugavpils railway line. It was a region populated mainly by Polish people and most of it was under the control of the anti-Soviet Polish Home Army. German garrisons were stationed in major cities and railway stations .

I was one of the few members of *Boevoi* who lacked the many basic skills required in battle. I had no formal military training, nor any experience in handling explosives. I was in an unenvious situation. I could not admit that I was ignorant, yet every mistake could cost me my life and place my battle comrades in danger . It took weeks of trial and error before I managed to acquire some basic combat skills. In battle situations I learned by observing and listening to older partisans and simply by using common sense. Before winter arrived I managed to acquire some partisan experience. On one occasion I participated in the mining of the railway tracks on the line running from Vilnius to Daugavpils, in Latvia. Our objective was to blow up a train with German military personnel and ammunition which was heading to the northern section of the eastern front. At that time, there were several methods of mining railway tracks in use. In certain circumstances, it was possible to dig a hole under the tracks, place a mine there, furnish it with a detonating fuse, and wait for the train to pass. The weight of the passing train would put pressure on the tracks, activate the detonator, and cause an explosion. This was the safest mining method. By the time the train passed the partisans were already far away and out of danger. But this method was not always successful. By the middle of 1943 most railway lines, leading to the front, were guarded day and night by German soldier. Bunkers, equipped with heavy machine-guns, were constructed, every several hundred metres, along the tracks and German soldiers patrolled the tracks day and night, watching for anything suspicious. Moreover, before a train with military personnel would pass, a locomotive attached to several wagons loaded with sand would cover a given stretch of the tracks and make sure that there were no mines. If a mine was planted, on the given stretch of the tracks, it would explode under the wagons with sand, and do little damage. Thus the old method of mining the tracks was no longer productive and it became necessary to devise new mining techniques. We applied one of them in our current operation.

On our way to the assigned location we marched several nights, hiding during the day in the forest. It was cold, but no fire could be set up, because the smoke could be detected by the Germans, or noticed by local inhabitants who could denounce us to the police. At dusk, we moved closer to the railway tracks. We selected a place where the tracks were running through the forest. Some fifty metres from the tracks, however, all trees were cleared to give German soldiers in the bunkers a good view of the area and make it possible to control the approaches to the tracks. This made our mining operation more difficult.

Late in the evening we approached the tracks as closely as possible, and waited on the edge of the forest for night. Our unit was composed of eight people. We split into three groups. Three of us moved some fifty metres to the right and another three to the left. Two partisans with the explosives remained in the middle. When the locomotive with the wagons of sand passed and the German patrol returned to the bunker signalling that the tracks were clear, the train at the railway station, several kilometres away, started to move. That was when the partisans with the explosives ran onto the track, placed the mine in front of the oncoming train, and ran back. The mine was equipped with a delayed action detonator, so that it would explode in the middle of the train, causing as much damage as possible. Otherwise the mine could destroy the locomotive, while the train would remain intact. Fortunately, the explosives were placed without complications and the mine exploded as planned. I was in the group of three to the right of the explosion. We were supposed to cover the retreat of those who placed the mine and help them reach the forest unharmed. Immediately after the explosion the blaze blinded us and machine-guns from the bunkers began to spew out fire randomly in all directions. But it was dark, and we were invisible. We opened fire from the sides to confuse the Germans and make the retreat of the other group more secure. By the time the fire caused by the explosion, subsided we were already more than a hundred metres deep in the forest, moving in separate groups in the direction of our agreed meeting point. At midnight we got together and continued our march until morning.

Several nights later we arrived at another section of the railway tracks to start preparation for our next act of sabotage. This time we applied a different mining method. It was more difficult and dangerous, but success was almost guaranteed. We had information that a train with military personnel and armoured vehicles was moving to the front. We positioned ourselves and waited for the train. But instead of placing the explosives and running away, we set the mine and attached a wire to the detonator. We sat some fifty metres from the tracks, waiting for the train to come. As soon as the passenger wagons approached the explosives on the tracks we pulled the wire and the mine exploded. Only then did we begin our retreat. The Germans placed a fire rocket in the air and it became bright as in day light. Surviving Germans from the train opened fire and tried to pursue us. Again, we opened fire from the sides and made the retreat of our mining group easier. As soon as we were in the forest, we felt relatively safe. The Germans would not risk going into the forest in the darkness.

After a successful tour of duty, lasting over a month, we returned to our base late in December 1943. In 1944 the focus of *Boevoi* operations changed gradually. Greater emphasis was placed on intelligence work. We operated mainly in outlying regions inhabited by Poles and Lithuanians. Intelligence work in this area required the knowledge of these languages, as well as an understanding of the workings of the local military and civil institutions. My experience of living under Nazi rule and my proficiency in the Polish, Lithuanian, and German languages, facilitated our work. I assisted in the process of planning intelligence operations and directed the work of several local civilian undercover agents. We made contact with representatives of a number of official and clandestine political organizations, including the Polish A.K., and the R.O.A., or the pro-Nazi Russian Liberation Army. We were also in communication with the Lithuanian political splinter group, headed by General Plechavicius. Our activity soon produced practical results. We were instrumental in organizing the defection of a large group of R.O.A. military personnel. With the help of our undercover agents we organized major acts of sabotage in German garrisons. We gathered information about the work of local Nazi collaborators and provided it to the Soviet security forces for future consideration. We participated also in direct combat endeavours. Our activities were becoming bolder. The Germans were busy transferring all manpower to the front and we had more freedom to act in the hinterland. In February 1944, one of our groups had a major encounter with a German army unit on the highway between Molodeczno and Vileika, in Western Belorussia. Some eighty Nazis were killed in battle.

In preparation to the Soviet offensive, in the spring of 1944, we were ordered to move most of our forces further westward. *Boevoi* was reorganized. Its main task was now to assist the Soviet army in its forthcoming offensive. That involved the destruction of military objects, lines of communication, military equipment, and army personnel. We were supposed to hamper the retreat of the German army and stop them from moving their plundered goods to Germany. The newly reorganized combat groups were despatched in different directions, closer to enemy garrisons. One unit operated near the railway station Podbrodzie, another one in the region of Molodeczno, a third group was active near Vilnius, and a fourth moved as far as Warsaw. Before our departure westwards we received new supplies of ammunition, sophisticated weapons, and explosives. In March 1944 Soviet planes twice visited the Narocz partisan base. Identification bonfires were set up in a clearing, deep in the forest. The planes arrived at night and dropped by parachutes all that we required for our new tasks.

In March 1944, I was transferred to a combat unit under the command of the officer Nedoboi. The unit had three groups, six-seven fighters in each. We were very well armed. Each group had two machine-guns and three submachine guns. There was also an abundance of explosives. Our base was near the town of Kobylniki, but we were all the time on the move. We were mining railway tracks, highways, and bridges. We were cutting communication lines and arranging ambushes. Yet our task was not an easy one. We operated in an area in which we had few friends. We were always in great danger, in case of confrontation with Germans or the A.K. There were no safe routes of retreat, nor the possibility of taking care of the wounded. The Polish A.K., which controlled much of the area, conducted little anti-Nazi activity. They were waiting for the Soviets to do the job. Instead, they were fighting other local political groups, trying to maintain their control in an area which they regarded as their domain.

On one occasion, early in the spring of 1944, a group of the Nedoboi unit, of which I was part, was given an assignment to blow up a train following to the front. Before we reached the object of operation we decided to gain some information about the movement of the trains. With that purpose we went to see one of our undercover agents who lived in a house on the shore of a small lake. The road to the house led first uphill and later down to the shore. It was early evening. After hiding the whole day in a bush, we decided to move. We approached a peasant and ordered him to harness his horse. We put part of the heavy explosives on the cart and followed in the required direction. Since we did not want the driver of the cart to find out about the clandestine anti-Nazi activity of his neighbour, I stayed behind with the cart, while the other members of our group tried inconspicuously reach the house of our contact man. After a while I saw from a distance, of over a hundred metres, my colleagues coming to join me. Suddenly they started making some puzzling motions, and running in crouching position back to the lake and into the bushes. I realized that something was wrong. I looked around and saw in disbelief German and Latvian SS soldiers moving across the field in my direction. It had become instantly apparent to me that the Germans saw me, but did not notice my colleagues.

There was no time to think. All I could do was run. The forest, some bushes, and a marsh were not far away, but I carried an automatic rifle, several grenades, and some explosives which I could not abandon. There was an unwritten law among the partisans that one can lose his rifle only together with his arm. And what would I do in the dark forest without a reliable weapon which was indispensable for survival? I was running as fast as I could and the Germans were chasing me. I was some fifty metres away from them. Suddenly they stopped and started shooting at me from a distance. I fell to the ground and waited. When the shots stopped I got up and ran. They started chasing me again. That procedure repeated itself several times. It was getting dark. Night was my salvation. But I was exhausted, my energies were depleted, my boots were full of water and each time it was more difficult to get up from the marshy land. The awareness, however, that a momentary delay might mean death prompted me to act. My will power forced me to muster all my remaining strength. I would get up each time and continue to run even faster than before. Finally I reached a little forest. To delude my pursuers, instead of running deeper into the forest, I changed directions and ran along the edge of the woods. The Germans lost track of me and I was saved, at least for a while.

My situation was desperate. I was all alone in the middle of the night in a dark forest. Our base was more than a hundred kilometres to the east, and I did not know even my exact location or my whereabouts. I knew that we had a contact man in this district, but the area was inhabited by unfriendly locals, and I had no idea how to find him. I decided to act fast. I walked for close to an hour along the edge of the forest, entered a village, and knocked on the door of the first house. The peasant was surprised and scared, but he did not suspect, at first, that I was a Soviet partisan. My first objective was to find out where I was and inquire about the directions and distance to our undercover agent. For fear of revealing his exact whereabouts I could not tell the peasant of the village I was looking for. I managed to learn, however, that the village I intended to reach was some twenty kilometres away. The peasant suggested that I should stay overnight and in the morning he would take me wherever I needed. I ordered the peasant to harness his horse and take me without delay. He hesitated. He obviously began to suspect that I was a Soviet partisan. While we were haggling I was keeping an eye on the village street. Suddenly I noticed people with rifles walking along the road. They obviously saw the light in the house and became suspicious. I did not know who the armed men on the street were, but I was certain that they were not Soviet partisan. Hence, I assumed that they were either members of the A.K., German soldiers, or local policemen. In a split second I had to decide what to do. I ordered the peasant to put out the light and decided to get out from the house before it was too late. Outside there was always a better chance to escape in the dark.

The house stood sideways to the street and the door faced the yard from the side. Rifle in hand I approached the door. I saw two individuals standing at the gate, leading to the yard. Their rifles were placed on the fence, aiming in my direction. I waited a few seconds, shouted something in half-Russian and half-Polish and spurted away behind the house. At the same moment two shots were fired in my direction. Fortunately, they missed the target. I fell to the ground and took out a grenade to be ready for any eventuality. I was lying and waiting. Seconds felt like hours. I was afraid that the armed men might try to get me from behind. I soon realized, however, that they were nowhere in sight, and vanished somewhere in the dark. They surely saw that I was armed and probably did not want to risk a frontal assault. I decided to act. I entered the house. The peasant was scared to death. He was praying, kneeling at the holy image, in the corner of the room. His wife and children were crying. I ordered him to get the horse and move immediately. Trembling, he begged that I should leave him alone, but I had no choice. Spring nights were short, and I had to move fast. I did not know the area and, besides by walking I would never reach the required location before daybreak. When I threatened to shoot and set his house on fire he relented. Soon we were on our way. Some five kilometres from the house of our undercover agent I let the peasant go and continued on foot. When I arrived our contact man knew already about my mishap. In times of war rumours spread fast. He gave me all the necessary information, supplied me with food, and prepared an itinerary for my long journey back to our base. I walked all alone for four nights, hiding in the day in forests and marshes. When I returned to our partisan base everyone was surprised to see me alive. They were sure that I was caught by the Germans. Rumours spread in the vicinity that the fateful evening the Germans caught a man and brought him to the garrison. My colleagues were afraid that under pressure of torture I might divulge partisan secrets to my interrogators. Indeed, the Germans did apprehend that evening a man, but that was the driver of the cart we requisitioned. My commanders did not doubt my story. They knew that since I was Jewish and had no family around, the Nazis would not try to engage me in any covert activity.

Partisan life was full of tension, unexpected shifts, and continuous danger. For close to a year I never went to sleep undressed. The only comfort permitted was taking off one's boots. My assault rifle and grenades were always at hand. Having a bath in a village sauna was considered a real luxury. There was seldom an opportunity to stay overnight in an ordinary bed. When instead of sleeping in a bunker there was a chance to stay over night in a peasant's house we usually slept on the floor, some straw under our heads, and barely covered with our greatcoats. Moreover, in times of military operation, we spent most nights marching in the dark, rather than sleeping. Whatever rest we could get was always in hiding and during the day. We had become accustomed to sleep standing, sitting, and walking, at any time, any place, and in any climatic conditions. Once, I remember, after walking a whole night I fell asleep under a tree. When I woke up in the afternoon I was all soaked, lying in a puddle of water. It was raining for hours, but I was so tired that it did not affect my sleep. We were young and strong, at that time, and could put up with many difficulties, yet there was a price to be paid in the future for everything. Partisan life strengthened our spirits, but it left a mark on our health and physical condition.

Nonetheless, partisan life had also its redeeming features. First of all, any Jewish partisan craved revenge and was elated at the sight of humiliated and suffering Nazis. In the spring of 1944, I was hiding, together with my group, in a forest, not far from a small lake. We were waiting for the night in order to move on to the object of our operation. We were tired, but bored. We could not set a fire to cook some potatoes, or boil water, because the smoke could reveal our whereabouts to suspicious local residents. I carefully ventured into the bushes, near the lake, to pick some berries. To my surprise I saw a German soldier, crouching behind a tree, and relieving himself. I ran quietly back to my colleagues to pass on the news. We instantly decided to catch the German alive. We approached him unnoticed from behind, and apprehended him before he managed to utter a sound. It turned out that our prisoner, together with another German soldier, came here from the nearby garrison to fish in the lake. We soon caught the other German, as well. We gagged and tied them up and all together we moved back to our base. The Germans were surprised and scared. We instructed them to obey orders and keep quiet and warned them that if they caused any trouble we would kill them without delay. It did not take long before all traces of their aryan pride disappeared and they were outdoing each other in their denunciation of Hitler and the Nazi regime. We delivered them to our headquarters safely. There, they were interrogated and assigned to do some menial jobs. When the Soviet army set Belorussia free from Nazi occupation they were transferred to a war prisoners camp.

June, the first month of summer, brought the usual sounds of thunder and the rains that followed. It also brought closer the thunder of artillery cannonades from the eastern front. They were the harbingers of freedom which were already close in sight. It was clear that the frontline was approaching. The German defences were shattered and their army in retreat. Residents of Belorussian villages and towns were exchanging the latest rumours about events on the frontline in whispers. No one knew who could be trusted. The Nazi administration was still in place, but everyone knew that its days were numbered. People were tired of war, devastation, and suffering. They craved freedom and peace. The sounds of artillery exchanges were growing louder and louder and the frontline seemed already not far away. One summer day, in the first week of July, the Soviet army liberated our area of operation and, suddenly, we found ourselves on Soviet territory, free from Nazi occupation. People hiding in the forests, including many Jewish men, women, and children, came out into the open for the first time in years. The German army, devastated and demoralized, withdrew in a hurry. The partisans made sure, however, that their retreat was not an easy one. Most roads and bridges were blocked and mined. The Germans were trapped. Small bands of German soldiers hid now in the forests and marshes which were until recently occupied by the partisans. They tried to withdraw and reach the frontline unnoticed, in order to unite with their comrades, but their efforts were futile. Most of them were caught, disarmed, and transferred to war prisoners camps.

As the frontline moved further west, our partisan detachment was assigned the task of clearing hiding Nazis from the local forests. It was a difficult job with many dangers. We were not qualified to fight regular army units. We lacked the necessary skills and equipment. One encounter with a German military detachment, roaming the Belorussian forests, was particularly memorable. It ended tragically and resulted in many casualties. Some of the best partisans became victims of these post-liberation confrontations. In one of these bloody battles with a German SS unit we lost eight men. One of those killed was lieutenant Grigor'ev. He was one of the original partisans parachuted early in the war. When the front moved westwards his wife came to the recently liberated areas, in search of her husband. But instead of meeting him in person, she was faced with the terrible task of burying his dead body. Her grief was enormous. When some of the Germans who killed her husband were caught and brought for interrogation, she was the first to demand revenge. Some of the SS men were executed on the spot by local peasants who attacked them with clubs and knives.

I stood and watched the scene from some distance in horror. I had no sympathy for the SS murderers, yet I was shocked by this gruesome sight. I had witnessed torture at close proximity, but in most instances atrocities were committed by the Nazis. In this case, overcome by an insatiable craving for revenge, peasants tied up and beat the Germans to death. Mrs.

Grigor'ev, overwhelmed with sorrow, became delirious. She ran around with a knife, cutting the bodies of the helpless victims. Hideous Nazi crimes made me believe that SS murderers did not deserve compassion or mercy. Yet it was nauseating to watch the half dead Germans swaying on their legs, their blood gushing all over. I appreciated the yearning for revenge, but I could not believe that the thirst for blood was so real; that the potential for evil was so great in every human being.

Earlier in my youth, when I was a boxer, I was taught that one should never hit an enemy who was down on his knees. War, however, was no gentlemanly game, and adhering to this rule could have cost me my life. In one of our partisan battles we chased a group of dispersed German soldiers in the forest. At one point, I stumbled upon a wounded German, hiding behind a tree. He had his hands up and begged me not to kill him. Surprised, I contemplated what to do with him, failing to see that he still had a gun in his hand. An older partisan who was next to me could not understand what happened. When I explained that the German beseeched me not to kill him, he laughed and shot him on the spot. He than admonished me that there was nothing partisans could do with a wounded German. There was no one to look after him and, besides, we had hardly enough medication for ourselves. Moreover, he pointed out, the wounded German, who was still armed, could have killed me. I realized then that I still was naive and inexperienced, and that war was a deadly game in which there was little room for sentiments. The partisan in question was called Zaitsev, but his real name was Zass. He was a Jew from Odessa. He served in the Red Army and was taken prisoner by the Germans. He managed to escape and join the partisans. Except for Max Begun, he was the only other Jew in *Boevoi*. He was very brave and respected by all partisans, including those who were anti-Semitic, but he was also one of the well known self-haters. He admitted to me that he wanted to escape his Jewish identity by any possible means.

The battles with the remnants of the retreating German army in the Belorussian forests marked the end of my partisan activity. Our detachment gathered and started its move towards the city of Minsk, the capital of Belorussia. We marched slowly. For the first time there was no need to rush, or hide during the day. On our way we observed the devastated landscape: burnt villages, destroyed towns, and blown up bridges and highways. The frontline was now to the west of us, on the border of Lithuania and East Prussia, as well as in Poland, not far from the shores of the Vistula river. As we moved we saw columns of war prisoners driven eastward. The Germans marched heads down, as if afraid of the light of the day. There was no sign of their former pride and sense of superiority. I compared them, in my mind, with the Germans I came across in my ghetto days. What a difference power made! Absolute power corrupts. It created terrible monsters out of ordinary human being, but the loss of authority turned them into nonentities.

We continued our march. For the first time in months there was no need to sleep fully dressed. Nor was there any need to carry a weapon all the time. It took a while before I got used to the notion that there was no immediate danger. I would wake up in the night, all in sweat, fearing that I was helpless, because my rifle disappeared. As we were moving with little haste I had time to contemplate my future. I was still nineteen, and I was sure that since the war was not yet over new challenges were certainly in store for me.

With the liberation of Belorussia and Lithuania from Nazi occupation, the Jewish partisan saga ended. Most Jewish partisans, former residents of Vilnius who joined the Lithuanian partisan brigade in the Rudnicki woods, as well as many of those who were scattered in different partisan combat detachment in the forests of Western Belorussia, returned to Vilnius after liberation. Most former partisans, members of the communist party and their sympathizers, stayed in the city. Most others, however, did not want to live under Soviet rule and left Vilnius as soon as possible. They moved to Palestine, or other countries in the West.

The fate of the members of the underground group to which I belonged in the ghetto varied. Several were killed on 12 Strashun Street. A few others perished while fighting the Nazis in partisan units. Those who survived the Holocaust and the war dispersed all over the world. The leader of our group, Ch. Rubanovich, lived after the war in France, several others, in Canada, but the majority moved to Israel.

The Jewish partisans, natives of Vilno, made a significant contribution to the anti-Nazi war effort. They acted boldly, faced the enemy valiantly, and avenged the suffering and humiliation endured by their brethren.

NOTES

[1]. Mark Shteinberg, "Tragediia i bor'ba," Novoe russkoe slovo, 14 October, 1994, 37.

[2]. Vladimir Levin, "Partizantskii nalet na istoriiu," Ibid., 18 November 1994, 33.

[3]. Ibid.

[4] I. Klimov, and N. Grakov, Partizany vileishchiny, 2d ed. (Minsk 1970), 322.

[5]. Ibid., 343.

[6]. Rimantas Zizas, "Armed Struggle of the Vilnius Ghetto Jews Against the Nazis in 1941-1944," in The Days of Memory, ed. by E. Zingeris (Vilnius 1995), 322.

[7]. Dov Levin, Fighting Back (New York 1985),184.

[8]. Vladimir Levin.

[9]. Tadeusz Lopalewski, Miedzy Niemnem a Dzwina, Ziemia Wilenska i Nowogrodska (London 1955), 244.

[10]. Yitzhak Arad, The Partisan: From the Valley of Death to Mount Zion (New York 1979), 150.

Gedimino (Mickiewicza) Street

The Old City

**Choral Synagogue,
Pylimo (Zawalna) Street**

Left:
Old City

Below:
**Sidestreet leading to
the Cathedral Square**

Below:
Antokolskio Street

The Ruins of the Great Synagogue in Vilnius in 1944

Above:
Rudninku (Rudnicka) Street

Right:
Strashun Library and the Gaon's House and Synagogue

Below:
The Blown up premises of 12 Strashun Street

The Choral Synagogue

Old City

Above:
33 Zawalna (Pylimo) Street

Right:
Monument at the Jewish Cemetary in Vilnius erected in 1991, to Leo Shneidman who died in the Ghetto in 1942

Left:
New monument to the Jews murdered in Ponary (Paneriai) erected in 1991

**Museum dedicated to the memory of the
Holocaust victims in Ponary (Paneriai)**

**Monument at the pit in Ponary where the
murdered victims were cremated en masse**

The Ghetto in Vilnius

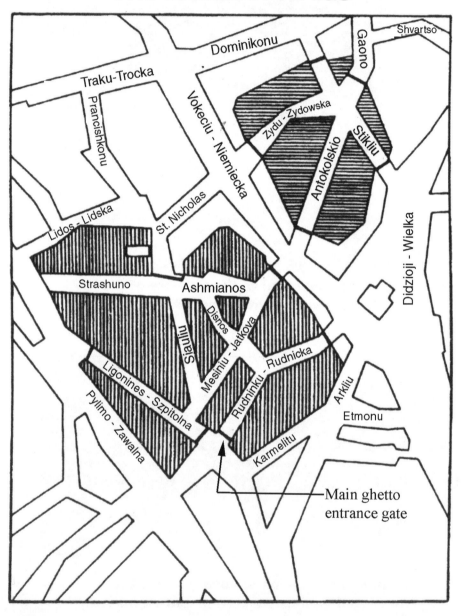

Main ghetto entrance gate

▨ First Ghetto: September 6, 1941 - September 23, 1943

▨ Second Ghetto: September 6, 1941 - October 21, 1941

CHAPTER THREE
THE SOVIET ARMY

Nazi occupation in Belorussia was over. Vilnius was also liberated, and the frontline was now deep in Lithuania. The former members of *Boevoi* were encamped in the village of Zatsyn, near the city of Minsk, the capital of Belorussia, and given several weeks of rest. In August 1944, most of us were called upon to appear for interviews with Soviet officials in Minsk to decide our future destiny. Those who were parachuted from the Soviet Union to Nazi occupied territory, as well as professional Soviet security officers, were given assignments in the Soviet hinterland. Some other former partisans, with secondary education, were sent to study in institutions of higher learning. Max Begun was one of them. He was admitted to an institute in Minsk to study medicine. The fate of the rest, myself included, was still in the air.

Step by step our camp in Zatsyn became empty, and it appeared that the few still remaining there were probably destined to join the Soviet army. I was one of them. I was a stranger and an outcast in Minsk. All other partisans of *Boevoi* were born, or lived before the war, in the Soviet Union, while I was a foreigner and a Jew. Most of my friends, and other Jews from Vilnius who managed to escape from the ghetto in time were already back in the city. When my turn came for an interview in Minsk it was suggested to me and several others former members of *Boevoi*, that we join the Marshall B. Tito partisans in Yugoslavia. This proposition did not thrill me, in the least and I looked for a way out. The prospects of becoming a partisan in a strange, far away land, was far from enticing. This time, however, luck was on my side. Salvation came from unexpected quarters. The Soviet Union was always a country of wonders and a miracle happened this time, as well. The General in charge of the Belorussian security forces, who was supposed to sign the order for our departure, was a Georgian, named Tsanava. It appeared that in some ways he displeased the Commander-in-Chief of the Soviet Army, J. Stalin, and he was unexpectedly arrested. Since no one was yet appointed to replace him, our departure to Yugoslavia was delayed. We decided then to try to escape this intended new partisan escapade by volunteering to join the Soviet army without delay.

Soon I was on my way to a reserve regiment, not far from Minsk. There, new conscripts were trained before their departure to the front. Life in this regiment was gloomy and austere. The food was poor and we were always hungry. Most soldiers in the regiment were middle-aged Belorussian peasants from areas recently liberated by the Soviet army. There were also some former partisans. The peasants were supplied with food by visiting family members, and were happy to remain in the camp for as long as possible. They were ready to delay their intended move to the front at any price, including bribery. Hungry former partisans, on the other hand, were eager to get away as soon as possible, hoping that at the front they would be, at least, well fed.

After several weeks of training, I was sent with a group of others to the third Belorussian front. I arrived at the former border between Lithuania and East Prussia early in October 1944. Several hundred of us were brought to the headquarters of an infantry Army, some ten kilometres from the frontline. The new arrivals could be divided roughly into three groups. There were the young former partisans, the old peasant farmers, and the "reconstructed ones," or soldiers wounded earlier in battle, now returning to the front after treatment and recovery in hinterland hospitals. At the Army headquarters we were lined up, inspected, and assigned to separate regiments and battalions. The young former partisans were sent to the most dangerous and burdensome positions. I, together with several other former partisans, were directed to a regimental reconnaissance platoon which was based approximately one kilometre from the frontline. Most of our work, however, was in no man's land.

We arrived at our new base in the evening. We were given a place to sleep in a cold dug-out. There were no pillows or bedding, just straw. It was late in the autumn and one could hardly fall asleep on the cold and damp earth. But that night there was little opportunity to sleep anyway. A barrage of heavy enemy artillery fire came down on our base without warning. It lasted most of the night. By the time it was over, early in the morning, dead and wounded bodies were scattered all over. Among them were some of those who had just arrived the day before, together with me. Experienced soldiers were joking that the families of those killed would receive standard notification forms telling that their relatives fell a heroic death, defending their motherland, in battle with the perfidious Nazi enemy. In fact, most of those killed had no chance of facing the enemy.

A regimental reconnaissance platoon was usually composed of some forty people. In my platoon there were hardly twenty. The commander, a sub-lieutenant, was wounded several times. In the beginning of the war he was a simple soldier. He had little education, but because of the lack of qualified officer personnel, he was promoted through the ranks. In regiments, facing directly the enemy across the frontline, reconnaissance was one of the most difficult and dangerous jobs. Soldiers seldom survived there for long. Those who could get away with a slight wound were considered lucky.

In November 1944, the frontline, near the former border of Lithuania and Germany, was stable. The Soviet army was entrenched and so were the Germans. Between the trenches was no man's land. It was mined from both sides and protected by barbed wire. Our regiment controlled a stretch of several kilometres. The duty of the regimental reconnaissance unit was to explore the enemy's defences and mining patterns in no man's land. The platoon was also charged with the task of penetrating into the German trenches in order to capture, disarm, and bring back a so-called "tongue," or German prisoner who could provide information about Nazi installations, fortification, and manpower in a given area. There was no question that catching a soldier off guard, capturing and gagging him in the German trenches, and finally bringing him alive to the Soviet side was a formidable and very risky undertaking. No wonder the casualty rate in reconnaissance platoons was one of the highest in the whole army.

Before any intended operation, we were given several days of rest and increased portions of food. We were also provided daily with 100 gr. of vodka, extra cigarettes, and chocolate. Since I did not drink or smoke I traded my vodka and cigarettes with other soldiers for chocolate, sugar, and bread. In fact, I did try to smoke at the front. I was told by some old soldiers that smoking helps fight boredom and it warms up the whole body, making it easier to cope with the long freezing winter nights. I soon realized, of course, that it was a cheap joke. I stopped this new adventure before becoming seriously addicted to tobacco. Moreover, I still remembered that my father's excessive smoking habits ruined his health and shortened his life.

Days before going into action, members of our platoon would observe enemy trenches and select a place of operation. In order to divert attention from the intended object of attack, during the night our artillery would open fire at an adjoining sector of the front. We could proceed only after field engineers removed the mines and cut the barbed wire near the Soviet trenches. We crawled then across no man's land, following the field engineers who were supposed to clear the approaches to the German trenches from mines and other obstacles and tried to enter the enemy trenches unnoticed. We usually acted on a moonless night. We moved after midnight, because that was when few soldiers were on guard, and vigilance was wanting. That did not mean that entering the enemy's trenches was an easy job. Whenever anything suspicious was heard, or observed, in no man's land, a fire rocket was instantly put up in the air, making all movement, even retreat, almost impossible.

I spent more than two months in the reconnaissance unit, and only once did we manage to enter the German trenches, overpower and gag a half-sleeping soldier, and bring him back to our staff command. We crossed no man's land without major obstacles and entered the German trenches unnoticed. It was dark and many Germans were asleep. When we stumbled upon one of them, who was standing on guard at a machine-gun aiming point, he mistook us for some of his own. When he realized who we were it was already too late and he offered little resistance. By the time the Germans noticed that something was amiss and that one of them disappeared, we were already close to our trenches. They immediately opened heavy machine-gun and mortar fire. They wounded one of our soldiers, but we managed to reach our trenches and escape. It was quite an exploit and I was proud to be part of it. But without a dose of good luck we could have never accomplished it. After we fulfilled this difficult task we were allowed to celebrate and rest for more than a week.

Life was so fickle at the frontline that no one made any far reaching plans. Every day, hour, or minute could make a difference between life and death. People were killed in most unexpected places and situation. There was no place, or time, that one was completely safe and secure. Our cook was killed by a stray bullet when he was delivering food to the staff bunker, far away from the frontline. Another soldier from our platoon was blown up by a shell together with the makeshift toilet where he was attending to his natural needs. Some old members of our platoon, who were at the front since the early days of war in 1941, were adept at avoiding dangerous situations. They did it in such professional manner that no one could suspect them of cowardice or disobedience. In one instance, when we were in the middle of no man's land, we were told to find safe cover in the field and wait. Suddenly we heard a small mine explode in the vicinity. It attracted the attention of the Germans. They opened fire, and it became impossible to proceed with our plan. We were forced to withdraw back to our trenches. The following week we were exploring the location for our next possible operation. Days later I learned that the mine which exploded during our failed operation was set up by one of our own men. He realized that there was little likelihood of success that night, and decided to abort the operation. Why unnecessarily risk lives? The platoon commander knew of it and approved. All that, however, was kept secret from senior staff officers and the political commissar. They could, of course, suspect that something was wrong, but had no definite evidence to prove it.

In general, most Soviet soldiers were brave, sometimes even reckless. They were overwhelmed by a daily barrage of patriotic and anti-Nazi propaganda, which encouraged acts of heroism. Every detachment had a political officer whose duty was not only to indoctrinate the rank and file, but also to watch and report of any sign of disobedience, pacifism, defeatist mood, or anti-Soviet activity. The above notwithstanding, even patriotic individuals were loath to die. Some would try anything to avoid danger. There were instances when soldiers were admitted to hospital with minor self-inflicted wounds. That was done with the purpose of escaping, at least for a while, the danger of death. When caught, however, such soldiers were court-marshalled, and executed for cowardice and treason.

The last, and only successful, escapade into the German trenches marked the end of my service in the reconnaissance unit. One morning the political officer arrived, lined up the by now halved platoon, and ordered all those who had completed secondary school education to step forward. I was the only one. All others, including the sergeants and platoon commander, hardly finished elementary school. War did its job. It deprived a whole generation of education. The officer invited me to the staff office and declared that soldiers with secondary education were recruited for admission to a military school which trained professional officers. The school was located somewhere on the Volga river, far away from the frontline. For that purpose I was ordered to proceed the following day to Army headquarters for a special interview. The prospect of becoming a Soviet professional officer and spend the rest of my life somewhere deep in Russia was not very enticing. But I could not refuse the chance of getting away from the hell at the frontline, at least for a while. Army headquarters were far from the frontline and rarely attacked by enemy artillery fire.   I left our platoon bunker on a high. I served in a unit which was the first to enter German soil and the personal appreciation expressed by the Commander-in-Chief of the Soviet Army, J. Stalin, was inscribed in my soldier's identification document. Moreover, I was lucky. So far I had managed to survive all danger and was slightly injured only once. But my good spirits were soon dampened. At the frontline, under constant enemy fire, a simple soldier was valued and respected by his superiors. At the staff office, away from the front, the intelligence officer who interviewed me, treated me with disdain. My service in the reconnaissance platoon did not impress him and my partisan activity, for which I was awarded a special medal, was suspect. He wondered how could I, a Jew, survive Nazi occupation, and he obviously suspected me of possible collaboration with the enemy. He recognized that I was unfit to become a Soviet officer and sent me back to the reconnaissance platoon.

Chance, however, willed a new turn to my fate. It was my good fortune never to be able to reach the reconnaissance platoon again. When I was approaching the sector of the frontline where our regiment was located, I learned that in the few days that I was away the whole infantry division, of which my platoon was a part, was transferred to Hungary and replaced by another military corps. I did not know what to do. Soldiers moving around near the frontline without reason, or proper documents, were usually suspect. They could be deserters or even spies. I approached the commandant of a nearby transfer point and asked for directions. The

137

following morning the commandant called me in, presented me to a sub-lieutenant, and told me to follow him. It turned out that I was assigned to a motorized battalion, attached to a cavalry corps, which was in the process of being transferred from Lithuania to Poland, from the third Belorussian front to the second.

We arrived north of Warsaw late in December 1944. We stayed there for several weeks getting ready for a major offensive the purpose of which was to drive a wedge between the German military forces and cut off East Prussia from Germany proper. In Poland Soviet soldiers were for the first time exposed to a foreign environment. Similarly, the Poles had no previous experience in dealing with Soviet people. By the end of the war, close to half of the Soviet rank and file consisted of members of national minorities, mainly from Central Asia and the Caucasus. They were unfamiliar with European traditions and way of life, nor did they speak Russian well. Some of them could hardly make a distinction between Germans and Poles and treated both equally, as enemies. Some of them plundered the local population, abused women, and offended those who resisted their advances. The Poles did not submit easily. They were just recently liberated from Nazi occupation and were already familiar with the brute force of invaders. They sought out Soviet commanders, complained of maltreatment, and demanded justice. Since I was the only one in our detachment able to speak Polish, many Poles came to me and asked for assistance. The political officer of our battalion became suspicious. He suspected that I could be in collusion with the enemy. I was soon summoned to the counter intelligence department at the corps headquarters for interrogation. I provided the officer in charge with information about my background, and submitted my partisan credentials. The colonel in charge said that the reliability of my testimony would be checked and that I would be informed of the results as soon as they would become available. I returned to my battalion, but I was aware that I was watched, and that my movements were restricted.

In the meantime the offensive began. Our tanks supported by artillery and air force moved first westwards, and later turned to the north into East Prussia, in the direction of the cities of Allenstein (Olsztyn) and Konigsberg. In the beginning, the German population retreated together with the German army, but at some point that had become impossible and, for the first time, Soviet soldiers encountered face to face German people. The rage of the Soviet soldiers was horrendous. There were few among them who did not suffer from the Nazi onslaught. Most lost relatives in the war and many were dispossessed of all their belonging under occupation. The anti-Nazi propaganda in the Soviet Army was so strong that every soldier was overwhelmed by an insatiable craving for revenge. The first Germans encountered on our way suffered most. Many civilians were indiscriminately killed, women raped, property destroyed, and German military warehouses plundered. Alcohol was available in abundance and Soviet soldiers got drunk, hardly able to perform their duties. Senior officers tried to keep the rank and file under control, but it was an impossible task. The officers themselves were affected by a mixture of different emotions, including those of exhilaration, hatred, and duty.

Our tank battalion was moved north, driving a wedge between the Nazi forces. We approached the Baltic Sea between the cities of Konigsberg and Danzig (Gdansk). As a member of tank-borne infantry, I was at the very thick of the battle. Step by step, German resistance was waning. Before the end of January 1945, East Prussia was cut off completely. It was only a matter of time before the German army in this region would have to surrender.

One winter day, in East Prussia, when there was a temporary pause in battle, I was approached by the political officer of our detachment and ordered to follow him to the intelligence department of the corps. When I arrived there I learned that my credentials were checked and my reliability was no longer questioned. I was told that I was transferred to the reconnaissance headquarters of the corps where I would work as an interpreter and translator. I was then attached to a small service platoon and given a new uniform. Instead of riding on a tank, under constant enemy fire, I was now riding a jeep, mostly with high ranking officers. That did not mean that I was completely out of danger, but life certainly became better and more interesting. I was called upon to assist in the interrogation of German officers, read and translate documents, and participate in the establishment of a civil administration in the newly liberated areas.

One winter day I was riding in a jeep with an officer in the region of Danzig. I observed scattered groups of Jewish women moving slowly southwards and away from the front line. I surmised that these were former inmates of a nearby concentration camp, just recently liberated from the Nazis. The women were poorly dressed, exhausted from hard labour and malnutrition. I looked into their faces from a distance. All looked alike. There was the same mark of suffering and humiliation in all of them. Only one face stood out more prominently. It was the face and figure of a young Jewish woman strikingly similar to that of a girl who attended the *Tarbut* secondary school in Vilnius, before the war, and was a classmate of mine. Our jeep passed the Jewish women rapidly. I had no chance to stop to make sure who she was. The officer in charge was in a rush and would have never agreed to that. But her image haunted me even after the war and brought back memories of my childhood and youth.

After the capture of the capital of East Prussia, Konigsberg, the birthplace of the famous philosopher Immanuel Kant (1724-1804), our corps moved south, back into Poland. We crossed the Vistula river and moved westwards into Germany proper. By March 1945 we were again driving another wedge into the frontline, to the north, reaching soon the Baltic Sea between the cities of Kolberg (Kolobrzeg) and Stettin (Szczecin). This time we cut off the German troops concentrated in Pomerania.

The war was nearing its end. According to an agreement between the Western allies and the USSR, the Elbe river was to serve as a boundary separating East Germany from the West, as well as the Soviet occupation army from those of the USA, Great Britain, and France. The German forces were demoralized and retreated in disarray. They were trying to escape Soviet war prison, preferring to surrender to the Americans or British. But it was a long way from Pomerania and East Germany to the Elbe river, and many German divisions had no recourse but to capitulate to the rapidly advancing Soviets. On 3 May 1945 I was at the approaches to Berlin and had an opportunity to witness its fall. The war ended on 8 May 1945. A day earlier our detachment reached the Elbe river in the vicinity of the towns of Wittenberg and Lenzen.

The last days of war were exhilarating and tragic at the same time. The soldiers abandoned all rules of vigilance, instilled in them over the years of war, and gave vent to their instincts. The last day of war, a victory celebration in one of our military detachments ended in disaster. Seven soldiers poisoned themselves with wood spirit. It was a truly tragic occurrence. We could hardly believe that after all the tribulations of war, one could face death at the hands of such insidious and covert enemy as alcohol. Nevertheless, relatives of the poisoned soldiers would surely receive official notes stating that their children or siblings fell a heroic death in combat with the treacherous Nazi enemy. Another soldier in our corps, the same day, was accidentally killed in the process of sorting military trophies.

By the end of the war the German army was totally destroyed. Nothing was left of the former posture, pretence, and arrogance of German officers and soldiers. Immediately after the war, however, Soviet military units were also in disarray. Discipline was on the decline. Alcohol, sex, and marauding had become a way of life. It took a while before special security units, brought in from the Soviet Union, were able to establish a semblance of order. The local German population was then taken under protection, and many military front line divisions were removed from Germany. After all, those representing the Soviet administration knew already then that the Germans residing in the eastern part of the country would soon become citizens of the so-called D.D.R., or German Democratic Republic, an "independent" pro-Soviet German socialist state.

Psychologically, however, the civil population of East Germany had a hard time in coming to terms with Soviet occupation. The German people were shocked by the collapse of the Nazi empire and by the sheer fact that from victors they have turned into victims. They were devastated because it was difficult for them to accept the domination of a people they had until recently regarded as inferior. Many German civilians, residing near the Elbe river, abandoned their homes and moved in haste, across the river, to West Germany. But not everyone was ready to forsake their homestead and many tried to adapt to the new conditions of life. An incident in Lenzen, in the neighbourhood where our detachment was stationed, made me realize that this adaptation process was extremely painful, and for some Germans, almost impossible. Some Germans preferred death to what they regarded as Soviet oppression.

One afternoon I was called upon to interpret in the interrogation of an elderly German. He led us to an attic in one of the houses around the corner. The sight in the attic was gruesome. Six people, three adults and three children, hung from rope, attached to a cross-beam. A seventh rope was ready and waiting. The whole family, grandparents, parents, and children were to commit suicide in order to escape Soviet humiliation and occupation. The grandfather assisted the others and was to commit suicide last. But after helping all members of his family to kill themselves, when his turn came, he failed to muster his will power and courage to end his own life. And now he was standing and telling this story to his Soviet interrogator. At that time, I still had little compassion for those who were part of the Nazi murderous machine, but I was touched by the picture of the innocent children killed for no reason whatsoever. Surely they were not responsible for the crimes committed by their parents.

Personally, the end of the war was a mixed blessing. I was happy to survive both the Holocaust and the war. But paradoxically survival, the main objective of life during this tragic war, lost its meaning for me. There was no longer any danger to my physical well being, but a terrible emotional emptiness set in to replace it. It was caused by the devastating sensation of complete loneliness. My fellow soldiers were in constant touch with their families and were waiting impatiently for the time when they would be discharged and return home. The high point in a soldier's daily life was the time when the mail was delivered. Everyone congregated at the mail room and waited for news from home. I had no home, no relatives, and no mail to receive. There was even no next of kin to report to, in case anything happened to me. I was like a stray animal, in a strange herd, with no place to return to.

After the war ended, our corps continued to stay in Germany for over four months. Every soldier was permitted to send a parcel of so-called war trophies to his family back home once a month. I had no family, but I had the address of my colleague from my partisan days, Max Begun, who lived and studied in the city of Minsk. I wrote a letter and sent a parcel to him. I was extremely happy to receive a reply from Max and to learn that the parcel arrived safely. It made me, in a sense, equal to other soldiers. It was a sign that I was not completely alone in this world. My second parcel, however, occasioned no happiness, but rather anguish. The reply this time was not from Max, but from a woman, a lab-technician at the institute where he studied. She informed me that Max was dead. He was murdered in his native town of Parafianovo, in Western Belorussia. He went to visit his home town, and also to look for some things, hidden by his family before the Nazi onslaught, only to be killed by those who appropriated their property and did not want to return it to its proper owners. Poor Max! He survived the war and the Holocaust only to be murdered by his former neighbours. Nazi propaganda and actions poisoned the atmosphere in the formerly occupied territories and a Jew was still regarded by the locals as a lower creature, and expendable. These terrible tidings had a shocking effect on me, not only because I was sorry for Max, but also because I realized that although the Holocaust and the war were over there was no end in sight to the real struggle for survival. Moreover, time dulled somewhat the pain caused by the recent Nazi atrocities, but it could do little to heal the wounds.

In September 1945, our corps was moved from Germany to the Soviet Union. On the way it was stationed for several months in the cities of Lublin and Zamosc, in Poland. One afternoon, walking on the main street in Lublin, I was surprised to encounter Tolia Krakovsky, a former schoolmate from *Tarbut*. He was the first to tell me that my sister, Lucy, was alive, and that he recently saw her somewhere in Poland. He also hinted that many Jewish soldiers in the Soviet army, in particular those who lived before the war in Poland and Lithuania, were deserting and escaping to the West, before their return to the USSR. My encounter with Krakovsky was brief. It was getting late and I had to return to my unit, but our conversation disturbed my peace and unsettled my existence. I surely wanted to meet the surviving members of my family who were currently somewhere in Poland and moving to the West, but I was stuck in the Soviet army and moving in the opposite direction.

The notion of deserting from the Soviet army, however, seemed to me, at that time, unpractical. I was totally isolated from the outside world and had no contact with anyone who could assist me in such endeavour. Moreover, I felt that it was treacherous to abandon and stealthily betray those who helped me survive the Holocaust. That did not mean, of course, that I intended to spend the rest of my life in the Soviet Union, but I decided that I would leave the country legally rather than as deserter. Years later, I realized that I was naive. I was brainwashed by Soviet communist propaganda to which I was subjected daily. I knew then litte about the Soviet totalitarian regime and the abuse of human rights in the USSR.

Before New Year 1946, we moved back to the USSR. Our corps was now stationed in the small Ukrainian town of Iziaslav, just east of the former Polish-USSR border. Early in 1946 I accidentally learned that former Polish citizens, those of Polish and Jewish nationality, could now be legally repatriated back to Poland. I started to make inquiries and contemplate my next move. Unfortunately, I learned soon that in order to be able to apply for repatriation I would have to be first discharged from the army. Only then, as a civilian, could I relinquish my Soviet citizenship, which was bestowed upon me without my asking, and move to Poland. In our detachment there was one Polish soldier who expressed the wish to be transferred to the Polish army and move to his native country. Instead of being sent to Poland, however, he was sent to continue his service to the Soviet Far East. No wonder I gave up the idea of repatriation for a while, and tried to bide my time by adapting to the life of a simple soldier in the Soviet army.

Sport came once again to my rescue. I was the only private to be a member of our corps' basketball team and to participate in the army championship in the city of Kiiv (Kiev), all the others were officers. Somewhat later I became the bantam weight boxing champion of the Carpathian Military Region. The championship took place in the city of Lviv (Lvov). I reached the final without much trouble, but there I was faced by a formidable opponent. He was a well trained, rested, and fed army captain stationed in Lviv. The boxing ring was the only place where a soldier could challenge the authority of a senior officer. All the same, it was a complicated task. The referees and judges were local people and they were biased in favour of my opponent. It was apparent that the captain knew them all. It was a difficult fight, but I was confident that the odds were in my favour, and expected victory. Unfortunately, the judges announced the captain champion. To my surprise the audience, composed mainly of simple soldiers, was on my side. They were greatly offended by the fact that one of them was treated unjustly and robbed by the judges of his deserved victory. The soldiers raised such a clamour that it was impossible to continue the competition. When the General in charge arrived to investigate, he was mobbed by protesting soldiers who demanded justice. Without much ado the General ordered that our fight be repeated later in the evening. The judges protested that it was against the rules; that no boxer was permitted to fight twice the same day. But the General was relentless. He just replied that Soviet soldiers were strong and could withstand any difficulty.

Late that evening I faced the captain again in the ring. I was exhausted. I hardly made it to the end. But this time the judges were apparently afraid of the soldiers' rage and I was announced the champion. I was thrilled not only by the awards and honour, but also by the realization that, despite my foreign sounding Jewish name, the soldiers supported me in my fight with a Russian officer. It appeared that in certain circumstances the expression of class consciousness could be stronger than national identification, and that despite the alleged unity and equality, preached continuously in the Soviet army, there was little common between soldiers and officers. The rank and file harboured little love for their superiors.

As an award for my sport accomplishments, I was granted a month furlough which I could spend in the location of my choice. May 9, 1946, I arrived in Vilnius. It was the first anniversary of the defeat of Nazi Germany. Most people were celebrating it, but I was overcome by a deep sense of sadness. I went to the house we lived in before the war, but it was occupied by strangers. I walked the streets for hours, but I did not see any one I knew. I spent most of my life before the war in Vilno, yet now I was a stranger there. I decided to leave this place, never to return again.

Chance, however, prompted a change in my plans. On my way to the railway station I stopped near the Choral Synagogue where Jews usually congregated in those days. I did not find any acquaintances there, but one woman recognized me. She worked in the days of the ghetto together with my father. She confirmed that my sister survived the war and she told me that, after liberation from concentration camp, she came to Vilnius to look for me. Someone told her, however, that I perished at the front and she immediately left for Poland. This woman also gave me the names of some old residents of Vilnius that I was acquainted with before the war. That was when I met the Brancovski family and some other youngsters who survived the war fighting the Nazis in the Lithuanian partisan brigade in the Rudnicki forest. I decided to spend my holiday in Vilnius with my newly found old friends. They accepted me like one of their own and they replaced me my family. After my furlough was over, I returned to my military unit in Iziaslav where I served until March 1947. Then I was discharged from the Soviet army and I returned to Vilnius to begin a new life.

CHAPTER FOUR

THE AFTERMATH.   VILNIUS TODAY

After the liberation of Vilnius from Nazi occupation the few surviving Jews, hiding in special bunkers, or sheltered by gentile friends, came out into the open. Some Jewish partisans and members of the Soviet underground also returned to the city. In August 1944, when a roll of the city population was taken, some 600 Jews registered. It was assumed, at that time, that another 500 failed to disclose their Jewish identity.[1] Half of those registered were Soviet born Jews who arrived with the new Soviet administration from the USSR, as well as surviving Jews from other cities and towns in Lithuania. Thus, immediately after liberation close to a 1,000 Jews resided in the city.

Until the summer of 1947, when the repatriation of Polish born Jews from the USSR to Poland was formally stopped, the composition of the Jewish community of Vilnius was in a flux and Jewish life in the city was in a state of transition. It became clear in the course of repatriation that most Jewish natives of Vilno, who survived the Holocaust, refused to live under Soviet rule, and those who remained in the city were mainly supporters of the Soviet communist regime. A few others were prevented from moving to the West by different circumstances of life. It appeared, thus, that while the Jewish population of Vilnius continued to grow by the influx of Soviet Jews, there were in the city no more than several hundred original Jewish residents, born in Vilno before the war.

Life in Vilnius after the war was vastly different from the life established in the city prior to 1939. The national composition of the population, its social structure, and economic base were changing rapidly. Before the war most inhabitants were Polish and Jewish. After the war the majority was formed by Lithuanians and Russian. Before the war Vilnius had few major industrial enterprises. After the war, under Soviet rule, a number of manufacturing plants were constructed, and thousands of new workers moved into the city, both from rural Lithuania, as well as from other Soviet republics. Moreover, the standard of living in the Soviet Baltic republics was much higher than that in the rest of the Soviet Union, and many Soviet citizens were enticed by the prospects of a better life. That did not mean, of course, that the standard of living in Vilnius was now higher than that before the war. It was just indicative of the harsh living conditions in Russia, itself.

Jewish life in Vilnius after the war changed beyond recognition. In fact, there was no such thing as Jewish communal life. As a constituent part of the Soviet state, Lithuania was subject to national, social, and cultural policy determined by Soviet political and ideological considerations and enacted in Moscow for the whole Soviet Union. The atheistic essence of Marxist dogma ruled out the possibility of Jewish religious expression of any significance and the anti-Zionist nature of Soviet national and foreign policy precluded any meaningful connection between Soviet Jews and their brethren in Israel, or in the West. A certain relaxation in the strict application of Soviet official religious and nationality policy was evident during the Second World War. In 1942, a Jewish Soviet Anti-Fascist Committee was created in Moscow. Its main purpose was to attract the support of the international Jewish community for the Soviet war effort, and contacts between the leaders of the Committee and representatives of North American Jewry were permitted.

The tolerant attitude of the Soviet leadership towards the feeble national and religious aspirations of national minorities was, however, a temporary phenomenon. As soon as the war was over, a new brand of Soviet Russian nationalism was unleashed by Stalin. In August 1946 the Communist Party Central Committee promulgated a decree about the work of several Soviet literary journals. The main purpose of this decree was to initiate a campaign of denunciation of the "decadent West," especially the United States, and the glorification of everything Russian and Soviet. It aimed at ferreting out those guilty of "servility before the West" to whom the term "rootless cosmopolitans" soon came to be applied. Jewish intellectuals, scholars, and writers were prime targets of these attacks. They were accused of double loyalty, and servility to the West.

In the late 1940s, however, the Soviet approach to Jewish issues was ambiguous. On the one hand, the Soviet government discriminated against its Jewish minority, depriving it of the few cultural and social benefits granted during the war, while on the other, it supported the partition of Palestine, recognized the newly created state of Israel, and voted for Israel's admission to the United Nations. The Soviet support for the creation of a Jewish state was by no means a humanitarian deed, nor an expression of Soviet political altruism. It was rather a calculated act the purpose of which was to introduce political and military discord in the Middle East, hastening thus the departure of the British from Palestine, and creating a window for Soviet infiltration.

The Soviets anticipated that the creation of an independent Jewish state would raise the national consciousness of Soviet Jews and provide them with a new sense of national identity. In order to preclude such a possibility, and instil fear among Soviet Jews, the government initiated a number of anti-Jewish policies. 1948 was the year the state of Israel was formally established. The same year marked the beginning of a concentrated attack on Soviet Jewish institutions and personalities. During the night of 12 January 1948 S. Mikhoels, the artistic director of the Jewish State Theatre in Moscow, and the chairman of the Jewish Anti-Fascist Committee, was murdered in an alleged "car accident," in the city of Minsk, in Belorussia. In November of the same year the Committee was disbanded altogether, and early in 1949 most members of its active leadership, among them a number of leading Soviet Jewish poets, writers, and intellectuals, were arrested. Many other prominent Jewish personalities were imprisoned and groundlessly accused of espionage and nationalistic anti-Soviet activity. In the summer of 1952 the Military Collegium of the USSR Supreme Court sentenced to death on trumped up charges, twenty-four Jewish poets, writers, and bureaucrats, most of whom were members of the Jewish Anti-Fascist Committee executive board. Among those executed were the well known poets Y. Fefer and P. Markish, and the diplomat S. Lozovskii. They were shot on 12 August 1952. The others were sentenced to various terms of prison and labour camp, ranging from five to twenty-five years of incarceration.

Several months later, on 13 January 1953, an official TASS announcement about the arrest of a group of medical doctors - alleged saboteurs, appeared in the Moscow newspaper Pravda (Truth), the official organ of the Communist Party Central Committee. It informed the Soviet people that a terrorist group, composed mostly of Jewish physicians, employed at the Kremlin medical centre, was involved in sabotage activity, aimed at undermining the health and shortening the lives of Soviet leaders. The doctors were accused, that under the cover of dedicated medical treatment, they conducted murderous activity and espionage. Show trials and public executions of members of the so-called "doctors' plot" were planned for March 1953. The government intended to instigate anti-Jewish pogroms, and then "save" the Jews from the wrath of the masses by deporting them to remote regions of Siberia. A public letter, signed by many well known Soviet Jewish political and cultural figures, was prepared well in advance, in which they begged Stalin and the Soviet government to save the Jews from the rage of ordinary Soviet people. Most Soviet Jewish senior bureaucrats, politicians, and intellectuals obliged out of fear and signed this ignominious document. Among the few who refused to acquiesce were the writers V. Kaverin and I. Ehrenburg, the General I. Kreizer, and the singer M. Reizen.

The death of Stalin, on 5 March 1953, saved the doctors from execution, and most Soviet Jews from deportation to Siberia. After the death of the tyrant, the doctors' trial was cancelled and most physicians arrested in connection with the trumped up charges were released. But the spiritual emasculation of Soviet Jewry continued. True, after Stalin's death the intensity of Soviet anti-Semitism somewhat diminished, but the anti-Jewish campaign was now replaced by a new wave of anti-Zionism, and anti-Israel propaganda. For all practical purposes, however, the distinction between anti-Semitism and anti-Zionism remained blurred, and ordinary Soviet citizens saw little difference between them.

Just as all over the Soviet Union, the Jews in Vilnius had to learn to live with the constraints of Soviet nationality policy. Immediately after the war some limited Jewish cultural activity was still permitted in Vilnius. A Jewish museum was established, and a monument in memory of the Jews murdered by the Nazis in the forest of Ponary was erected. Soon, however, in 1949, the museum was closed, and the monument in Ponary was destroyed in 1952. Until the death of Stalin, in March 1953, and in particular until the Twentieth Communist Party Congress in 1956 at which N. Khrushchev uncovered Stalin's crimes and denounced the atrocities committed by his henchmen against his own people, most Jews in Vilnius lived in fear.

I arrived in Vilnius after I left from the army in the spring of 1947. It was a time when social pressure, Russian nationalism, and anti-Semitism were on the rise. I did not intend to remain in the USSR for long and I immediately applied to the appropriate authorities with a request for repatriation to Poland. Unfortunately, it was too late. The repatriation process was already completed and my application was rejected. Thus, I had no choice but to remain in Vilnius, now again the capital of Soviet Lithuania.

Life in Vilnius in 1947 was not easy. Food was still rationed, good jobs were scarce, and, besides, I had no profession or trade. When the war started in 1941 I was sixteen years old, barely out of school. In the army my movements were limited and my choices were restricted, but I was provided with food, shelter, and other necessities. Life as a free man burdened me with a number of new concerns such as housing, employment, education, and food on the table. My situation was alleviated by the kindness and extreme self-sacrifice of my friends Misha and Fania Brancovski. They opened the doors of their small two-room flat and accepted me as a member of their own family. Only those familiar with the conditions of life in the Soviet Union, after the Second World War, could appreciate their generosity of spirit. They admitted a total stranger into their crammed quarters and provided me with a home.

My integration into the new, non-military, existence was hampered by the fact that I was not a member of the communist party, that I was a Jew, and that I survived Nazi occupation. Any one who lived, even for a short time, under German rule was regarded as a potential spy and was suspect. It did not matter that the Nazis murdered all Jews indiscriminately, regardless of their political affiliation. The sheer fact of survival placed the

Jew in one category with all others who were suspected of collaboration with the Nazi regime. Since most positions of consequence in the Soviet national economy, education, or administration required security clearance, any Jew who lived under Nazi rule and was not a party member had a hard time in securing a proper job.

Again, as in the past, my situation was mitigated by the fact that I was a well known sportsman. Soon after my arrival in Vilnius a rumour spread in the city that I was back from the army and different sport clubs began to vie for my services. Soviet sport operated, in those days, on the labour-production principle and each sport association represented a certain branch of the national economy, army, or internal security forces. I joined the sport club *Spartak* the membership of which was composed mostly of those who were members of Soviet industrial producers' co-operatives (arteli). *Spartak* provided me with a job where I had little to do and a lot of free time to participate in sport activities. Soon I was a part of a basketball team that won the championship of Vilnius, as well as first a member, and later the head, of the Lithuanian *Spartak* hockey team.

In 1947 a Soviet national hockey league was formed and teams from the Baltic republics were invited to participate. Until then the Soviets played a version of hockey different from the one popular in Canada. It was called hockey bandy. It was played with a short stick, a small ball, instead of a puck, and on a rink the size of a soccer field. Teams from the Baltic states were the only ones who had some previous experience of playing hockey with a puck. The other teams in the league were from Moscow, Leningrad, and Kuibyshev. Hockey in the Soviet Union was a winter sport. There was, at that time, not a single artificial rink, or indoor arena for hockey, anywhere in the Soviet Union. All competitions were conducted outdoors and the schedule was always at the mercy of the weather. It did not take long before the Soviets mastered the skills of the new game and, by 1949, the Lithuanian *Spartak* hockey team was relegated to a lower league, and soon disbanded altogeter.   That was when I decided to devote most of my time to boxing. I became the champion of Vilnius, and a member of the Lithuanian national boxing team. At the same time I coached the *Spartak* boxers and I was appointed to the position of associate chairman of the Lithuanian national *Spartak* association. The chairman was a demobilized officer from the Soviet army who knew nothing about, nor was interested in, sports. After the end of the war many party members, former officers, were appointed to positions for which they had absolutely no qualifications. They simply acted as figureheads and they watched over the political reliability of the staff. We, as Nazi occupation survivors, were little trusted by those in power.

In 1950 I left the Lithuanian branch of *Spartak*, and transferred to *Zalgiris*, a Lithuanian national trade union sport association. I was appointed principal of its central sport school and head coach of the boxing section. At the same time I was the head coach of the city of Vilnius selects and of the Lithuanian national boxing teams. By that time I stopped participating actively in boxing competitions and devoted all my time to coaching and administrative responsibilities. Our club produced a number of outstanding athletes, including USSR, Europe, and Olympic medal winners. In 1956, I was invited, among others, to coach the USSR national boxing team in preparation to the 1956 Olympic games in Melbourne. R. Murauskas, a member of our club in Vilnius was awarded a medal at the games in the light-heavy weight boxing division.

It did not take long, however, before my involvement in sport competition on the highest level raised in my mind a number of ethical questions. It became obvious to me that amateur sport had lost much of its former relative "purity." As early as in 1947 I witnessed, for the first time, death in the ring. When I returned to the dressing room, after my victorious final light-weight bout for the championship of Vilnius, I saw one of the participants in an earlier fight lying unconscious, unattended and ignored by most passers-by. The boxer in question soon died, but the sight of this helpless youngster unsettled my tranquillity and spoiled my victory celebration. Moreover, it haunted me during all the years of my practical involvement with the sport of boxing.

Soon it became clear to me that even in amateur boxing murder in the ring was a common occurrence. It often happened that a boxer could not recover from a brain haemorrhage, caused by numerous punches to his head, but the fight would continue even after the boxer was groggy, no longer in control of his actions, and unable to defend himself. I soon realized that boxing was an extremely dangerous sport and I began to question my involvement in it. Moreover, I became aware of the fact that the emphasis on the political ramifications and the commercialization of sport, in which monetary and political gain was stressed at the expense of health, fitness, and education, had emasculated sport competition of the attributes associated with the true meaning of sportsmanship. Winning at any price became the motto, and athletes were prepared to go to any extreme to abuse their bodies and break the rules of competition, in order to achieve their cherished goals.

Sport in the Soviet Union was a highly politicized affair, and the government did not spare any effort, or financial resources, to make sure that Soviet athletes were victorious in world and Olympic championships. This was to illustrate the alleged superiority of the Soviet system of government over those in the West and to attract the recognition and admiration of young people all over the world. Hence, the social status and economic well-being of leading coaches and athletes in the Soviet Union were far above average. Olympic, world, and even USSR champions and their coaches were national heroes and they were treated and rewarded accordingly.

Theoretically all Soviet athletes were amateurs. In practice, however, all members of Soviet national teams, as well as members of upper league clubs in sports such as soccer, hockey, or basketball were pseudo-amateurs. They were all paid secretly by the government and did nothing else, but train and participate in competitions. There was only one difference between western professionals and Soviet pseudo-amateurs. The former operated in a free market and could sell their services to the highest bidder. The latter could not haggle and were forced to accept whatever was given, because the government was the only employer. In order to encourage high performance, a secret system of monetary awards was established, whereby both the athlete and his or her coach were rewarded for success. When in 1955 and 1956 members of my club R. Juskenas and R. Murauskas respectively, became champions of the USSR, I received in each case a bonus of 5,000.00 rubles. This amount was equal, at that time, to a worker's annual salary.

For quite a while I was happy to bask in the fame and adulation of the fans. I enjoyed seeing my picture in the daily press and I was proud to be recognized instantly by passers-by on the streets of the city. Nonetheless, I knew that one cannot be a productive athlete all his life and that the fate of coaches, managers, and other sport personalities was fickle, at best. They were usually good as long as they were lucky and could produce champions. At all other times, they were dispensable. To avoid the possibility of an unexpected downfall, I embarked in 1949 on an extensive programme of study to prepare myself for any eventuality. I graduated in 1954 from the Minsk State Institute for Physical Culture, and the same year enroled in a graduate programme in sport physiology at the Moscow Scientific Research Institute for Physical Culture. Work and study, at the same time, was extremely difficult. The more so since I had to commute often from Vilnius to Minsk and Moscow to attend lectures and pass exams.

Except for the few instances when I was exposed to blatant anti-Semitic discrimination, my life in the Soviet Union was productive and fulfilling. I enjoyed a living standard well above average. I received a higher education, I married, and had good friends. Nevertheless, I never forgot my roots, and always yearned to be reunited with my family. After the death of Stalin, the new Soviet ruler, N. Khrushchev, in 1956 revived the old repatriation agreement between Poland and the USSR, and former Polish citizens could again relinquish their Soviet identity and move back to Poland. I did not hesitate long and decided to leave my home, most of my possessions, my friends, and the relative security of life in Vilnius, and venture into a new life which was still associated in my mind with our family existence in the non-Soviet environment of my childhood.

I arrived in Warsaw in the spring of 1957, but my stay there was short. My sister Lucy, the only surviving member of my immediate family, was by that time already in Toronto, Canada. Initially I moved from Warsaw to the port city of Gdansk, because I hoped there to take a boat going directly to Montreal. In Gdansk, I coached for over a year the local internal security boxing team *Wybrzeze*. As a token of appreciation for its success I was provided with a foreign passport, which was otherwise almost impossible to secure. Thus, after a short interlude in Poland I landed, together with my wife and baby daughter, on 19 September 1958 in Quebec, Canada to begin a new life.

After my departure from Vilnius the situation in the Soviet Union changed little and Jewish life in the city continued to stagnate. Social organization in the Soviet Union was based on class rather than nationality principles and no Jewish social, intellectual, or even cultural groups or associations were permitted to function. Any sign of national awareness was suspect. Jewish social life in Vilnius was a private matter and Jewish cultural activity was limited to occasional amateur dramatic or artistic variety performances.

After the six-day war in 1967, the USSR severed diplomatic ties with Israel and initiated a drive in support of Arab and communist adversaries of the Jewish state. The Soviet Union refused to recognize Zionism as a national liberation movement, and supported the United Nations Organization's resolution which equated Zionism with racism. A special Soviet anti-Zionist committee was formed in Moscow with the aim of conducting anti-Israel and anti-Zionist propaganda among the Soviet people. In an obvious attempt to stress the difference between anti-Semitism and anti-Zionism, the committee included many Jewish pro-communist intellectuals, scholars, and bureaucrats.

In the 1970s, during the years of L. Brezhnev's rule, the Soviet anti-Israel campaign bolstered anti-Jewish feelings in the country and many Jews were frustrated by semi-official discrimination. This new situation raised the level of Jewish national awareness and many Jews began to identify more openly with their brethren in Israel and in the West. This, in turn, led Jewish activists to open dissidence and fostered Jewish emigration from the USSR. Those employed in enterprises producing military hardware, or having access to Soviet state secrets, were usually refused permission to leave. They were often denied employment or residence permits in major cities, and were accused of parasitism and anti-Soviet activity.

The relative success of the state of Israel, and the growth of anti-Semitism in the USSR, stimulated the revival of the Jewish national spirit and prompted an interest in Jewish history and Jewish religious and cultural values among Soviet Jews. The example of Lithuania influenced Jews residing in other major Soviet centres and encouraged the development of a clandestine system of Jewish education.

Whether for political, economic, or national reasons the drive of many Soviet Jews to leave their native land reached excessive proportion. It soon became an important issue of international dimensions. American Jewish leaders supported Soviet Jews in their urge to emigrate. They issued a call "let my people go," and exerted pressure on American politicians urging them to support the cause of Jewish emigration from the USSR. The interest of American Jewish leaders in Jewish emigration from the USSR was twofold. On the one hand they wanted to assist in the national revival of Soviet Jewry and effect a positive change in Soviet anti-Zionist and anti-Israel policies. On the other, with the declining levels of immigration to Israel from North America and the West, they viewed Soviet Jewish immigration to Israel as an important source of manpower which could bolster the demographic, political, and economic situation of the Jewish state.

The Soviet government resisted pressure from the West. It did not want to submit to blackmail and attempts to interfere in, what it regarded as, internal Soviet affairs and it refused to open its borders to all Jews wishing to leave. Moreover, it did not want to set a precedent which could provide other Soviet national minorities with a notion that they could request permission to abandon their fatherland as well. Furthermore, Arab states pressured the USSR to stop Jewish emigration, because it would strengthen the political and military might of the Jewish state. Indeed, between 1948 and 1970 Jewish emigration from the USSR was an individual matter. Only 25,200 Jews were provided with exit visas and most of those permitted to leave went initially to friendly socialist countries, members of the communist block. The situation changed drastically in the 1970s. Between 1971 and 1980 248,900 Soviet Jews left the USSR, 62.8 per cent of that total arrived in Israel. In the 1980s and early 1990s the level of Jewish emigration from the USSR fluctuated. Between 1981 and 1986, at the height of the cold war, only 16,900 Jews were permitted to leave. But in the years of Gorbachev's *perestroika*, the numbers grew rapidly. In 1987-1989

100,000 left the USSR,[2] in 1990 - 201,300, and in 1991 - 194,000.[3] With the growth of Jewish emigration from the USSR, however, the number of those opting to settle in Israel began to decline rapidly. In 1985 30 per cent of all Soviet Jewish emigres went to Israel. In 1986 22 per cent, in 1987 25.1 per cent, but in 1988 only 11.1 per cent, and in 1989 a mere 10.2 percent.[4]

The choice of destination, selected by Soviet Jewish emigres, was determined by a variety of reasons. Most Jewish natives of Lithuania and Vilnius emigrated from the Soviet Union directly to Israel. Education, culture, and national and religious affinity helped determine their choice. Under Soviet rule Jewish life in Vilnius was always more active than in most other cities of the former USSR. Many Jewish natives of Vilnius, still residing in the city, before the war were educated in Jewish schools and continued to speak to each other and to their children in Yiddish rather than Russian or Lithuanian. As late as in 1989 37.5 per cent of all Jews in Vilnius still declared Yiddish as their native language.[5] Russian and Ukrainian Jews, on the other hand were seldom exposed to Jewish education and upbringing and lacked the background acquired by the natives of Vilnius or Kaunas in their Jewish environment. Thus, since Jewish culture and the Hebrew and Yiddish languages were alien to them, the cause of their emigration was primarily economic, with national considerations playing a minor role, and they preferred to settle in the USA, Canada, or Western Europe.

Emigration decimated the Jewish population of Vilnius. According to the official Soviet census in 1959 there were 16,534 Jews in the city, but by 1979 the number declined to 10,723, or 2.3 per cent of the total city population. By 1989 the number diminished further to 9,109, and today there are 5,600 Jews in Lithuania, and less than 4,000 in Vilnius. Between 1989 and 1994 of the total of 12,400 Jews in Lithuania, 6,122 left the country. 5,059 went to Israel.[6]

11 March 1990 the Supreme Council, or the parliament of Lithuania, proclaimed its independence from the Soviet Union. Initially the Soviets refused to recognize Lithuania's independence. The August 1991 anti-Gorbachev coup in Moscow, however, led to the disintegration of the Soviet Union and the creation, in December 1991, of a Commonwealth of Independent States, composed of former Soviet republics. The Baltic states refused to join this new Commonwealth. In 1991 independent Lithuania gained diplomatic recognition from most Western countries, and in September 1991, it was admitted to the United Nations. This change in the fortunes of Lithuania affected also the destiny of the Jews still remaining in Vilnius. Their fate was no longer subject to internal or foreign Soviet policy, but rather to the vicissitudes of life in independent Lithuania, and its

place in the fellowship of free nations.

The struggle of Lithuania for secession from the USSR, in the late 1980s, was accompanied by the growth of national consciousness among the Jews of Vilnius. Many continued to view emigration as their only possible option and used the political situation, connected with M. Gorbachev's policies of *perestroika* in the Soviet Union to hasten their departure. Others, however, decided to stay. Family circumstances, age, and economic considerations determined their choice. They actively supported the cause of Lithuanian independence, trying at the same time to revive Jewish life in the city.

As early as in 1988 a Jewish Cultural Society was established in Lithuania. In 1991 this society had been transformed into a Jewish Communal Council which officially represents, today, the interests of the Jews of Lithuania and Vilnius. Its offices are located in the former premises of the *Tarbut* secondary school, on 4 Pylimo (Zawalna) Street in Vilnius, which also houses a number of other Jewish organizations.

Despite its relatively small size, the Jewish community of Vilnius is vibrant. It supports amateur dramatic circles, a concert brigade, and a Jewish People's Theatre. It sponsors a society for legal assistance, a public medical centre, an association of scholars and intellectuals, a youth centre, and a sport club, *Maccabi*. B'nai Brith and a Zionist Organization are active in the city, as well. The Jews of Vilnius are served by a regular Jewish radio broadcast and a monthly fifteen minutes Jewish television programme has been on the air since February 1992. Several hundred children are enrolled today in the Jewish national school, named after Sholom Aleikhem. There are two streams in the school. In one, Lithuanian is the language of instruction, in the other one - Russian. But Hebrew and Jewish studies form an important part of the curriculum. A new religious orthodox school opened its doors in the fall of 1996.

In 1989, *Yerushalayim de'Lita* (Jerusalem of Lithuania), a Jewish monthly in the Yiddish language, with occasional pages in Lithuanian, Russian, and English, began to appear. By 1994, the periodical ran out of money and stopped publication. In April 1995, with the financial backing of former and current Jewish residents of Vilnius, it resumed publication. Since July 1996 the newspaper appears bi-monthly in Yiddish and Russian. Occasionally it publishes also in English and Lithuanian. The lack of money forced it to curtail operation again.

Until the incorporation of Lithuania into the USSR the Faculty of Humanities of the Vilnius University had a well established department of Jewish studies. In 1940, with the advent of Soviet rule, this department was closed. In 1990, after fifty years of banishment, the department of Jewish studies has been re-opened. A Free University for the study of Jewish culture is also in operation in Vilnius since 1992. Lithuanian authorities have helped the Manhattan based Institute for Yiddish Culture to acquire copies of a part of the original *YIVO* archives, still available in Vilnius. Risking his own life, Antanas Ulpis, the former head of the Lithuanian State Book Chamber, managed to save some of the *YIVO* materials in the days of Nazi occupation and Stalinist rule.[7]

In general terms, Vilnius today resembles little the city remembered by those who were born there before the war and who left immediately after. Its population has more than doubled and its boundaries moved to the north, east, and west. The history of the Jewish community is mostly connected with the old part of the city, particularly the former Jewish quarters, the district where the ghetto was located. Much of this area was devastated by war and Nazi occupation and much of whatever could have been saved was subsequently destroyed by the Soviets. The Great Synagogue, for example, caught fire just before the city was liberated by Soviet troops, in July 1944. It was damaged extensively, but not beyond repair. It still could have been saved. Jews were still praying there during the high holidays of 1944 and 1945. But the ruins of the Great Synagogue soon disappeared from sight. The side of Vokieciu Street (Nemiecka, Muzejaus), where the synagogue courtyard was located, was levelled to the ground and, in 1964, a kindergarten facility was opened at the very same spot.

By 1990 a number of religious institutions became active in the Jewish community. The Choral Synagogue, on 39 Pylimo Street, the only surviving Jewish house of worship in Vilnius, was opened again to the public. A Rabbi arrived in Vilnius from England to serve the religious and ritual needs of the faithful. Rabbi David Smith was born in Great Britain, but his grandparents were natives of Lithuania. In 1996 Rabbi Samuel Kan arrived from England to replace him. The new Rabbi continues, however, to live in London and visits Vilnius only from time to time. In his absence a local layman conducts services. In 1993 another rabbi, delegated by the Chabad-Lubavitch movement in the USA, arrived in the city. Rabbi S.B. Krinsky, a young man of twenty-seven,[8] just recently ordained by the Central Lubavitch Yeshiva in New York, initiated a number of programmes with the purpose of attracting the secular Jews of Vilnius and their young children. The Lubavitch organization opened Sunday schools for religious education, as well as separate summer camps for boys and girls. They arranged communal celebrations of Jewish holidays and festivals, such as Passover, Chanukah, and Purim. They constructed and put in operation, a *mikvah*, or ritual bath. Rabbi Krinsky serves also as a *shochet*, making kosher meat available to Lithuanian Jews.

It is evident that the activity of the Lubavitch *Hasidim* does have fruit, but it introduces also strife in the small Jewish community of Vilnius. The Lubavitch *Hasidim* try to gain total control of Jewish religious life in the city, including the Choral Synagogue. Many local Jews resent it. They are not ready yet to make the abrupt leap from atheism and complete secularism to orthodoxy and are more comfortable with the modern version of Judaism, promoted by the rabbi from England. As it is, the small Jewish community in Lithuania consists today of three different segments, each trying to control Jewish life. There is the modern Jewish religious community, the *Hasidic* community, and the third, largest group, includes all secular Jews who still constitute the majority. The discord in the Jewish community and the attempt to control Jewish Life in Lithuania by religious organizations is vehemently opposed by the Board of the Jewish Community Council in Lithuania. It has recently come out with a declaration which states bluntly that it "does not back up the proposal to establish republican religious Jewish communities,"[9] in Lithuania.

The leadership of the Jewish community, with the assistance of local authorities, does its utmost to protect Jewish historical monuments in the city and commemorate appropriately important dates in the history of the Jews of Vilnius. In this respect, the Jewish State Museum in Vilnius, located in a small wooden structure at 12 Pamenkalnio Street (Portova, Uosto, P. Cvirkos), plays an important role. It has managed to retrieve and exhibit some objects from the old Jewish museum, closed by Soviet authorities in 1949. It also displays recovered relics from the Great Synagogue, as well as from other pre-war synagogues and Jewish institutions in Lithuania. It arranges, from time to time, thematic public exhibitions devoted to the history of famous personalities and Jewish and Hebrew educational institutions, as well as to the effects of the Holocaust on Lithuanian Jewry. It organizes also scientific conferences, and publishes books on relevant subjects.

The Jewish community of Vilnius today resembles little the pre-war Jerusalem of Lithuania. It is a faint shadow of its glorious past. Nonetheless, it tries slowly to retrieve its roots, and recapture its history. In June 1991, a new monument, with inscriptions in Yiddish and Hebrew, in memory of the Jews murdered in 1941-1944, was erected in Ponary. Small commemorative rocks, with special inscriptions, were placed at the pits in which the victims were cremated en masse. A small museum, next to the monument to the Jewish victims, also functions in Ponary.

In January 1992 a commemorative plaque was installed at 8 Rudninku (Rudnicka) Street (previously no. 6) where the Vilnius ghetto Judenrat had its offices, and where on 3 November 1941, during the so-called action of the "yellow certificates," some 1,200 Jewish victims were assembled for transportation to Ponary. Another plaque was installed at 3 Lydos (Lidska) Street in memory of the 2,000 Jews who were assembled there on 7 September 1941, just before the ghetto was established, for deportation to Ponary. In 1993, fifty years after the liquidation of the ghetto in Vilnius, an appropriate monument was erected in the public square, near the former main entrance to the ghetto on Rudninku Street. At the same time a monument was erected near the two buildings which housed, during the war, the H.K.P. labour camp on Subaciaus (Subocz) Street. Several other plaques, in memory of well known Jewish personalities, were also placed in different appropriate locations throughout the city.

There are few cities in the world where the names of streets have changed as frequently as in Vilnius. In the course of history, all local authorities, except for the Nazis, have recognized the contribution of Jews to the culture and economy of the city and named streets after important Jewish personalities. Before the war there were streets named Zydowska (Zydu, Jewish) and Gaona (Gaono, Gaon). The Soviets joined these two streets into one and united it with Stikliu (Szklana). Today these streets have reverted to their original names and are called, again, Zydu and Gaono, respectively. Before the war there was a street named after the well-known philanthropist and book collector M. Strashun. Under Soviet rule, the library was closed and the street renamed to Zemaitijos. Despite the fact that most Jews in Vilnius refer to it, even today, by its old name, officially the street is still called Zemaitijos. Other streets in the city are named after S.I. Finn (1818-1890) the author of the first book in Hebrew, published in Vilna in 1860, and the Jewish sculptor M. Antokolski (1843-1902).

One of the important responsibilities of the Jewish Community Council is to look after the Jewish cemetery. According to unofficial sources, the first Jewish cemetery in Vilnius was established in 1487.[10] The first recorded information about it dates back to 1592. The graveyard where the Gaon of Vilna was originally buried was located on the north-west side of the Neris river (Vilja), across the Castle Hill (Gora Zamkowa). It was closed in 1830, and totally dismantled in 1949-50.[11] A major sport facility and an indoor swimming pool were constructed after the war at this location. In 1828 a new Jewish cemetery was opened at Uzupio (Zarzecze) Street which was active until 1943. By the early 1960s it was completely destroyed. Most tombstones were removed and used by the Soviets for various public construction projects.

The new Jewish cemetery is located in Seskiniai (formerly known as Dembowka, near Wilkomirska or Ukmerges Street). The first to be buried there in 1941 were the victimized inhabitants of the Vilnius ghetto. The new cemetery has been in operation for over fifty years. It reflects well the recent history of the local Jewish community. The remains of the Gaon of Vilna were first transferred from the shore of the Neris river to the cemetery on Uzupio. Today his remains, those of his wife, and son, as well as the relics of Count Valentin Potocki - or the so-called *Ger-Tsedek* (righteous proselyte) - who converted to Judaism and by decree of a catholic church court was burnt on the stake in 1749[12] are stored in a special vault at the new cemetery in Seskiniai. The remains of the pre-war spiritual leader of Vilnius Jewry, Ch. O. Grodzienski, and of some other important Jewish personalities were also transferred to the new cemetery. Recently monuments have been erected there to former Jewish political leaders, to the children who perished in the ghetto, to members of the Jewish underground murdered by the Nazis, to pre-war and ghetto Jewish teachers, as well as to some of those who were buried there anonymously during the Nazi occupation. The significance of the Jewish cemetery in Vilnius is not only practical, but also symbolic. At the time when all Lithuania is covered with nameless graves of Jewish martyrs, the cemetery in Vilnius reflects, at least in part, the long history of the local Jewish community.

The current Lithuanian government makes a considerable effort to raise the profile of its Jewish community by sponsoring and assisting in the organization of a number of cultural and commemorative events, connected with the history of Jewish life in Lithuania and Vilnius. In October 1993 a major International Conference, in commemoration of the 50th anniversary of the liquidation of the ghetto in Vilnius, took place in the city. During 3-4 May 1995 Vilnius was the place of a sitting of the Committee on Culture and Education of the European Council's Parliamentary Assembly which was held jointly with an International Conference on Yiddish Culture. In April 1997 a special International Arts Festival was organized in the city to mark the 55th anniversary of the foundation of the Jewish theatre in the Vilnius ghetto. And, in September 1997, the 200th anniversary of the death of the Vilnius Gaon, or the Genius of Vilna, was observed. President A. Brazauskas appointed a special committee, chaired by the Minister of Culture, to organize the commemorative events which included an International Scholarly Conference, exhibition, the unveiling of a new monument, and other functions.

The collapse of the Soviet empire has affected the relationship of Jews with their non-Jewish neighbours in many different ways. Before, anti-Jewish and anti-Zionist activity was directed and controlled from Moscow and the spread of racial hatred by individuals was forbidden. The Soviet press and the media conducted a covert anti-Jewish campaign by attacking the state of Israel and Jewish leaders in the West. It attempted, however, to project an image of impartiality by stressing the difference between anti-Semitism and anti-Zionism. With the advent of *glasnost* and *perestroika* in the Soviet Union, which entailed freedom of expression, the abolition of censorship, and a rapprochement with the West, official anti-Jewish propaganda ceased. The new freedom of speech, however, gave rise to a new wave of anti-Jewish propaganda incited by formerly clandestine Russian nationalistic and fascist groups.

In Lithuania the situation was somewhat different. Prior to independence most Lithuanians regarded themselves as oppressed by the Soviet state and showed some sympathy to the Jews who were also a minority tyrannized by the regime. They even took pleasure in the accomplishments of the state of Israel, if only because it irked the Soviet leaders in the Kremlin. In the late 1980s, when Lithuania expanded its struggle for independence, its leaders tried hard to assure the international community that an independent Lithuania would comply with international human rights laws, and that it would protect and treat its national minorities with respect, tolerance, and understanding. Soon after Lithuania proclaimed its independence, Vytautas Landsbergis, the Chairman of the Supreme Council and head of State, declared that the republic of Lithuania would not tolerate any displays of anti-Semitism.

On the surface, everything appeared to be fine. Jewish deputies were elected to the Lithuanian national parliament. Full diplomatic relations have been established between Israel and Lithuania and a Lithuania-Israel Friendship Society began its activity. But the shadows of the past hover over the relationship of Lithuania with its Jewish minority. Official policy was, in this case, not always tantamount to the situation in real life. For many years, under Soviet rule, the complicity of many Lithuanians in the anti-Jewish Nazi crimes was covered up by the general designation of collaboration with the Nazi regime and anti-Soviet activity. No special reference to the participation of Lithuanians in the mass murder of Jews, during Nazi occupation, has ever been made. When Lithuania was liberated from Nazi occupation, by the Soviet Army, many Lithuanians who collaborated with the Nazis escaped to the West. Some, who did not manage to flee, went into hiding, facing, for a while, the new local authorities with armed resistance. In time, most of them were apprehended by Soviet security forces, put on trial, and convicted to lengthy prison terms in the Soviet GULAG. Even those who did not go underground, but were accused of minor anti-Soviet offenses, at the time of occupation, were arrested and convicted to prison terms. Hence, under Soviet rule there were few Lithuanians in Vilnius who might have served the Nazi regime in any capacity. Some of those jailed, and condemned by the Soviets, were permitted to return to Lithuania after their jail terms expired. Most of them, however, preferred to remain inconspicuous, and kept a low profile.

After Lithuania gained independence from the USSR, the situation changed drastically. Those who were arrested by the Soviets for their collaboration with the Nazis and were, in most instances, members of auxiliary para-military and police units, concerned primarily with anti-Jewish activity, all of a sudden have become anti-Soviet freedom fighters, who allegedly joined the Nazis with the sole purpose of fighting against the Soviet occupation of Lithuania. From criminals they have been turned into victims, martyrs, war veterans, and national heroes.

On 2 May 1990 the Lithuanian government passed a Law on the "Rehabilitation of Persons Repressed for Resistance to the Occupying Regime," and soon after state authorities began the process of indiscriminate rehabilitation of all those who were jailed and convicted by the Soviets. Those responsible for implementing the Law either ignored the war records of the applicants, or adopted an incredibly liberal definition of the term "participation in genocide." How otherwise could one explain the rehabilitation of self-confessed murderers of Jews?[13] The rehabilitation of former war criminals in Lithuania legalized, in a sense, the mass murder of innocent victims, most of them Jews.

Several days later, on 8 May 1990, the Supreme Council of the Republic of Lithuania adopted a "Declaration Concerning the Genocide of the Jewish Nation in Lithuania During the Period of Nazi Occupation." The Declaration condemned explicitly, and without reservations, the murder of Jewish citizens in Lithuania, yet it remained vague on the issue of Lithuanian participation in the Nazi atrocities,[14] and left the decision about the fate of alleged Lithuanian Nazi collaborators in the hands of bureaucrats in the department of justice.

The case of Aleksandras Lileikis, one of those expelled from the USA, is instructive. During the war Lileikis was the head of the Lithuanian secret police of the Vilnius region, actively participating in the extermination of local Jews. After the war he entered the United States under false pretences. Recently, incriminating evidence on his wartime activity was discovered in German archives. Despite the fact that Lithuanian officials were lax in providing additional evidence required, the eighty eight year old Lileikis was stripped of his U.S. citizenship because he lied in his application when he was admitted to the country. He left for Vilnius in June 1996, because he was due to face a deportation hearing any day.[15] In Vilnius, however, justice officials were slow in taking legal action against Lileikis. They were allegedly busy checking rumours that Lileikis was during the war a member of the Lithuanian anti-Nazi underground, and that he joined the local police

163

with the purpose of conducting anti-Nazi subversive activity. Lithuanian bureaucrats were thus advancing the absurd notion that the mass murder of Jews was required to conceal covert anti-Nazi activity. It is clear that those in charge of Lithuanian justice were biding their time. They were waiting for Lileikis, and other Nazi collaborators, to die a natural death, hoping that they will be spared the trouble of having to organize war criminal trials.[16]

The Jews of Lithuania are bewildered and outraged. They have started a campaign against the rehabilitation of those who served the Nazi regime and participated in the mass murder of Lithuanian Jews. They demand that all those who assisted the Nazis in their heinous crimes be put on trial. The justifiable indignation of the few remaining Jews in Lithuania has been faced, however, with an outburst of rage by surviving Nazi accomplices, their friends, relatives, and current supporters. They accuse the Jews of having supported the Soviet regime and of having assisted in the deportation of many innocent Lithuanians to Siberia. According to them, the Jews themselves were to blame for the wrath of the Lithuanian people and the vengeance they meted out against their Jewish neighbours.

These charges of the Lithuanian anti-Semites are, of course, preposterous. Indeed, a number of Jews in Lithuania supported the Soviet system and some worked in the Soviet security organs, but a greater number by far was victimized by the Soviet regime. It is well known that the number of Jews, expelled by the Soviets to Siberia, was in relative terms much higher than that of indigenous Lithuanians. Close to 30,485 Lithuanian citizens, or 1.4 per cent of Lithuania's total population, were expelled to Siberia in the third week of June 1941. Among them were approximately 7,000 Jews, or three per cent of the total Jewish population in Lithuania.[17] It is evident from the above that, on average, the Jews suffered more from the ferocity of the Soviet regime than most other inhabitants of Lithuania. Nevertheless, today many Lithuanians attach to all Jews a collective responsibility, accusing them of genocide and complicity with the Soviet regime.

The outrage of Jews, and the reaction in the West, over the indiscriminate rehabilitation of former collaborators with the Nazis, somewhat slowed down this process. There are indications today that the Lithuanian government is prepared to take a closer look at the past of every individual concerned. A joint Lithuanian-Israeli commission of inquiry to review the rehabilitations granted has been established, and "six rehabilitations unjustly granted to Nazi collaborators had been cancelled."[18] Unfortunately, this issue brought into the open with new force the lingering anti-Semitism prevalent in certain segments of Lithuanian society.

The Lithuanian government tries to discourage the spread of anti-

Semitism in the country, but it cannot deter the local press from disseminating virulent anti-Jewish propaganda. In a report, in the weekly Europa, about the commemoration of the destruction of the Jewish community of Kaunas, attended by President A.M. Brazauskas, the writer A. Krasauskas pokes fun at the President and the few old Jews present. He does not hide his distress that so many Jews have managed to survive the Holocaust.[19] Anti-Semitic sentiments expressed in the Lithuanian daily press encourage hoodlums to overt anti-Jewish activity. Thus, the Jewish cemetery in Vilnius was recently desecrated on several occasions.

The anti-Jewish attitude of certain representatives of the Lithuanian press affects also the relationship between the Jews born in Lithuania, currently residing in other countries, and their native land. The Association of Lithuanian Jews in Israel issued recently a Proclamation, stating that the Jewish community in Lithuania "had the highest Jewish victimology rate during the Holocaust, a fact due in no small measure to the zealous collaboration of numerous Lithuanians with the Nazis," and that "any meaningful reconciliation between Jews and Lithuanians must be preceded by a candid admission of the guilt of numerous Lithuanians in the murder of Jews."[20]

Indeed, on 22 September 1994, prior to his October 1994 visit to Israel, the Prime Minister of Lithuania, Adolfas Slezevicius, appeared on television to urge Lithuanians to acknowledge and repent for the heinous actions of their brethren. He declared that "despite the fact that the Holocaust was the realization of Nazi policies... we should recognize that hundreds of Lithuanians took direct part in the genocide. This obliges us to repent and ask the Jewish people for forgiveness." Moreover, he stated that "the Government of Lithuania assumes responsibility for prosecuting those who participated in murder."[21]

The above notwithstanding, a cursory examination of the current Lithuanian press makes it clear that many Lithuanians resent being reminded today of the misdeeds of their fathers and the few remaining Jews in Vilnius are a constant irritant to those who prefer to forget about the Holocaust in Lithuania. Instead of assuming responsibility, they blame the victims who refuse to forget their humiliation and suffering. By denying their guilt of complicity in Nazi crimes, some Lithuanians want to erase these shameful pages from their history, escaping thus, if not physical, then at least, moral retribution.

There is no question that the discussion of Nazi occupation and the participation of Lithuanians in Hitler's crimes is a sensitive issue which cannot be kept under cover forever. It is unfortunate, however, that the new climate of freedom in Lithuania, which makes possible to expose and air in public grievances, cooped up for years, also fosters a revival of a latent anti-Semitism which makes the life of the small Jewish community in Vilnius even more difficult.

Late in February 1995 the President of Lithuania, Algirdas Brazauskas, visited Israel. He met there with leading Israeli political personalities, including President Ezer Weitzman and Prime Minister Yitzhak Rabin. He visited the Yad Vashem Holocaust Memorial and Museum and addressed the Israeli parliament, the Knesset. In Israel the President of Lithuania offered a public apology to the Jewish people for the complicity of many Lithuanians in the mass murder of Jews during Nazi occupation of Lithuania. He also declared that he had just signed a decree which provides for the proper verification of each individual's wartime activity, before one could be rehabilitated.[22]

The reaction of the Lithuanian Jewish community in Israel to the statement of President Brazauskas was positive. It appeared that a new beginning in the tense relationship between the few surviving Lithuanian Jews and their native land was possible. Unfortunately, the response in Lithuania was different. The President's opponents berated him for his actions. They attempted to cover up and justify the crimes of Lithuanian Nazi collaborators by accusing the Jews of all possible misdeeds against the Lithuanian people. During the discussion in the Lithuanian parliament of the bill "About the Urgency of the Struggle with Racism, Xenophobia, anti-Semitism, and Intolerance", just prior to the departure of Brazauskas to Israel, Z. Shlichite, a professional lawyer and the associate chairperson of the parliamentary Committee on Issues of State and Law, accused Jews of anti-Lithuanian activity and declared that on his trip to Israel Brazauskas should demand from Israeli authorities the names of all Jews, currently Israeli citizens, guilty of carrying out the genocide of the Lithuanian people.[23]

After the return of Brazauskas from Israel, a new wave of virulent anti-Semitic propaganda appeared on the pages of the Lithuanian nationalistic press. Referring to the activities of pro-communist Jews at the time of Soviet rule, Juozas Tartilas, another member of parliament, declared that instead of apologizing to the Jews he hoped "to live to hear the apology of the President of Israel, E. Weitzman, for the participation of his compatriots in the genocide of Lithuanians."[24] Even more disappointing was a letter published in *Respublika* by Jonas Avyzius, a leading member of the Soviet Lithuanian cultural elite and one of the best known Lithuanian prose writers who was awarded in the past the prestigious Soviet Lenin Prize for Literature. Avyzius castigated Brazauskas for his apology to the Jews without demanding, in return, that the President of Israel apologize for the alleged crimes committed by Jewish supporters of the Soviet regime.[25] The Chairman of the Lithuanian Union of Nationalists, R. Smetona, was even more outspoken. He claimed that no one had the right to atone, or apologize, in the name of all Lithuanians. There could be no collective guilt nor collective apology. Foreign countries have no business in telling Lithuanians how to treat their citizens.[26]

It is rewarding to know that in the past not all Lithuanians collaborated with the Nazis and that, today, many seek reconciliation with the small Jewish minority. In fact, during Nazi occupation many Lithuanians, risking their own lives, protected and saved their Jewish neighbours from the Nazis. It has been reported that only in 1943 ninety-five Lithuanians were arrested for disobeying anti-Jewish Nazi laws.[27] Moreover, some Lithuanians were executed by the Nazis for hiding Jews.[28] Two hundred and thirty representatives of Lithuania were awarded the Yad Vashem medal for "Righteous People of the World." Over a hundred Lithuanians were presented with the "Cross for Saving Perishing People" established by the Lithuanian government.[29]

Some Lithuanians are prepared today to acknowledge the role of Lithuanian collaborators in the Nazi anti-Jewish crimes and to view the President's demarche in Israel as a positive step in Lithuanian-Israeli relations. Thus, in an open letter published in the Lithuanian press, Darius Birzinis claims that the objective of the new wave of anti-Semitism in Lithuania is to cover up the crimes of Lithuanian Nazi collaborators. Birzinis emphasizes that some leading members of the catholic church supported the Hitler regime and approved of its anti-Jewish policies. He points out that the indiscriminate murder of Jews in Lithuania, by Lithuanians, started even before the German army captured the major Lithuanian cities. Birzinis concludes by saying that "one cannot identify the hundreds of Lithuanians who participated in the mass murder of Jews... with the Lithuanian nation, just as one cannot identify Jews, members of the Soviet secret police, with the Jewish people.... One should not justify the bloody murderers, members of one nation,... only because the nation which was subjected to genocide had its own villains."[30]

It is clear from the preceding discussion that the approach of the Lithuanian government to issues affecting its Jewish minority is at best confusing. On the one hand, it denounces anti-Semitism and the participation of some Lithuanians in Nazi crimes, and it proclaims its desire for good relations with its Jewish minority and the state of Israel. On the other, it fails to prosecute Lithuanian war criminals, expelled from the USA and presently residing in Lithuania, and it does nothing to curb the dissemination of anti-Jewish hate propaganda by local journalists and politicians. It is obvious that the government of Lithuania finds itself today in a quandary which is the result of its attempt to appease both, its Jewish minority and the nationalistic fringes of Lithuanian society, at the same time.

In the meantime life in Lithuania is not easy. The economic situation improves very slowly, and corruption pervades most sectors of the economy and public life. It may take years before the living standard in the country reaches again the 1989 pre-independence level. The average income of a worker is just above $100.00 US a month, and old age pension is on average a mere $35.00. There are some who have become exorbitantly rich in the new conditions of the market economy, but the majority of Lithuanians can hardly make end meets, and the disparity between the rich and the poor is growing, from day to day.

The Jews of Lithuania have a rich history, but it is doubtful whether the future holds much in store for them. Despite the recent revival of Jewish life in Vilnius the number of Jews in the city continues to dwindle and the future of its Jewish community is bleak. Many of those who are active in Jewish community affairs are, relatively speaking, old. One third of all Jews in Lithuania are pensioners and the average Jewish resident of Lithuania is today 43.5 years old.[31] Among the young, who still remain in the city, more than a third have non-Jewish spouses.

The small Jewish community of Vilnius continues to cope with its problems of daily existence. The young are biding time, wondering what the shaky future holds in store for them, while the few Holocaust survivors who are still around are continuously reminded of their difficult past. For all practical purposes, the old Jerusalem of Lithuania is dead, and the few remaining Jews in the city are the keepers of its graveyards and a memorial of its glorious past.

NOTES

[1]. G. Agranovskii, and I Guzenberg, Litovskii Ierusalim (Vilnius 1992), 7.

[2]. Sidney Heitman, "Soviet Emigration in the 1990s: A New 'Fourth Wave'?" Soviet Jewish Affairs 21, no. 2 (1991), 12.

[3]. Sidney Heitman, "Soviet Emigration, Jewish and Non-Jewish: Trends and Projections," Viewpoint XX, no. 4 (Toronto 1992), 3.

[4]. Sidney Heitman, "Soviet Emigration Under Gorbachev," Soviet Jewish Affairs 19, no. 2 (1989), 18.

[5]. Sidney Heitman, "Jews in the 1989 USSR Census," Soviet Jewish Affairs 20, no. 1 (1990), 28.

[6]. Jerusalem of Lithuania (Vilnius), no. 7 (58), October 1995, 3.

[7]. Emanuelis Zingeris, "Knygu Hebraju ir Jidis Kalbomis Fondai Lietuvoje," Knygotyra, 13(20) (Vilnius 1987), 97.

[8]. Lubavitch International (1994), 17.

[9]. Jerusalem of Lithuania (Vilnius), no. 6 (57), September 1995, 4.

[10]. Agranovskii, Guzenberg, 4.

[11]. Ibid., 64.

[12]. Israel Cohen, Vilna (Philadelphia 1992), 416.

[13]. Efraim Zuroff, "The Memory of Murder and the Murder of Memory,"The Days of Memory, Emanuelis Zingeris, ed. (Vilnius 1995), 399.

[14]. Ibid., 397.

[15]. The Globe and Mail (Toronto), 20 June 1996, A16.

[16]. Litovskii Ierusalim (Vilnius), nos. 7-8 (67-68), July-August 1996, 1-3. It appears that despite procrastination and many legal maneuvers Lileikis my finally face trial. See Canadian Jewish News, 28 August 1997, 36; and 5 March 1978, 40.

[17]. Obzor (Vilnius), September 1997, no. 37, 14.

[18]. Zuroff, 401.

[19]. Europa (Vilnius), 29 July-5 August 1994, no. 22 (98), 1.

[20]. Gachelet (Tel-Aviv), August 1994, 1.

[21]. New York Times International, 23 September 1994.

[22]. Ierusalimskie vesti, 12 March 1995, 5. According to a note, published in Lietovos Rytas, 5 May 1995, close to a 1,000 applications for rehabilitation, from citizens of Lithuania victimized by the Soviet regime, have been rejected due to the participation of those concerned in the genocide of Jews. See Jerusalem of Lithuania, no. 5(56), August 1995, 3.

[23]. Ekho Litvy (Vilnius), 28 February 1995, 4.

[24]. Vechernie novosti (Vilnius), 7 April 1995, 3.

[25]. Lietuvos Jeruzale (Vilnius), no. 1 (52), April 1995, 3.

[26]. Literaturnaia gazeta (Moscow), 15 March 1995, 9.

[27]. Michailas Erenburgas, "The Specific Character of Help to Nazi Victims in Lithuania (1941-1944)," The Days of Memory, Emanuelis Zingeris, ed. (Vilnius 1995), 432.

[28]. Algirdas Jakubcionis, "Lithuanian Attitudes Towards Jews, the Vilnius Ghetto, Its Inmates and their Fate," Emanuelis   Zingeris, ed., The Days of Memory (Vilnius 1995), 388.

[29]. Jerusalem of Lithuania (Vilnius), no. 7 (58), October 1995, 1.

[30]. Ekho Litvy, 28 March 1995, 4.

[31]. Jerusalem of Lithuania (Vilnius), no. 7 (58), October 1995, 3.

CONCLUSION

The history of the Jewish community of Vilnius is a tale of growth, accomplishment, even glory, but also one of privation, destruction, and annihilation. Vilnius was founded early in the fourteenth century and, soon after, Jews have established a firm presence in the city . The evolution of Jewish life in Vilnius progressed over the years gradually. It was largely conditioned by the political situation in the country and the generosity of its rulers. By the middle of the nineteenth century, Vilnius was one of the main centres of Yiddish and Hebrew secular and religious learning, as well as of Jewish social, cultural, and political activity in the diaspora.

Vilnius was the home of Elijah, the Gaon of Vilna (1720-1797), and, among others, of the great Hebrew poet J.L. Gordon (1831-1892). The most productive Jewish printing plants and publishing houses, anywhere in the world, were located in the city. Jewish public libraries, including the one named after, M. Strashun (1817-1885), were famous for their exquisite collections of original materials in a variety of languages. The *YIVO*, or Jewish Scientific Research Institute, established in Vilno in 1925, centred its activity on the investigation of current Jewish problems, and the struggle against anti-Semitism. It promoted Jewish linguistic and literary studies and fostered the revival of the national consciousness of Jews. Vilna was the cradle of Jewish socialism and one of the main centres of Zionist activity.

Under Russian tsarist and Polish rule Jewish life in Vilno was insulated from major outside influences, yet it was vigorous and vibrant. Anti-Semitism hampered economic life, but it also intensified Jewish self-awareness, and fostered identification with Jewish religious, social-democratic, and Zionist ideals.

The incorporation of Vilnius into the USSR, in the summer of 1940, had far reaching consequences for the Jews in the city. All forms of Jewish national, cultural, religious, or political expression were banned, and the teaching of Hebrew was forbidden. Many leading Jewish political, social, and business personalities were exiled to Siberia. The capture of Vilnius by the Germans in June 1941 changed the face of the city forever.

Under Nazi occupation the Jews of Vilnius were exposed to the most heinous crimes of torture and murder. Nazi SS-men and their Lithuanian collaborators executed, en masse, thousands of innocent Jews in the Ponary forest, just outside the city boundaries. For two years the surviving Jews of Vilnius were confined within the walls of a ghetto. Deluding themselves that service to the Nazi war machine would save their lives, they had no choice but to work and hope. Few, however, trusted the sincerity of the Nazis, and gave no credence to their promises. In September 1943 the ghetto in Vilnius was liquidated and its residents were deported to concentration and death camps.

Early in 1942, a Jewish armed resistance organization, the so-called F.P.O., was formed in the ghetto. Its initial plan to stage an uprising within the walls of the ghetto, however, failed. The F.P.O. lacked the necessary determination to wage battle. Moreover, it could not muster the support of most ghetto Jews who still believed in the possibility of survival. In the end most F.P.O. fighters escaped into the nearby forests and joined the pro-Soviet partisans. Vilnius was liberated from the Nazis, by the Soviet Army, on July 13, 1944.

Nazi occupation decimated the ranks of the city's Jewish population. Most were killed in Ponary, or in the death camps of Treblinka, Majdanek, and Auschwitz. In addition to those who were exiled, or managed to escape to the USSR, no more than 3,000 Jews, or between four and five per cent of the pre-war total Jewish population of Vilnius, survived the Holocaust. Close to one third of all survivors managed to escape the Nazi clutches by joining the partisans in the Belorussian and Lithuanian forests. Others were saved by friendly gentiles, or liberated in concentration and death camps by advancing allied forces.

Most Jewish natives of Lithuania who survived the Holocaust refused to remain in their native land. Their memories of the recent past were too painful to ignore. The wounds were still fresh and few wanted to be reminded daily about their humiliation and suffering. Most Holocaust survivors moved to Israel, the USA, and other countries in the West. In 1995 no more than approximately 1,000 former Lithuanian Jews continued to reside in their native land. No more than 200 Holocaust survivors live today in Vilnius.

After the Second World War, and until 1990, when Lithuania proclaimed its independence from the USSR, Jewish life in Vilnius was determined by Soviet political and ideological considerations, and by policies enacted in Moscow for the whole Soviet Union. The atheistic essence of Marxist dogma and the anti-Zionist nature of Soviet national and foreign policy ruled out the possibility of any meaningful Jewish religious, political, or social expression. After Lithuania regained its independence, the small Jewish community of Vilnius, decimated by emigration, has undertaken the difficult task of recapturing its past. Today, Jews are again free to practice their religion and derive spiritual strength from their rich heritage. The future of the Vilnius Jewish community, however, is clouded. The repudiation of the recent indiscriminate rehabilitation of former Lithuanian war criminals, by Jewish organizations and western public opinion, has stimulated the resurgence of anti-Semitism in Lithuania. The growing influence of right wing and nationalistic political parties and clans poisons the atmosphere in the country and encourages Jewish emigration. The dwindling number of Jews, still remaining today in Vilnius, serve as a memorial to the glorious past of its Jewish community.

The destruction of the Jewish community of Vilnius and the tragic destiny of East-European Jewry are well documented recent historical events. And yet, there are today many unscrupulous individuals who deny the very existence of gas chambers and death camps in Nazi occupied Europe. They take advantage of the ineffectiveness of the research tools of the historical sciences and abuse the gullibility of ordinary people. Guided by narrow political and ideological stimuli, they manipulate facts, fabricate evidence, and use statistical documentation selectively in order to concoct a picture of reality which has nothing in common with the truth. Some Holocaust deniers, former Nazis and their collaborators, refuse to acknowledge their gruesome deeds in order to gain absolution for their crimes. Others, are driven by a guilty conscience and the desire to clear the name of the German nation and its fascist allies. In most instances, however, the denial of the Holocaust is an expression of the current revival of racism and neo-fascism and a calculated attempt to malign, denigrate, and abuse the Jewish people. It is gratifying to know, however, that reliable and serious historians treat the subject of the Holocaust with empathy and understanding. Those who survived the Holocaust, and are still around, add a personal touch to the historical accounts of this inscrutable tragedy.

The fall of Jerusalem of Lithuania marked not only the destruction of its communal, social, religious, and cultural institutions. It implied also individual murder of all those who nurtured Jewish life in the city. No single Jewish family in Vilnius survived the Holocaust intact. Before the war my immediate family was comprised of my parents, myself, and my sister. I had thirteen aunts and uncles. Most were young or middle-aged, and in good health. Only two of them survived the Holocaust. One was crippled by torture and died soon after liberation. The siblings of my parents had many children, but only one of my cousins survived. Among the close to one hundred Jews residing in our house, no more than seven young people managed to escape slaughter. Five survived in concentration camps, and two in the forest. All others perished. In the spring of 1941, there were thirty-five students in my class. Only nine survived, including the three who escaped to the Soviet Union before the arrival of the Wehrmacht to the city. In view of the above, all exhortations of Holocaust deniers sound ridiculous. Surely all these residents of Vilnius, my relatives, neighbours, and friends are not hiding somewhere for the last fifty years. They are all dead. They were brutally murdered by the Nazis and their local henchmen.

173

The history of Vilnius and the destruction of its Jewish community are closely intertwined with my own past. I was born, matured, and educated in the city. I lived there until September 1943. I escaped from the ghetto just prior to its liquidation and joined the anti-Nazi partisans in the Belorussian forests. I returned to Vilnius in 1947, after having served three years in the Soviet Army. I continued to live in the city until 1957. In 1958 I joined my family in Canada. Over the years, I have visited Vilnius more than a dozen times. I am still drawn to the city by the few remaining old friends, by the gravestones of my family members buried there, as well as by the memories of my youth.

I lived an eventful and stirring life. I faced a Nazi firing squad at the age of sixteen and spent two years in a ghetto. I did battle for a year in the ranks of a Soviet partisan unit and I served as a private in the Soviet Army which invaded Germany. I was among those who reached the outskirts of Berlin early in May 1945, and several days later joined hands with American and British soldiers on the shores of the Elbe river. I did my duty and served in the army with distinction. I was awarded several orders and medals for my contribution to the anti-Nazi war effort. Yet I do not regard myself as a hero. I passed through all circles of hell and survived. Only once was I slightly wounded in combat. I survived not because I was wise or more courageous than others; not because I was cunning or treacherous; not because I was hiding in the dark, or killed many enemies. I survived because I was lucky. I witnessed how chance rules human destiny. Indeed, my difficult life tempered my body and spirit, but I survived because I was always fortunate to be in the right place at the right time. The Nazi plague was equal to a natural disaster of the greatest magnitude and there were no special prescriptions for individual Jewish survival. Danger and death lurked all over, and no one knew when or where one would be stricken.

The life of each individual is different and peculiar. It is suggested that every human being who lives to maturity can produce at least one book, telling his, or her, own life story. Every Holocaust survivor and war veteran has many stories to tell, because surviving during the war, each day at a time, was a miracle. The survivors' life after the Holocaust is pervaded by the constant sensation of irretrievable loss and by nightmares and memories of the horrible past. It is also, however, an experience of overcoming uprootedness, adaptation, reassertion, and vindication. During the Holocaust every survivor was faced with the tragic realization that one is all alone in this world and that there is nowhere to turn for assistance. This awareness and the acutely felt loneliness stirred a spark of life in the deadened souls of most survivors, and helped them become independent, industrious, self-reliant, and responsible citizens. Today, just as most other people, some Holocaust survivors may experience periods of anxiety, depression, and emotional paralysis. Most Holocaust survivors, however, are successful in their endeavours. They tackle the problems they face with confidence in their ability to surmount most new challenges of daily life. The contribution of Holocaust survivors to the economic, cultural, and social life of the communities they have joined after the war illustrates the above proposition convincingly. That is, however, a different subject which deserves special and undivided attention.

APPENDIX

CHRONOLOGY

IX cent. B.C. The region of Vilnius ihabited

1009   The name Lithuania first mentioned in German chronicle

1323 City of Vilnius founded by Grand Duke of Lithuania Gediminas

1326   First Jews settle in Vilnius

1387   Lithuania adopts Christianity

1440   First Jewish house of worship built in Vilnius

XIV-XVI centuries.   Jews granted charters, by Lithuanian Grand Dukes and Polish Kings, to live and trade in the city

1569   Formal unification of Lithuania and Poland

1573   First official permit to build synagogue in Vilnius

1579   University established in Vilnius

1635   The Great Synagogue constructed in Vilnius

1655 Muscovites and Cossacks invade Vilnius and devastate Jewish community

1720-1797 The Gaon of Vilna Elijah ben Solomon Zalman. Vilna centre of strife between Misnagdim and Hasidim

1791   Jewish pale of settlement established in Russia

1795   Polish-Lithuanian Kingdom partitioned between Russia, Germany, and Austro-Hungary

1825-1855 Rule of Nicholas I in Russia

1827   System of cantonment for Jewish boys introduced in Russia

1892   Strashun Library established in Vilna

1894   Choral Synagogue constructed

1897   "Bund" established in Vilna

1902   "Mizrachi" organization founded in Vilna

1903   Theodor Herzl visited Vilna

1905   October. First Russian revolution

1914-1918 First World War

1916   "Tarbut" secondary school established in Vilna

1917   February revolution in Russia

1917   October revolution in Russia

1918   Yiddish Real Gymnasium founded in Vilna

1918 November. Poland and Lithuania regain their independence

1918-1920 Vilnius changes hands nine times between Lithuania, Poland, and the Bolsheviks

1919   Jewish Historical and Ethnographic Society and Museum

founded
1920   October-1939 September. Vilno under Polish rule
1925   YIVO - Jewish Scientific Institute - founded in Vilno
1931,   10 November.   Anti-Jewish pogrom in Vilno. Polish student
stoned to death by members of the Jewish resistance
1939,   1 September. Nazi Germany invades Poland from the west.
1939   September. Soviet troops invade Poland from the east
1939,   18 September-28 October. Vilno in the hands of the Soviet Army
1939,   28 October-1940 July. Vilnius in the hands of independent
Lithuania
1939,   31 October. Anti-Jewish pogrom in Vilnius
1940   August-1941, 23 June.   Vilnius incorporated into the USSR;
becomes capital of Lithuanian Soviet Socialist Republic
1941,   22 June. Nazi Germany invades the Soviet Union
1941,   24 June-1944, 13 July. Vilnius under Nazi occupation
1941   Early July. Mass murder of Jews in the Ponary forest begins
1941,   July-August. Members of "Ypatingas Burys," or the so-called
        "catchers," round up and murder young Jewish males
1941,   31 August-5 September. Pre-ghetto Nazi extermination actions
1941,   September-November. Early ghetto extermination actions
1941,   6 September-1943, 23 September. First ghetto in operation
1941,   6 September-29 October. Second ghetto in operation
1941   October. Life "saving," so-called yellow, certificates issued   to
selected residents of the first ghetto
1942,   21 January. Beginning of anti-Nazi armed resistance in the
ghetto. F.P.O. established
1943   April.   Ghetto fighters begin moving into the forest to join
Soviet anti-Nazi partisans
1943,   16 July. Y. Wittenberg, head of the F.P.O., surrenders to   the
Nazis and perishes in prison
1943   August.   Deportation actions from the ghetto to labour camps
in Estonia
1943,   1-5 September. New deportation action to Estonia
1943,   1 September. Armed encounter with the Nazis in the ghetto
at 12 Strashun Street.
1943,   5-23 September. Many young people and members of the Jewish
underground manage to escape to the forest
1943,   14 September. Jacob Gens, head of the ghetto in Vilnius,
killed by the Nazis
1943,   23 September. Final destruction of the ghetto in Vilnius.
Ghetto residents deported to concentration camps.

1944,   13 July. Vilnius liberated from Nazi occupation

1944,   July-1990, March. Vilnius again capital of Lithuanian Soviet Socialist Republic. Jewish life stagnant

1985-1990   Accent of M. Gorbachev to power and beginning of liberal reforms in the USSR

1988   Jewish Cultural Society established in Vilnius

1989   Yerushalaim de'Lita, Jewish monthly newspaper established in Vilnius

1990,   11 March. Lithuania declares independence from the USSR

1990   Department of Jewish studies opened at the Vilnius University

1990,   2 May. Law on the "Rehabilitation of Persons repressed for Resistance to the Occupying Regime" passed by the Lithuanian government

1990,   8 May. "Declaration Concerning the Genocide of the Jewish Nation in Lithuania During the Period of Nazi Occupation" passed by the Lithuanian government

1991   Jewish Cultural Society transformed into Jewish Communal Council

1991,   June. New monument to commemorate the Jews murdered in Ponary erected

1991,   September. Lithuania admitted to the U.N.

1991,   December. Dissolution of the USSR

1993,   September. Fiftieth anniversary of the destruction of the ghetto in Vilnius commemorated publicly

1995,   May. International Conference on Yiddish Culture, together with a sitting of the Committee on Culture and Education of the European Council's Parliamentary Assembly, takes place in Vilnius

1995,   February. President of Lithuania, Algirdas Brazauskas, visits Israel

1997,   September. Commemoration of the 200th anniversary of the death of the Vilnius Gaon

POPULATION OF VILNIUS-VILNA-VILNO

YEAR	TOTAL	JEWS
1645	12,000	2,620
1662	4,476	415
1818	33,568	14,097
1832	35,737	20,646
1860	60,040	24,448
1875	82,668	38,882
1897	154,532	63,996
1905	161,904	80,000
1910	186,461	63,800
1913	230,738	77,533
1914	235,000	98,700
1916	140,840	61,263
1917	138,787	57,516
1919	128,476	46,507
1923	167,454	58,186
1931	193,337	55,007
1933	207,300	58,500
1939	215,200	60,000
1941.IX.		40,000
1941.X.		25,300
1942.IV.		18,500
1943.IV.		20,192
1944.XII.		800
1959	236,078	16,534
1979	481,000	10,723
1989	576,000	9,109
1991	580,000	4,000
1996	584,000	3,800

Population list compiled from the following sources: Leyzer Ran, comp., Jerusalem of Lithuania (New York: Album Committee 1974); Israel Cohen, Vilna (Phladelphia: The Jewish Publication Society of America 1992); G. Agranovskii, and I Guzenberg, Litovskii Ierusalim (Vilnius: Lituanus 1992), and J. Jurginis, V. Merkys, A. Tautavicius, Viliaus Miesto Istorija (Vilnius: Mintis 1968).

BIBLIOGRAPHY

1. Agranovskii, G., and I. Guzenberg. <u>Litovskii Ierusalim</u>. Vilnius: Lituanus 1992.

2. Arad, Yitzhak. <u>The Partisan: From the Valley of Death to Mount Zion</u>. New York: The Holocaust Library 1979.

3. _____. <u>Ghetto in Flames: The Struggle and Destruction of the Jews in Vilna in the Holocaust</u>. Jerusalem: Yad Vashem 1982.

4. Arendt, Hanna. <u>The Human Condition</u>. Chicago: University of Chicago Press 1958.

5. Bauer, Yehuda. <u>They Chose Life: Jewish Resistance in the Holocaust</u>. New York: American Jewish Committee 1973.

6. _____. <u>A History of the Holocaust</u>. New York: F. Watts 1982.

7. Bendzius, A., J. Kubilius, J. Ziugzda, eds. <u>Vilniaus Universitetas</u>. Vilnius: Mintis 1966.

8. Braham, Randolph L., ed. <u>Contemporary Views of the Holocaust</u>. Boston: Kluwer-Nijhoff 1983.

9. Bettelheim, Bruno. <u>Surviving and Other Essays</u>. New York: Knopf 1979.

10. Choron, Jaques. <u>Suicide</u>. New York: Scribner 1972.

11. Cohen, Israel. <u>Vilna</u>. Philadelphia: The Jewish Publication Society of America 1992.

12. Dawidowicz, Lucy. <u>The War Against the Jews. 1933-1945.</u> New York: Holt, Rinehart and Winston 1975.

13. _____. <u>From that Place and Time: A Memoir, 1938-1947</u>. New York: W.W. Norton 1989.

14. Dobroszycki, Lucjan, and Jeffrey S. Gurock. <u>The Holocaust

in the Soviet Union. Armonk, N.Y.: M.E. Sharpe 1993.

15. Eckman, Lester E., and Chaim Lazar. The Jewish Resistance:
    The History of the Jewish Partisans in Lithuania and White
    Russia During the Nazi Occupation, 1940-1945. New York:
    Shengold Publishers 1977.

16. Encyclopeadia Judaica. Jerusalem: Encyclopeadia Judaica 1971.

17. Fleming, Gerald. Hitler and the Final Solution. Berkeley:
    University of California Press 1984.

18. Frankl, Viktor . Man's Search for Meaning. New York:
    Washington Square Press 1985.

19. Gerutis, Albertas, ed. Lithuania: 700 years. New York:
    Manyland Books 1969.

20. Greenbaum, Masha. The Jews of Lithuania. A History of a
    Remarkable Community. 1316-1945. Jerusalem: Gefen Publish-
    ing House 1995.

21. Grobman, Alex, and Daniel Landes, eds. Genocide: Critical
    Issues of the Holocaust. Chappaqua, N.Y.: Rossel Books 1983.

22. Grossman, Vasilii, and Il'ia Erenburg, eds., Chernaia kniga.
    Vilnius: Yad 1993.

23. Gutman, Yisrael, and Livia Rothkirchen, eds. The Catastrophe
    of European Jewry. Jerusalem: Yad Vashem 1976.

24. Harrison, E.J. Lithuania Past and Present. London: T. Fisher
    Unwin Ltd 1922.

25. Hilberg, Raul. The Destruction of the European Jews. New York:
    Holmes & Meier 1985.

26. Jewish Resistance During the Holocaust. Proceedings of the
    Conference on Manifestations of Jewish Resistance. April
    7-11, 1968. Jerusalem, 1971.

27. J. Jurginis, V. Merkys, A. Tautavicius. Vilniaus Miesto
 Istorija. Vilnius: Mintis 1968.

28. Kalmanovitch, Zelig. Yoman be-geto Vilnah. Tel Aviv: Moreshet
 bet - 'edot' 1977.

29. Klimov, I., and N. Grakov. Partizany vileishchiny. 2d ed.
 Minsk: Belorus' 1970.

30. Korchak, Reizl (Ruz'ka). Lehavot be'efer. Merchaviia, Israel,
 1946.

31. Kowalski, Isaac. A Secret Press in Nazi Europe. The Story of
 the Jewish United Partisan Organization. New York: Central
 Guide Publishers 1969.

32. Lazar, Chaim. Destruction and Resistance. New York: Shengold
 Publishers 1985.

33. Learsi, Rufus. A History of the Jewish People. Cleveland, Ohio:
 The World Publishing Company 1966.

34. Levin, Dov. Fighting Back: Lithuanian Jewry's Armed Resistance
 to Nazis, 1941-1945. New York: Holmes & Meier 1985.

35. Levin, Vladimir. "Partizanskii nalet na istoriiu." Novoe
 russkoe slovo, 18 November 1994, 33-4.

36. Lopalewski, Tadeusz. Miedzy Niemnem a Dzwina. Ziemia
 Wilenska i Nowogrodzka. London: Tern (Rybitwa) Books 1955.

37. Ochmanski, Jerzy. Historia Litwy, 2d ed. Warsaw: Ossolinski
 Publishing House 1982.

38. Pinkus, Benjamin. The Jews of the Soviet Union. Cambridge:
 Cambridge University Press 1990.

39. Ran, Leyzer, comp. Jerusalem of Lithuania, 2 vols. New York:
 Album Committee 1974.

40. Rindzyunski, Aleksander. Hurban Vilnah. Tel Aviv: Bet Lohamei ha-geta'ot 1987.

41. Sachar, Howard Morley. The Course of Modern Jewish History. New York: Delta 1963.

42. Schopenhauer, Arthur. The World as Will and Representation. Translated from the German by E.F.J. Payne. New York: Dover Publication 1966.

43. Shteinberg, Mark. "Tragediia i bor'ba." Novoe russkoe slovo, 14 October 1994, 37-8.

44. Shutan, Moshe. Geto un vald. Tel Aviv: Ha-mehaber 1971.

45. Sutskever, A. Fun Vilner geto. Moscow: Der emes 1946.

46. The Universal Jewish Encyclopedia. Ed. by Isaac Landman. New York: Universal Jewish Encyclopedia 1969.

47. Trunk, Isaiah. Judenrat: The Jewish Councils in Eastern Europe Under Nazi Occupation. New York: Stein and Day 1977.

48. Vaitkevichius, B., ed. Istoriia Litovskoi SSR. Vilnius: Mokslas 1978.

49. Yahil, Leny. The Holocaust: The fate of European Jewry 1932-1945. New York: Oxford University Press 1990.

50. Zingeris, Emanuelis. "Knygu Hebraju ir Jidis Kalbomis Fondai Lietuvoje. 1904-1981." Knygotyra, no. 13 (20)(Vilnius 1987), 86-103.

51. _____, ed. The Days of Memory. Vilnius: Baltos Lankos 1995.

52. Zinkus, Jonas., ed. Lithuania. An Encyclopedic Survey. Vilnius: Encyclopedia Publishers 1986.

INDEX

Québec, Canada
1998